MAUREEN DOWNEY

WHO IS
My Mother?

WHO IS MY MOTHER?

PROMINENT
BOOKS
EDGE

5830 E 2nd St, Ste 7000 #9983
Casper, WY 82609
USA

Some people come into your life for a reason,
Because your turn has come to share, grow or learn
They bring you an experience of peace or make you laugh.
They may teach you something you have never done.
They usually give you an unbelievable amount of joy.
Believe it, it is real.
But only for a season.

Anon.

Table of Contents

PART I

And Then We Were Five

Chapter One

There was nothing unusual about the way the summer of 1973 began but by the time Labour Day rolled around, our lives had been changed forever. A chain of unexpected events caught us by surprise. Well, that's not exactly true. If you asked everyone in the family how it started, all fingers would probably be pointed in my direction.

That summer began much as usual. When school 'got out' in the latter part of June, the Kerry family shouted a collective "hooray" and began tidying up the house and stuffing things into duffle bags etc., in preparation for the annual exodus to our summer cottage at Sandy Bay. Both cars were packed to overflowing with bags, beach towels, the guinea pigs in their cage, books, Rascal (our tabby cat), Tessa (our Australian shepherd dog), raincoats, swimsuits, etc., then off we drove to the line-up at the ferry terminal.

I suppose you would describe the Kerrys as a 'typical' family, at least up until that summer. Dad, Steve, accounting consultant in his early 40's, mum, Maura, in her mid-thirties (part-time paralegal and part-time mother), son Ben (age 8) and daughter, Amy (age 6). We were doing okay financially, having in 1972 replaced our first little overcrowded house with a five-bedroom, split level with a view, on the North Shore of Vancouver. The summer cottage at Sandy Bay was the icing on our cake - a gift from Steve's stepmother fondly referred to as Auntie Lou. We all loved Vancouver Island and from the time the children were born, we always spent our holidays there. When Auntie Lou discovered this rather quaint 'cottage' and made it possible for us to have our very own getaway at Sandy Bay, we were overjoyed.

Summers at Sandy Bay were the best of times. The ferry trip to the Island took about 90 minutes, then a quick 30-minute drive up the highway, and a right turn at Manders Road where we veered off down a narrow lane which we always referred to as 'the panhandle', coming to a stop where the trees parted at our back porch. On the left-hand side of the panhandle was an older wooden bungalow set in a pretty English-style garden. This was the residence of our closest neighbour, Mrs Glen. At the time, we all considered Mrs Glen to be extremely old. Rumour had it that she was at least 80! Rumour also had it that Mrs Lane had at one time owned all the land from where her house stood all the way down to the beach. Apparently, this redoubtable lady had been widowed twice, and as a consequence became the owner of some desirable real estate. We were given to understand that, during both marriages, Mrs Glen had suffered very poor health and had been nursed lovingly by her deceased spouses. According to local legend, upon the demise of spouse number two, she had made a miraculous recovery and had enjoyed excellent health ever since! All we knew was that circa 1973 when we moved into the neighbourhood, Mrs Glen took an afternoon nap in her sunroom after lunch every day and could quite regularly be observed walking down to the beach for her daily swim, using a large pole as a walking aid, much like Moses in The Ten Commandments. Mrs Glen was a most convivial neighbour, and her garden became a daily retreat for our cat, Rascal, who napped there after lunch because (as Mrs Glen pointed out to me), it was the only place where he could escape from the neighbourhood dogs.

On the right side of the panhandle was another little house, occupied by Lily and Albert Jones. Lily was a housekeeper at one of the large, high-end houses overlooking the golf course. She was the sister of Iris, wife of Tommy; as well as sister of Rose, wife of Alec whose houses were to the left of us and opposite us! We were surrounded! All six of them were retired and enjoyed chatting with us at every opportunity! But before I forget, the best feature of the panhandle was a pear tree, growing in the middle. It was an unimpressive looking tree, but it produced the most heavenly tasting winter pears which we all shared, picking and putting them in brown paper bags where they kept beautifully and were in great demand for as long as they lasted --- which wasn't long!

2

Into this idyllic place came the Kerry Family, their guinea pigs, cat, dog and, from time to time, visiting children, for another wonderful summer of fun, frolic and good times. Mum Kerry would hold the fort from Monday to Friday, and Dad Kerry would arrive from work on Friday evenings and leave on Sunday evenings, except for the week or two when he took his "real" holidays.

As for the house itself, the term 'cottage' should be interpreted loosely. It began its life as a somewhat square-shaped shed that grew. At some point it was one big room, then a wall was added, still leaving a fairly big room on one side and creating a kitchen on the other side. Cupboards, sink, stove, fridge etc. were added to the kitchen, as well as a big picture window comprised of many rectangular panes of glass. On the opposite side of the cottage, some steps, a verandah and a front door were added, as well as a false front. When you approached the house from that side, it looked more like the outside of a saloon in a western movie. We never used that side of the house because there were no gutters and constant dripping from all the pine trees had rotted the verandah.

Later, a bathroom and two bedrooms were created on the west side, at a lower level, so we had to go down two steps into each bedroom. The bathroom consisted of a bath, toilet and washbasin. On one side of the bathroom, there was an odd little door that opened into a narrow, rectangular room? about 14 ft long x 5 ft. wide, with a small window. We never did figure out why it was there, but on several occasions, we managed to set up a rollaway bed in it, to accommodate an extra body, and Rascal used the tiny window (which we always left open for bathroom ventilation) to exit the house if the back door was shut!

As a result of the addition of the bedrooms and bathroom, the roof on that side of the cottage sloped downwards at quite an angle. The master bedroom had single beds and we squeezed two sets of bunk beds and a chest of drawers into the other bedroom. It even had quite a big closet where Ben once fell asleep for three hours behind the suitcases, causing great panic because we feared he had wandered off down to the beach and been drowned! Fortunately, he awoke and staggered out onto the back porch before we dialed 911.

The living room was enormous, with two folding day beds, a huge old couch, a couple of comfortable chairs, and in one corner at a window overlooking the verandah, a desk and 3 wall shelves beside it. We and even room for our black and white television which had 2 channels (at night only). But with so many other distractions, who needed a television anyway?!!

Underneath the main floor and accessible from outside via a door below the kitchen, was an unfinished (dust floor) cellar where we had clothes lines for dripping swimsuits on rainy days when the outside line was of no use. Eventually, as we converted to 'luxury' status, we acquired a used washer and drier and an electric lawn-mower, etc. At the rear of the house, we even had a tool shed and a homemade shower head, attached to a hose and suspended from a tree outside the tool shed – providing a shower where we could wash the sand off our feet etc..

Perhaps the greatest asset of our wondrous "cottage", was the fact that it occupied a corner at the back of our 2/3-acre lot which was surrounded by forest. We had room for everything! There was a horseshoe pitch, a volleyball net, a ping pong table, a croquet lawn; a vegetable garden, some flower beds and even a pen and run for our guinea pigs. At the back door, which was the only door we ever used, there was a small, covered porch with a broom cupboard and steps down to a large concrete patio where we had a picnic table complete with umbrella, chairs, barbecue grill, etc. Our big kitchen window faced the garden and a large, fenced jungle of trees owned by some 'newspaper people' who had a house overlooking the beach further down, and who, we were told, did not intend to remove the trees-- hooray for us – we loved the trees!

From our garden to the east, all we had to do was open our rustic gate and walk down the tree-lined road past two houses (behind trees to the left) veer left around a corner and skip down a steep hill. The road ended right at Sandy Bay, a wide, crescent-shaped beach that stretched on and on forever. The beach at Sandy Bay sloped away so gradually and so far out, that it was safe for little children; and when the tide came in over the sand on a hot day, the water felt like a warm bath.

Sometimes, we would walk down to the beach. At the top of the hill on a quiet morning, if you called out, there was a wonderful echo. We had a lot of fun with that echo, hollering and hooting as our voices bounced back. Sometimes, we brought our lunch down to the beach, sometimes we hiked back up to the house, and sometimes 'good old mum' would hike up by herself and bring lunch down in the car. We could paddle, swim, skip sand dollars, dig for clams, play 'kick the can', read, dig spaceships in the sand, sunbathe, play with friends who often came over to visit with us, watch Tessa chase seagulls, collect shells, play beach games, or just sit and do nothing at all. We had a great time! Each summer passed by in a flash. Then came the summer of 1973 when our lives changed in a most unexpected way.

Chapter Two

That summer, we arrived at the cottage and, as usual, tumbled out of the car in a flurry of anticipation. I began sorting out the kitchen while the children unpacked the guinea pigs and began setting up their run. In due course, the beds were made, clothes put away in drawers, etc., radio volume turned up somewhat loud, all the usual stuff. After supper, as per usual, we all took a stroll to the beach, noting any changes along the way. It was a lovely evening, there was a gentle breeze, the tide was coming in with tiny waves making a swishy-crunchy sound as they frothed onto the shingle. Everything was just about perfect.

Next morning, the children took off on their usual 'neighbour-hood tour' while I was busy in the kitchen. After an hour or so, I heard laughter on the back patio. It sounded as if they had met up with our neighbour's grandchildren who often came to visit. I popped out to say 'hello'. But no, it wasn't the Martin kids - it was a little girl I had never seen before. I was surprised, but what surprised me even more was how attractive she was. Older than Ben or Amy, she was sitting on one side of the picnic table engaged in a lively dis-cussion. Wavy blonde hair cascaded down to her shoulders, framing such a pretty face. As I walked down the steps, she turned to see me, and I found myself gazing into the most incredible violet eyes. At twelve years of age, Gina was totally lovely, with a happy, vivacious personality to match.

Amy introduced us: "Hi mom, this is Gina". So I introduced myself to Gina who had no difficulty at all with conversation. We learned that she lived opposite our house, down a long leafy lane on the other side of Manders Road in a house overlooking the sea. That's how Gina came into our lives.

In the afternoon, we all went down to the beach. Gina enjoyed being with Ben and Amy. The three of them got along well. Later, when we hiked back up from the beach and the children washed all the sand off their feet, it seemed perfectly natural that Gina should stay for supper. When I asked her if that would be okay or did, she need to check with home, Gina said she was staying with her grandparents, and she was allowed to stay out for supper. After supper, she went home.

In the morning, the sun was shining. Usually, I got up early before the children. I suppose you could say that it was to enjoy a kind of "mother's quiet time" before the Daily Action began! I opened the kitchen window a crack, to start a flow of fresh air. As soon as I did that, there was a thump directly outside the door as Rascal, who slept on top of the broom cupboard after his nightly rambles, jumped down to come in for his breakfast! I fed him and then took my portable breakfast outside so that I could eat it and admire the scenery at the same time. To my surprise, who should be sitting at the picnic table but Gina! We said good morning to each other and when I remarked that Ben and Amy weren't up yet, she asked if she could wait. So I invited her into our monster big living/family/activity/all-purpose room. My typewriter, sitting on a table in a far corner, caught her interest. So I showed her how to wind the paper in and left her to it while I finished my breakfast.

About twenty minutes later, when I returned to the kitchen Gina came to ask me if she could look at the books on the shelf beside the typewriter. Mostly they were storybooks for the children. When I peeked in a while later, she was sitting on the couch busily reading, with four of the books piled up beside her. By the time Ben and Amy appeared, Gina had read all four books and had started on another two. I watched her with the books. It was as if she was devouring them. I thought, "this child is starved for books". And I wondered why.

For the remainder of the week, Gina appeared on the steps every morning. She was there before I got up and she went home when I told her it was time to go. By this time, I was becoming somewhat curious, so I began asking questions. On Thursday when it was too windy for the beach, I took the children to Cedar Creek, one of our favourite picnic spots, for the afternoon. When I suggested that, since we were going a distance in my car, perhaps Gina should go home or call her grandparents to get permission, she said that it really was okay. Her grandmother worked at the drug store and her grandfather read books a lot, and if she went out and didn't come home until later, they always left food for her in the fridge. So we all went to Cedar Creek and enjoyed the hike down to the river and our picnic. The children had a great afternoon swinging from a rope into the river and sliding down the rapids to where the river widened. But my level of concern was growing. Here was a child who was free to roam the wild beaches and the surrounding forest where anything could happen to her and no one would know. It worried me.

We had a great summer together, especially Gina. One day, she told me that she wouldn't be staying with her grandparents forever because her mother would be 'coming back'. She said that her mother was 'back east' and told us that she also had a little brother, Scott (about 3 years old), and a little sister, Lucy (about 2 years old). When we left, just before the Labour Day weekend, I hoped that Gina's mother and siblings would soon return. As we said goodbye, with hugs and high fives, it felt like saying goodbye to a member of our own family – which indeed Gina had become, if only for a summer.

But that summer proved to be just the tip of the iceberg! We hadn't imagined what was to come.

Chapter Three

My father, who had been in failing health for some time, died quite suddenly in January of 1974 and in May, my mother came from Ottawa for a visit. She had never seen the cottage, so we decided to take her over to Sandy Bay for a few days over the long weekend in May. The weather was warm and sunny, and we took long walks on the beach and sat outdoors for supper. My mother loved it. To our surprise, Gina turned up to greet us as we were unpacking the car. We introduced her to Grandma Dorrie and exchanged all our news. Gina was still staying with her grandparents 'down the lane'. Her mother and little brother and sister hadn't yet returned... but hopefully soon. In the meantime, she invited us to attend her school year-end concert. Gina was acting in a short play. She was anxious for us to see her. When I remarked how proud her grandparents and aunt Sarah must be of her, we were dismayed when Gina told us that they were all "busy" and couldn't come! It seemed that no one was coming to see Gina. Well, of course, the Kerry family attended the concert! We all agreed it was fun and Gina was 'the best'! After that, Gina spent almost all the time with us, right up until we left for home. I told her we would be back in June as usual, and "see you then".

June arrived. School was 'out'. The usual packing up and loading of cars ritual took place. The Kerrys arrived at Sandy Bay! We expected Gina to turn up at our door within an hour of our arrival, but there was no sign of her. Nor did she turn up that evening, nor the next day nor the next. We assumed that her mother had returned, and

Gina was now busy at home. We missed her. The summer rolled along and it was mid-August before we knew it. Still no sign of Gina.

All of us missed Gina and talked about her a lot. One day I happened to chat with Mrs Glen (our brown bungalow neighbour), who was out working in her garden. When she commented that she had noticed Gina playing with Ben and Amy, I confided my curiosity about the grandparents who had never contacted me all that summer. Mrs Glen had quite a lot to say about that. As it happened, she had been a neighbour of Gina's grandparents for many years and had known Julia, Gina's mother, as a child. "That girl, was a handful from the very beginning", she told me, "she expected everything to be handed to her on a platter! One day when I met Lillian with Julia and her sister Sarah up in the village, I bought each of the two little girls ice creams. Sarah thanked me right away, but not Julia, and when Lillian asked Julia to say thank you, she just glared at me and she absolutely refused to do it. I remember how embarrassed Lillian was. But that was the way Julia always acted." Mrs Glen added that Julia, who was very pretty, had apparently been Miss Sandy Bay of 1960, and it had "gone entirely to her head".

I got quite an earful from Mrs Glen. Julia had married a nice fellow named Max Niemann, but the marriage had broken up soon after Gina was born and Julia being Julia, had gone her own way. There were rumours about drug use and roaming around with hippies, and there were "more little children", but Julia had disappeared from Sandy Bay and not much more was known, except that for some reason the grandparents, Henry and Lillian had been looking after Gina for the past year. It was clear to me that Mrs Glen didn't approve of the entire Spencer family.

Not long after this conversation, when I was in the village drug store, where Lillian worked, I made a point of mentioning to her that we were "missing seeing Gina this summer".

"Oh yes", Lillian replied, "Gina has been away visiting. She's with her dad now and we're hoping that he will keep her because we're having company in September and we just don't have room for her any longer".

I left the drugstore in a kind of semi-dazed state with Lillian's words whizzing around in my thoughts: 'hope he will keep her', 'we just don't have room for her any longer." I couldn't get my head around that at all.

The weather that August was just beautiful, Steve took his two-week break and we spent days at the beach, having picnic lunches, going out in our dinghy, taking long walks out to the headland, watching Tessa chasing seagulls, reading books and sunbathing --- usually an idyllic, carefree time. But not this year ... at least not for me. I couldn't get Gina out of my mind. "No room for her!". What if her dad doesn't want her? Where does she go? All of this kept going around and around in my head until one day I found myself thinking "what if", "if there is no room for her and if her dad doesn't want her, then what if Gina comes to live with us?. We love her. We want her. Then I thought, I guess we will have to go to her grandparents and ask them if we can have her? That's a bit bold, isn't it? Suppose they are insulted? Well, the worst that can happen is that they will kick us(me?) out? Just a minute, if I go and ask them, then I will need to discuss it with Steve and Ben and Amy. How will they feel about the idea of having Gina come to live with us?"

I began to make a plan – at least in my head. I gave a lot of thought to the matter of my own family. Steve was an orphan who grew up in an institution, so I believed he would be entirely sympathetic to Gina's situation. I knew that Gina and Ben and Amy got along very well together and had done so over a reasonably long period. I felt that our family would be okay with it. SO WHY NOT?!

The first thing to do was talk to Steve. As we sat on the beach one day, I shared my thoughts with him and asked him what he thought of my idea and he agreed! So the next evening, in my shorts, t-shirt and best flip-flops, hair carefully combed, lipstick on straight? I marched down the leafy lane to the very proper Spencers' lovely bungalow with its perfectly clipped and manicured garden, overlooking the Bay. Heart pounding, I knocked on the kitchen door. It was opened by Lillian Spencer!

Chapter Four

As I stood there, confronted by Lillian Spencer in the flesh, I had a panic attack. "Maura", I said to myself, "what do you think you are doing here? You must be crazy! Time to make some excuse, any excuse, and get out of here." Instead, I found myself saying, "Hello, Mrs Spencer, I wonder if I could have a word with you about a matter that concerns us?" "Of course, of course, do come in," Lillian ushered me into the kitchen.

I took a deep breath and launched into my little speech. "Well, as you know, Lillian, Gina has been spending a lot of time with us over the past year. She gets along well with Ben and Amy and we enjoy having her around. Well, I've been thinking about what you said when I was in the drugstore the other day, about not having room for Gina anymore and possibly her father won't be able to keep her. You see, we really care for Gina and we want to see her happy, so if it turns out that her father can't keep her, then we would be happy to have her come to live with us."

As I paused to catch my breath, Lillian walked out of the kitchen and down the hall where she opened what I presumed was the living room door and called "Henry – oh Henry, can you come into the kitchen for a moment." After a brief pause, a bespectacled Henry Spencer appeared, book in hand, and Lillian led him into the kitchen, "Henry", Lillian continued, "this is Mrs Kerry – you know -the Kerrys where Gina has been spending a lot of time --- well Mrs Kerry has come over to say that if Max can't keep Gina, then the Kerrys would be happy to have her come to live with them..:" I waited tensely for Henry's reply. "Oh, I say, Mrs Kerry," said Henry smiling quite benevolently, "how jolly decent of you!". " Of course," said Lillian, "we will need to call Max. If it's agreeable to you, we'll call you after that". I could see that Henry wanted to get back to his book, so I quickly gave Lillian our telephone number and I left for home,

Walking back up the leafy lane, I tried to work out how I felt. I was relieved that the Spencers had not kicked me out as an interfering busybody, yet for some inexplicable reason, I felt a bit sad. Possibly that was because they hadn't kicked me out?! At any rate, nothing was decided, and nothing could be decided until the Spencers spoke to 'Max'. And of course, I wouldn't discuss anything with Ben and Amy until we knew definitely what Max's decision was. In the meantime, his holiday now over, Steve left for home and the office.

Two evenings later, Lillian called. Max had decided that he couldn't keep Gina and he was sending her back on the ferry on Friday evening. The Spencers wanted to discuss my proposal further, so I invited them over for a "cup of tea".

Lillian and Henry Spencer arrived at our back door the next afternoon while Ben and Amy were visiting a neighbour whose friendly sheepdog had just produced 9 puppies.

Ever the 'absent-minded professor' type, Henry was wearing grey flannels, a white shirt, and a blazer with the Sandy Bay College emblem embroidered on the breast pocket. He was a big man with piercing black eyes behind his thick-rimmed glasses, bushy white eyebrows and somewhat tousled, longish hair. By contrast, in her sixties, Lillian Spencer was still an attractive woman, with finely chis-eled features, a wide mouth, blue eyes, and wavy shoulder-length greying hair that resembled Gina's. Neatly clad in white slacks and a matching tailored blouse, Lillian was one of those women who always look smart.

I showed them into our somewhat untidy living room where we all sat in rather awkward silence. How to begin? Finally, I said, "So I gather Max is Gina's father and he lives in Vancouver?"

Lillian began, "Yes, Mrs Kerry, Julia married Max in 1963 when she was 19 years old. Max used to come over to Sandy Bay in the sum-mer. Anyway, they lived in Vancouver. Max works at the hospital."

"Yes, Mrs Kerry", Henry interrupted, "Julia was much too young when she married Max. She had planned to continue her education...."

"Gina was born in 1962," continued **Lillian**, "The three of them used to visit every summer. Gina was a lovely baby."

"Yes, indeed, she still is lovely", I said.

"Unfortunately, their marriage broke up in 1967 when Gina was 5 years old", Lillian continued, "Gina visited with Max quite often. Julia had a difficult time, though --- with being a single mother, I mean. She had a few part-time jobs.

"She should have started taking night courses and continued her education. That's what she needed to do....", Henry commented.

"Julia moved around a lot," said Lillian. "Anyway, around about 1970, I think it was, she moved to Winnipeg. We more or less lost touch with her for quite a while. I think she had a boyfriend who moved there for work. While she was living there, she had the other two little ones --- Scott and Lucy" Lillian concluded.

"Yes," I said, "Gina has mentioned them to us. I think she said Scott is three or four and Lucy is two. I understand they are all still in Winnipeg. Gina told me that her mom isn't well."

"Yes, yes," said Lillian, "It has all been rather a problem. We didn't know a thing about it until we received a call from Social Services in Winnipeg when Julia was in hospital.

"And they needed a place for the three children until Julia was better", said Henry. "Of course, we have never met the other two children," he continued, "so we weren't comfortable with taking them. They were only one and three at that time, you see. But we did decide to help out by taking Gina."

"So Henry flew to Winnipeg and brought Gina back here", said Lillian.

"And that must have been the summer that we met Gina!" I spoke.

"Yes, well, as you know, she IS our granddaughter, but we are long past the age of bringing up children, so it hasn't been easy," Lillian explained.

"But we've jolly well done our best", added Henry.

"Of course, we never imagined that Gina would be with us for such a long time" Lillian continued. "but it seems that poor Julia had been having to manage on her own and she had become very depressed and run down as a result. I'm afraid they don't feel that Julia can take the children back yet."

"Yes. While school is in, having Gina with us was quite manageable, but given the situation, we were at a loss as to how to manage the summer," said Henry. " That's when we decided that it was time for someone else in the family to take Gina on. This past summer, we sent Gina to see her Grandmother Niemann in Langley."

"That didn't work out at all," said Lillian. "She sent her back after 10 days. Gina was much too active for her."

"After that, we sent her for a couple of weeks to Jeff and Gwen – he's our son --- they have two children and a ranch up in the Cariboo. I think Gina loved it there, but apparently Gwen found Gina hard to handle --- so she came back to us", Henry added.

"Really", said Lillian, "sending her to Max was our best hope. He remarried a couple of years ago and we thought that if they kept Gina, it would make a nice little family. But that hasn't worked – unfortunately."

And then you walked in and offered to have her and solved all our problems for us!" exclaimed Henry jovially.

Yes, I'm sure Gina will be just fine with you. We'll let Social Services know and they can get in touch with you to do the paperwork. There should be no problem with that," Lillian reassured us.

"Well," I ventured, "what about Gina? Will she be okay with it?"

"Oh, my dear," Lillian exclaimed, "we've already told her over the phone, and she is thrilled to bits!"

There wasn't really too much to add after that. Just the routine stuff. As soon as Gina returned, the Spencers would help her pack her things, and send her over to our house, just in time to return to the mainland and get ready for school.

After that, we shared a cup of tea, discussed music (Henry was retired and played the organ at the Sandy Bay Anglican church) and agreed that the weather had been lovely that summer.

There was a kind of aura of unreality to the evening's events, but perhaps that was just the way I felt? Tomorrow I would call Steve and then I would sit down to talk about their new 'sister' with Ben and Amy.

Gina bounced onto our doorstep within minutes of arriving back from visiting her father on the mainland. Right away, she wanted to know when could she bring all her 'stuff' over, and could she spend the last few days of the holidays with us? "Well," I said, 'if it's okay with your grandparents....". "Oh yes, Mom, it's fine with them". It seemed somehow natural that she would call me "mom".

We had two sets of bunk beds in the children's bedroom, and Gina was soon installed in one of the lower ones, with her "stuff" piled high on the upper bunk. The remaining days of August quickly vanished. I brought out the lists of school supplies and the kids and I made a shopping trip to nearby Nanaimo, finishing the day with supper at Grant's Cafe where the lemon meringue pie was 'to die for'.

The car stuffed to the roof and house locked up, we returned to the mainland just before Labour Day and began sorting books and labelling clothes for 'back to school'. Ben and Amy showed Gina around the house. Upstairs was the master bedroom, Ben's room and Amy's room. The main floor had an entrance hall, living room, dining room, kitchen, laundry room and washroom (with shower). On the lower level was the family room, a spare bedroom and storage room. The spare bedroom now became Gina's. "My very first bedroom of my own!" she informed me ecstatically.

Our life together as an 'expanded' family now really began, and over the coming weeks and months, we began to learn that when you unexpectedly add another child to your family, and when that child is older than the existing children, there is going to be a period of adjustment for all concerned. We were no exception.

PART II

The Kerry Rules

Chapter Five

The period of adjustment began on Day One of 'back to school'. Off went the three of them, bright-eyed and bushy-tailed, to Pine Park Primary School, five blocks away down a very steep hill. Amy began Grade 1, Ben was now in Grade 3 and Gina was registered in Grade 6. As usual, Ben and Amy arrived home just after lunch (because it was the first day back), told me it all went well for Gina and thumped down to the family room. But there was no sign of Gina. Ben said he had noticed her talking with a group of girls, so I wasn't particularly concerned until she hadn't returned by the time I began preparing supper. At that point, I made a few calls to friends who had children around Gina's age, but they hadn't seen her. I began to feel stressed. Then, just as I was thinking about calling the police, the door opened and Gina walked in!

"Hi, Mom" She smiled.

"Oh, Gina, thank God you're okay. Where have you been?" I demanded.

"Oh, some of the girls took me down to show me the park at the pier", she replied. "It's nice there".

"But I was getting worried when you didn't come home after school", I said. I think by my tone of voice, she realized that I was quite stressed.

"I'm really sorry, Mom," she said, "was I supposed to come home after school?"

Then I realized -- of course, she didn't know! How could she know? Before she came to live with us, Gina had been able to come and go as she wanted. The idea that someone else might be concerned and want to know where she was going and also might set a time when she should return, was almost completely unknown to her. I should have thought about that sooner. She would have to learn about that. Someone would have to teach her!

So it began, the 'education' of Gina. And it wasn't without its problems. As the self-appointed 'chief educator', I was the one who had to introduce Gina to what could only be described as "The Kerry Family Rules". When you grow up in a family, very little 'formal' training is needed because you learn them from mom, dad, teachers, etc. as you go along. Now I was finding out how difficult it is to adjust your life to live by a set of "rules" when you have been living for twelve years with hardly any. I also began to realize that when you have been living with such a degree of freedom, you have no way of developing a true sense of time. If you can do something when you wish, at any time you wish, the actual time of day simply doesn't matter.

For both Gina and myself, in particular, it was rough! Think of all the rules in a reasonably structured family lifestyle. Rules about: Time to get up, time to eat meals, time to go to school, time to be home after school, time to tidy up your room, time to wash and brush your teeth, time to watch TV, permission to go somewhere and with who, time to return from outings, We were used to all of the rules, but for Gina, it was a whole new way of living and it wasn't comfortable. For instance, there was a long struggle to get Gina to pick up a bunch of pencils from the family room floor. She had been doing a diagram and when they fell on the floor, Gina simply hadn't noticed. When I asked her to pick them up, she didn't feel like doing so. Picking up things from floors was a new idea for Gina. When I explained my reasons, Gina just glowered back. There was an argument. Finally, she picked them up and put them away. You might, of course, argue that picking up pencils from a floor was hardly worth creating such a big issue, but when two younger children are observing whether or not the eldest is required to keep the rules, then how the matter is finally resolved becomes extremely important. Time had to be spent explaining why it was important for all of us to keep these rules. Why? Because we ALL wanted to live together happily; and if one of us didn't keep the rules, it wasn't fair to the others. Anyway, that was my reasonable explanation and they accepted it!

It was a big load to put on a 12-year-old. Gina did her best. Some days were good and other days were difficult. At times there was friction because Ben and Amy felt that Gina was expecting everyone to reorganize around her wishes. So we had to work on that also. Steve was pretty good about it, but he got impatient. He felt that Gina wasn't grateful and should do more to help in the house. Somehow, his attitude wasn't at all what I had expected because Steve himself had grown up without the benefit of living in a family. My mother's attitude was similar to Steve's. This came as a shock. I began to realize that somewhere at the back of my mind, I had just assumed Steve and my mom would feel exactly as I did and support me all the way. Not so. This realization left me feeling 'out there on my own' but it never in any way changed my original wish to provide a stable and happy home for a lonely child. With perseverance, little by little, as family life became easier for Gina, it became happier for us all.

As the weeks went by, I was contacted by Family Services and interviewed by our Case Worker, Mrs Mercer, a middle-aged lady, who was starting the process of approving us as a foster family. I learned that Gina's grandparents were approved foster parents and had been receiving financial support from Social Services. As part of the approval process, Mrs Mercer visited us, looked at our house and Gina's room, chatted with Gina and obtained information from me about our family situation, etc. Everything went well and we expected to be officially approved by Christmas. I also received a call from Max Niemann, Gina's father, who wanted Gina to spend a weekend with him and his wife, Laura. I already knew that Gina enjoyed visiting her dad, so we made arrangements .I met him for the first time when he came to pick her up on a Friday evening.

I liked Max from the beginning. Slim and medium-height, he had dark, curly hair, sharp features, and kind, brown eyes. "I feel really bad that I couldn't keep Gina," he said, "but I'm married again and to be frank, I really want to have a peaceful family life." He continued, "Since Julia and I divorced, Gina has come to visit from time to time and each time her behaviour has been worse. With Julia, she was used to running wild. The last time she visited, she was light-fingered and began stealing change out of my coat pockets.

That bothered me. At one point I spoke to Julia about maybe having sole custody of Gina. I thought that if Gina came to me, she might settle down and Julia would be able to manage the other little ones better. But it was useless."

"What happened?" I asked.

"Julia got angry and said that she would never give me custody of Gina. She even said that if I tried to apply for custody, she would tell the court that I wasn't Gina's real father. It's a lie – but that's the kind of thing Julia does. Look, I'm sorry I can't step in to take care of her, but if I can help in other ways – like if she needs a bicycle or school stuff --- things like that – then I hope you'll let me know and I will help out."

Max lived up to his offer and I respected his honesty. He was manager of the laundry at a large hospital. It was clear that he genuinely cared about his daughter and wanted to be a positive influence in her life. Laura was supportive, too. Gina was always happy when she spent time there. That was important.

In the meantime, Gina and I were becoming closer, and from out of this closeness she began to share with me a lot of confidences and tell me things she had never before shared with anyone at all.

PART III

Confidences

Chapter Six

Starting, I suppose from the time they began talking, I began a kind of bedtime ritual with the children. After bath time, I would sit on the edge of the bed, tuck each of them in, and then we would have a little chat about such things as how their day had gone, maybe they would tell me about something that had happened at school, or perhaps they had a question that needed answering. Whatever the conversation, it was a one-to-one quiet, sharing time before sleep; we would finish with a simple prayer for our family and thanks for all the blessings we shared. Then it was time for lights out and goodnight.

When Gina joined us, I began this bedtime ritual with her. Because she was the eldest with no one else to follow, there were fewer time constraints. So from these nightly conversations, little by little, Gina shared her story with me.

One of our first conversations was all about friends. I had asked Gina how things were going at school. After all, she was a new girl, and I hoped that she was getting along well with her teacher and making some new friends.

"Oh yes, mom. Mrs Brown is very nice to me and helps me when I get a bit stuck, and I've met a girl called April Duncan. She is nice and she wants me to play at her house after school, but she has to ask her mom first."

"That's great," I said, "and of course you have to ask me if you can go. Right?". "Right," said Gina, "But mom, there's something I have been wondering about a lot and could I ask you about it".

"Okay," I said, "tell me what it is".

"Well, it's like this," she said, "When I was at school in Sandy Bay after I came to live with my grandparents, I was a new girl there, and I had a lot of trouble making friends".

"Oh," I said, "what was the problem?'

"Well, that's just it, mom, I never could work out why. There was this one girl, Gail, that I really liked and when I asked her if we could be friends, she just said, 'oh, no, I can't be friends with you!". Gina continued, "But when I asked her why not, she just said 'that's for me to know and you to find out', but, mom, I never did find out. Why couldn't she be my friend? I liked her so much".

As I listened, I had the sudden sinking feeling most of us get when confronted by unkindness. I could guess why Gail couldn't be friends. In a small place like Sandy Bay, Gina's mother's history was well known and there are always small-minded people in the world who consider themselves superior and above associating with anyone they believe to be inferior to them. That had a lot to do with why Gail couldn't or wouldn't be friends. How could I tell Gina this hurtful truth? Not right here, not right now. She was far from ready for that.

So I said, "Some kids have parents who decide what friends their children can have and sometimes this is not what their children want, but in the end, they have to do what their parents say. So don't feel bad if this kind of thing happens to you again. I'm sure you would have been a good friend, so they are the losers. And I hope YOU will never say that kind of thing to anyone who wants to be your friend. Just remember, the best way to have a good friend, is to be a good friend. Okay?"

"Okay, mom"

"Feel better now?"

"Yes, mom" And then it was a prayer and lights out.

Then there was the matter of schoolwork. After Gina joined our family and had begun Grade 6 at Pine Park, I had a short meeting with her teacher, Mrs Brown, to find out how Gina was getting along. Mrs Brown said that Gina was doing well, that she enjoyed class, got along well with others, had a bright and sunny nature, and liked to contribute to discussions. She did remark, however, that in some areas of math and particularly in reading, Gina struggled. No, Mrs Brown didn't feel Gina had any learning disabilities, but for some reason, she had difficulty in those areas.

Gina knew that I was meeting with Mrs Brown so of course at bedtime she asked me, "What did Mrs Brown say, mom? Am I doing okay?"

"Yes, Gina, Mrs Brown says you're getting along well and that you are a good student. But she did say that you're having a bit of difficulty with some of the math, and also with your reading, but she's sure you'll catch up."

"Yes, mom, I know. I've had a lot of trouble catching up. Ever since I started school in Winnipeg."

"Was there a problem with your teacher?"

"Well, my teacher was nice, but the biggest problem I had was that I was always in trouble!"

"In trouble? Why?"

"Well, you see mom, before we went to Winnipeg, we moved around a lot, so I didn't start school at all until we moved to Winnipeg. Then I think someone told my mom that I should go to school, so I went to Phillips Primary. But they didn't understand that I had never been to school before, and they put me in Grade 3. I didn't know how to read at all and I tried to explain that I had to stay home and help with Scott and Lucy, but they just didn't believe me."

"But didn't your mom write a note? And didn't your mom read stories to you and Scott and Lucy?"

"No, my mom didn't write a note. You see, my mom doesn't allow books. She says they have wrong ideas. We never had books at home. That's why I just loved all the books in your house at Sandy Bay. You have so many great books!" (And I remembered Gina sitting on the couch and reading them all!)

"So what happened at school in Winnipeg?"

"Well, mom, we finally got another teacher and she listened to me. She made time for the two of us to stay after school so that she could help me learn and catch up my reading."

"So, you were 8 years old when you began school. Is that right."

"Yup".

Well Gina, considering all the catching up you've had to do, I would say that you are an amazing girl! Take a bow! Woohooo for you. And Gina...... just keep on doing well. I'll explain this to Mrs Brown and I know she'll understand and help you all she can".

"Good night, mom"

"Good night big brain!! "(Giggles)

And of course, the topic of trips came up during one of our bedtime conversations.

"Trips are great,' expounded Gina. "I enjoyed all my trips this summer."

'What trips?" I asked.

"Well, I didn't see much of you this summer because I was away on trips," said Gina.

"Oh, yes."

"First I was invited to visit my Nona. That's my other grandma – my dad's mom. She is an artist and when I stayed with her she taught me a lot about painting and we went to the park to sketch, and to art galleries."

"Did you like it?".

"Oh yes," it was all very interesting. I wanted to stay longer but my Nona got tired, so I had to go back to Sandy Bay. Then I got invited to visit Aunty Gwen and Uncle Jeff. They have a ranch up north. It was great. Their kids are older than me and I **suppose** we argued a lot. But I got to ride horses and even gallop. I loved it. But I could only stay two weeks because they had to go to Calgary to visit cousins."

"It sounds like a lot of fun.

"After that, I went to visit my dad and Laura in Vancouver. Laura is nice. My dad and I really get along. Every time I visit them. I have a great time."

"And after that?"

"(**Deletion**)After that my grandparents called my dad and said that you had come along and wanted me to live with your family."

"So................," I said.

"And the rest is history", she smiled back.

"Good history, I hope?"

"Yup!"

"Good night, Gina"

"Night, mom".

She had no idea at all that those 'trips' were actually "test runs" to see if either Nona, her aunt and uncle, or her father would 'keep' her; nor did she know that she'd received a universal thumbs down. I sincerely hoped she would never find out.

There were many of these bedtime conversations, each one revealing the happenings in her life, as seen through the eyes of a twelve-year-old girl. Confusion, stress, anxiety with no outlet for expression, no ears to hear, no one to explain. For the most part a struggle. Just when I began to feel that I had a really good understanding of Gina's prior life and where she was 'coming from', we had a bedtime conversation that revealed her feelings in a whole new light. Once again, we were talking about life in Winnipeg, and about things that happened when she was looking after Scott and Lucy. When I asked her how she had kept them amused, Gina said: "Oh, you know how I like making up games. Well, I made up easy little games that even Lucy could play, and we sometimes drew pictures...."

"So you all got along well, then?" I asked.

"Well, when it was just Scott and Lucy and me, it was fine. But when my mom was at home, it wasn't so good."

"Didn't she like the games?".

"Well, my mom was sort of moody."

"Maybe she was tired after working all day."

"Maybe, but sometimes it was really scary."

"Scary? How do you mean?"

"Well, mom, one night I woke up because my mom was screaming and screaming..."

"Screaming! What was wrong?"

"I just don't know. I got up and went into the bedroom and she was yelling and throwing things and when she saw me, she got really mad and told me to "get out! Get out!"

"So did you go back to your room."

"Well, no, you see I didn't have a room. There was one bedroom and my mom and Scott, and Lucy slept in there."

"But where did you sleep?"

Just near our front door, we had a big cardboard box and that was my bed."

'So did you go back there."

"No, I didn't. I was worried about Scott and Lucy because they were in the bedroom with my mom, and she was making a lot of noise and I was afraid they would wake up and be scared."

"What did you do?"

"I went back to the bedroom to see if Scott and Lucy were okay."

"And......"

"And my mother started yelling again and telling me to get out and go away."

"So...."

"So, I was really scared, and I opened the door and went out onto the sidewalk."

"Where did you go?"

"I had a friend, Lori, who lived about 3 houses away and they had a basement door, so I decided to go there."

"Did Lori help you?"

"Well, it was the middle of the night and everyone was asleep. But the door was open, and they had a couch in the basement play-room, and I found a blanket and fell asleep there".

"All night.................?"

"Yes, all night. I woke up very early, though, and then I thought I should go home and see if Scott and Lucy were okay. And maybe my mom was asleep. So, I went back out onto the street and started walking back to our basement."

"And were things okay when you got back?"

"Well, mom, that's just it. A police car came along and saw me on the sidewalk, and they stopped me."

'They did?"

"I guess it was because I was still in my nighty. They wanted to know what I was doing outside in my nighty and bare feet....it was all snowy and twenty below......."

"I see."

"So, they put me in the police car and I showed them where I lived."

"What happened?"

"I had to stay in the police car. One policeman went inside and after a while, he came out and an ambulance came. And then they brought my mom and Scott and Lucy out. My mom was still mad. She shouted at me and Lucy started to cry, and then they got into the ambulance and drove away."

"Didn't you go, too?"

"No. The police took me to Social Services, and I think they called my grandpa because I spoke to him and he said he was coming to get me and bring me home with him."

"And what happened to your mom and the kids?"

"**(DELETION)**I think my mom went to hospital and Scott and Lucy went to care. I don't know."

"And your grandfather came and took you back to Sandy Bay?"

"Yes"

"So, you didn't see your mom before you left Winnipeg?"

"No. But I know she was still mad at me."

"Mad at you?' Why would she be mad at you?"

"Because it was all my fault!"

"All your fault?"

"Well, if I hadn't been walking along in my nighty and the police hadn't found me, nothing would have happened."

"Oh, Gina, I'm sure your mom doesn't think it was your fault."

"Oh yes, she does. She even yelled at me when they put her in the ambulance. And she has never called me since my grandpa came and got me, or written a note, or anything."

Tears glistened.

"Well, Gina, I think you just might be wrong about that. Your grandma and grandpa love you. Ben and Amy love you, we ALL love you. And I'm sure your mom loves you. You are a great girl!"

"Do you think so, mom?"

"Yes, I do. I KNOW so!"

We said our usual goodnight prayer. I hugged her close. Afterwards, I went downstairs and began folding laundry and I cried into Ben's big yellow T-shirt!

As the days and weeks passed and Gina began settling into daily life in what I at least considered a relatively normal family, there were ups and downs. None of us is perfect, but thanks to the good nature of the rest of my family, we made progress. My mother and Steve complained at times about what they called Gina's 'lack of appreciation'. I agreed that to some extent, they were right. On the other hand, from my point of view, what was happening had nothing whatsoever to do with 'appreciation'. It was all about helping a disadvantaged, unappreciated small girl to feel wanted and loved, and providing a 'friendly ear' to listen. I had become that 'friendly ear'. Mine was the ear that shared the outpourings of a little girl's heart.

PART IV

Uprooted Again

Chapter Seven

In November, we decided to get out of the rain and cold and go to Hawaii for Christmas. This would be the first trip overseas by air for all three children and there was great excitement. We were scheduled to visit Maui, leaving on December 19 and returning on January 3. We would stay in a condo, Steve would do some golfing and the kids and I would enjoy the beach and whatever else was interesting.

December arrived, and all the excitement of Christmas and preparations for our Hawaiian holiday began. Since we were leaving on the 19th, we dispensed with putting up a tree and lights and concentrated on keeping up to date with chores and working on little gifts for the friends and family left at home in 'cold' Canada.

Everything was going well. We seemed to have gotten over the initial 'hump' with Gina, who was now used to the family 'rules'. Since September, we had dealt with a lot of 'stuff' and now it was time to kick off our shoes and hit the beach. Excitement reigned; at least it reigned until the second week in December when the telephone rang. I answered it.

A low, quiet voice spoke: "Hello, Mrs Kerry, this is Julia. I understand that Gina has been living with you since September?"

"Yes............", I was speechless!

"It's good of you to have Gina stay. I'm back home now at Sandy Bay. Could I speak to Gina? Can you put her on the phone?"

When I called Gina and told her who it was, her face lit up with joy. She grabbed the phone, "Hi Mum", where are you. How are Scott and Lucy?. There was a pause, then **(DELETION)** "I guess so. Okay." She handed the phone back to me.

"My mom's back at Sandy Bay!" she said, "and she wants me to come home. When can I go?"

I spoke to Julia: "Gina tells me you want her to come home. I'll have to get in touch with Social Services here and ask them to contact you..."

"Good", said Julia, "please talk to them as soon as possible. I want her to come home before Christmas".

"Fine. I......." "Before I could finish my sentence, the line clicked shut.

This was something none of us had expected. It was a surprise. It was also quite a shock to see the joy that enveloped Gina. All of this, despite everything in the past. I think that was the moment when I learned a very valuable thing: ALL CHILDREN LOVE THEIR MOTHER, NO MATTER WHAT! Often incredible, but always true. But alas when something in that mother/child relationship goes wrong, it's a real tragedy for any child. Although I had children of my own, I hadn't known that before.

I called Mrs Mercer and made arrangements for her to pick Gina up so that she could be returned to Sandy Bay where her mother, Scott and Lucy were living in a small motel across the road from the public beach. Four days later, all thoughts of Hawaii happily forgotten, Gina packed her bags, gave each of us a big hug, promised to write, and left for Sandy Bay. And three days after that, the Kerry family left for the warm sunshine of Maui.

We had a great time in our condo, cooked a butterball turkey for Christmas dinner, drove to the town of Hana over 100 bridges, spent a lot of time at the beach trying to snorkel, met neighbours from home who were also spending Christmas in the sun, and generally enjoyed our holiday. It did feel a little odd going back to having two children. Gina had been a very lively addition that was now noticeably absent. I hoped that going 'home' would turn out as happily as she expected, but I felt uneasy. Oh well, no longer our problem. Right?

We returned to damp and fog: Nasty old January! School and the daily routine resumed as did my part-time job. I worked Monday through Friday, leaving the house after the children and returning just after they got home from school. It was ideal – giving me interesting work and extra money for trips and other extras for the family.

My employer was also very understanding, giving me the summer months off so that we could continue to spend them at Sandy Bay.

Around mid-January, after a heavy fall of snow, I went to the mailbox and found an envelope in Gina's writing. It was a sad little letter!

Gina wrote: "December 28: Dear Mom, I hope you get this letter soon and that you all had a great time in Hawaii. We visited my grandparents on Christmas Day but my mom had an argument with my grandma and we didn't stay for dinner. Things aren't going very well since I got back. My mom keeps me home a lot from school like before, so I help with Scott and Lucy but I don't want to get behind again with my schoolwork and I don't know what to do. Could I come back to live with you again? I miss you all so much. Do you think you could ask Mrs Mercer to bring me back over to you? Love, Gina xoxoxoxoxox to everyone. PS, Please let me know something soon."

My heart sank. Julia had custody of Gina. I didn't think there was any chance that Gina could be returned to us. What could I do? I stewed over it for a day, trying to work out a plan. Finally, I called Mrs Mercer, read Gina's letter to her, and asked her if maybe some help could be given through the school counsellors at Sandy Bay.

Then I decided that maybe I could take the ferry over and visit Gina for a day at Sandy Bay. The motel had no phone, but I could call Lillian and ask her to help arrange something. Hopefully, Lillian could talk to Julia. I thought that if I took Gina out, we could have a meal and talk and I could explain about her mother having custody, and, hopefully, I could encourage her to make the best of the situation. I could also tell her that I was trying to get help through the school counsellors.

At least I had a plan!

Chapter Eight

Arranging a day visit and outing with Gina wasn't easy. First of all, I called Lillian, told her that I had received a letter from Gina and I would like to go over to Sandy Bay and arrange to take Gina out for the day. From what Lillian said, I gathered that she didn't have a great deal of communication with Julia but she said that she would try to talk to her. I gathered that they weren't on friendly terms. Apparently, it would depend on Julia's mood when asked, so I needed some luck!

After that, I called Mrs Mercer and told her I was arranging to spend a day with Gina at Sandy Bay. Mrs Mercer confirmed that as long as there were no serious problems, there was no basis to interfere with Julia's custody.

And then I waited.

A week or so later, Lillian called to say that Julia was agreeable to me visiting Sandy Bay the following Saturday, and I could take Gina out for the afternoon. Ben and Amy sent along some "Hi Gina" cards and I took the Saturday morning ferry, arriving at Sandy Bay just before lunch. Hobbit Court Motel had a straight row of older cabins just across the highway and facing the angle parking at the main public area of the Sandy Bay beach. She must have been watching for the car because Gina came running down the steps of Cabin 4 as I pulled up outside. There was no sign of Julia or the other children. I jumped out, expecting to finally meet Julia. "Mum's gone to the store with Scott and Lucy," said Gina, giving me a joyful hug. "I have to be back by 6 o'clock".

Gina was all smiles and seemed at first to be her usual vivacious self. As we turned onto the highway, I wondered aloud where would she like to go, what would she like to do..............?" She had worked that out in advance. "Please, mom, can we go to the steakhouse in Nanaimo."

I smiled. Her top pick was still a big, juicy steak! As we headed for Nanaimo and the TeeBone steakhouse, she opened their "Hi Gina" cards, and we talked about Ben and Amy and what we did in Hawaii. Then we fell silent. After spending an hour or with her, I was noticing that Gina was quite pale, her lovely wavy hair was dull and straggly, her clothes were soiled and crumpled. She was nothing like the happy girl who left us just over a month ago.

In the warmth of the steakhouse, out of the cold January day, while she attacked her steak with great pleasure, I asked Gina how it was going at home.

"Not good, Mom", she mumbled through a mouthful.

"So, tell me about it".

"Well, Mom, it's my mom. She gets mad if I want to eat meat...." She waved her loaded fork at me.

"What do you eat, then?", I asked.

"Oh --- just whatever seems to come into my mom's mind. Sometimes she asks Scott what we should eat for supper, and if he says 'bananas', then we have bananas! ----- Mom, can you please take me back with you. I just can't live with my mom any longer. I thought when she came back and wanted me to come home that things would be different, but they're not."

I tried to explain the matter of custody to Gina, that her mother had a lot of problems and that Gina must try to understand and help more. I told her that I couldn't help but that I had spoken to Mrs Mercer about the problem of getting to school and Mrs Mercer was going to try to help through school. But all the time I was talking, that pale little face and those still-beautiful violet eyes looked up at me and I just felt helpless. It was clear that Gina wasn't getting a healthy diet. I was worried about her, but I tried not to show it.

We made the best of our day together. This included a trip to the supermarket where Gina stocked up on energy bars and other 'treats' She told me some people had given them a gift of a television set, but her mother had thrown it out "into the garbage can". Then we discussed some books she might be able to find and read in the library at school.

Around 5:30 p.m., we arrived back at Hobbit Court and we hugged goodbye. Julia came to the top of the steps and waved. Even from a distance, I could see a resemblance. She had the same wavey blonde hair. I was too far away to see her eye colour, but she was a good-looking woman, and it was clear to me that Gina was going to be even more attractive than her mother.

As the ferry 'rocked' its way back to the mainland, I tried to console myself. "Well, anyway, we would be back at the cottage by June, and we would all see Gina then. That was something to look forward to, wasn't it?

Chapter Nine

The next morning, I called Mrs Mercer, described my concerns and asked what she could do to help. She said she would have Social Services at Sandy Bay check out Gina's living conditions. And she would contact Gina's school. After that, I waited. Three weeks went by and still nothing from Mrs Mercer and nothing from Gina. I was anxious. Then, on the Saturday of week four, the telephone rang. Amy answered it.

"Here, mum, it's Gina's grandma," Amy handed the phone to me.

"Hello", I said in surprise.

(We were always formal): "Oh, Mrs Kerry," came Lillian Spencer's voice, "I'm sorry to bother you, but it's ...Gina...."

"Is she okay?" Every time I heard from Lillian Spencer, I got alarmed.

"Well, no, not exactly. It's just that it's happened again...."

"What's happened again?". Now I was alarmed.

"It's Julia. She's gone."

"Gone? Gone where?" I was incredulous.

"We don't know," said Lillian, "When Gina came home from school yesterday, Julia and the little ones were gone".

"What about Gina?", I wondered aloud.

"Well, Julia left all her things in a box in their kitchen, and Gina didn't know where to go so she walked over to our house." (short silence) "She wants to come back to you......."

"And you still don't know where Julia and the little ones have gone?".

"No, we don't. Julia didn't say anything to Gina. She just came home after school and they were gone and her things were there in the cardboard box."

My mind was whirling around. "Is Gina there? Can I talk to her?".

Then Gina spoke. It was a quiet little voice. "Hi mom, can you come and get me? I'm all packed."

"Well, okay, Gina. Dad's away on a business trip, but Ben and Amy and I will come over to Sandy Bay…. I guess tomorrow…….. on an early ferry. Okay?"

"That's very okay!", the voice was a little brighter.

"Can you put your Grandmother back on for a minute", I asked.

Then, to Lillian, "Lillian, the kids and I will come over on the ferry tomorrow. Have you have notified Social Services? Gina **can** come back to us, but after what's happened, I want some assurance that she won't suddenly have to return to Julia after a couple of months. It's not fair to her or our family."

"Yes, I agree," she replied, "I've already spoken with Social Services. They tell me they will apply for a temporary order to place Gina in your custody, but it's the weekend and you'll probably need to stay for a day or so and wait for a judge."

"Great, then we'll be over tomorrow. I'll call you then."

Ben and Amy were happy at the idea of a ferry trip and bringing Gina back to live at our house. We were up and away to the ferry terminal early next morning, however, the entire trip became a bit of a nightmare because we had a heavy snowfall overnight, the roads were a mess and the ferry line-up was horrific. This meant I had to arrange a dog-sitter for Tessa because Steve was away and I didn't want a damp, hairy dog in the car. So we muffled ourselves up in our ski jackets and snow boots and made it to the ferry terminal in record time. There was a lot of snow to shovel when we arrived at the cottage but we worked fast; Ben carried in some wood from the shed, and we were soon sitting in front of a roaring fire.

After I called Lillian, she dropped off Gina and her belongings about half an hour later. We had a joyful reunion. I made some hot chocolate and we all sat together around the fire, the kids chatting and laughing, me feeling pretty tired. Gina looked even paler than when I had last seen her just over a month ago. She had some kind of ear infection, there were dark circles under her eyes and from time to time, she coughed. The cough didn't sound at all good and she had lost a lot of weight. She had also developed an odd kind of hobbling gait. When I asked her about it, she said that she had burned the backs of her heels when she put them in the oven of the iron stove in the motel kitchen to warm herself on cold nights, so she couldn't walk properly on the back of her heels! I decided I needed to take her to a doctor when we returned home. Despite all of that, Gina was in great spirits. Her old sparkle was beginning to return. That was so good to see.

We toasted marshmallows. Then Ben and Amy went to get ready for bed and I had a one-on-one chat with Gina. She said that after my visit her mother had become very restless, kind of like when they were in Winnipeg. Gina tried to take Scott and Lucy out for walks with the hope that if her mom had some peace and quiet, she might be calmer. It didn't help. She still felt like her mother was angry with her. And then, finally, she came home from school and they had all left. At first, she thought that maybe her mother was just in one of her moods, but when she looked and saw that absolutely all of Scott and Lucy's things were gone and only her things remained, Gina decided her mom had really gone away for good. The only place Gina could go was to her grandmother's house ---- but really, she just wanted to come back and be in our family again. In a sad little voice, Gina said, "I just can't live with my mom anymore".

On Sunday afternoon, Lillian called to say that she had heard from Social Services and they would be applying for a temporary custody order but we would have to wait. Being a rural area, there was a Circuit Court that served many of the small communities, including Sandy Bay. The next Circuit Court was on Wednesday, so we would have to wait until after morning court, when, all going well, all four of us could return home to the mainland.

Time for a new family experience at our Sandy Bay cottage. What do you do at a summer cottage in winter when the beach is all covered with snow and it is freezing cold outdoors? Well, you stay indoors beside a warm fire. You read books, do jigsaw puzzles, play games, make popcorn, tell ghost stories, make plans for when you return, and hope you will be able to catch up quickly at school. Gina stayed close to me, we sat beside the fire with our arms around each other, we all cuddled up, laughed and giggled together; there was such a good, 'family' feel to it. Perhaps it was because of the cold outside, or the cozy warmth inside, or perhaps it was, simply, one of those rare moments that come unexpectedly, when the true spirit of belonging manifests its healing power. Whatever it was, nothing quite like it had happened before.

Wednesday morning arrived. We packed up the car and headed for the small, square provincial courthouse in nearby Felton. All we had to do was sit in the chilly courtroom while the social worker, Ms Thompson, described what had happened and asked for a temporary order of custody. The order was granted, pending further investigation into the whereabouts of Gina's mother, making it official for Gina to remain with us. After that, we headed to Nanaimo and the ferry for Vancouver.

Now we could get back to a normal life. At least that was the plan. But, as it turned out, 'temporary' was what it was until early April when Lillian Spencer called again. This time, the message was: "Mrs Kerry, so sorry to bother you, but she's back .... Julia's back........ and she wants you to return Gina."

Chapter Ten

When I contacted Social Services, Mrs Mercer was as surprised as I was! Communications with Social Services at Sandy Bay did little to clarify the where, when and why of Julia's return. I spoke again to Lillian Spencer who could only tell me that Julia was staying with friends in a commune at Ash Creek, a rural community about 5 miles away, but Social Services finally managed to locate her.

Towards the end of April, our telephone rang once again. This time it was Mrs Mercer who advised me that a court date had been set for May 26th, at Hilliers, to deal with custody and whether or not to extend the temporary order for her to remain with us. Both Gina and I would have to attend.

"But I won't have to go back to my mom, will I?" was Gina's first response to this news.

"Well, Gina, the judge put you in our care on a temporary basis when your mom went away, but now that she has come back, it will be up to the judge to decide what is best for you and for everyone," was the best reply I could give.

In the intervening period, Julia called several times and spoke to Gina. All the conversations were similar. She told Gina how much they missed her, how they were making little presents for her, how they were looking forward to all being together again. Scott and Lucy took turns on the phone saying "hi". In other circumstances, it would have been a happy time for Gina; but in these circumstances, I could see the tension they were creating, the sense of guilt. I wished the calls would just go away, but regardless of how much they worried me, the truth was that I was just a temporary foster parent and it was the social workers who decided what should happen.

After such a call Gina often would ask: "Will I be able to see my mom and Scott and Lucy?"

"I think so. Your mom will be at the hearing and maybe she will bring them along."

"I'd like to see them, you know. I miss them."

"I know that. So we'll let Mrs Mercer know and ask her if she can arrange it."

"Oh, good", Gina sounded relieved, "I don't want to go back there to live. I just want to see Scott and Lucy and see if they are okay."

I could understand that. After all, for a long time, Gina had played the role of default mother to them.

May 26th fell on the Tuesday following the May long weekend, so Gina and I left together for the cottage on the previous Sunday, while Ben and Amy stayed at home with Steve and Dorrie, my mother.

On arrival at the cottage, we had barely lit the fire and made our beds, when the phone rang. Gina answered, "It's my mom," she said, looking my way, "she wants to pick me up tomorrow and take me to visit with her and Scott and Lucy. Can I go?".

I had to think quickly about this. I didn't have any idea where Julia was living or who was going to do the picking up, because Julia had no car, as far as I knew. And anyway, we were about to have a court hearing and I didn't think it was a good idea to expose Gina to any further emotional pressure.

I said, "Gina, please explain to your mother that I'll have to contact Social Services to see if this is okay. Can she call back later when I've had a chance to do that?"

After the call, I contacted Social Services. I also decided to tell them about the numerous calls Julia had made to Gina since her return. Social Services decided that no visits should take place until after the hearing had concluded. This came as a relief to both Gina and me. Julia wasn't pleased.

The sun peeked out for a while on Monday, so Gina and I took a walk on the beach and popped in to say 'hello' to Henry and Lillian. When I told them Julia had wanted to see Gina, they seemed quite relieved that Gina didn't go. It was clear that Henry didn't approve of Julia's lifestyle and the overall impression I got was that Julia was a giant headache for them. Indeed, the Spencers showed no desire to see either Julia or the little ones. They were happy to see Gina, though!

Chapter Eleven

It was pouring with rain as Gina and I parked outside the old, red-bricked Sandy Bay courthouse early the next morning. We were met by Ms Thompson of Social Services, who took Gina out into the narrow hall, telling us that it wasn't customary to have an underage child who is the subject of a hearing, present in court during the proceedings. I walked in and took a seat at the back of the room which had a pleasant smell of cedar and old leather. There was no sign of Julia. Ms Thompson spoke to a colleague who disappeared outside (to find Julia, I presumed).

Judge Wilson, short, slim and eagle-eyed, entered and took his seat. Still no sign of Julia! A couple of minutes ticked by. Ms Thompson approached the Bench. The judge banged his gavel and asked: "I understand this is your application for custody of the minor child Regina Niemann? Are you ready to proceed Ms Thompson?"

"Yes, Your Honour. Social Services are ready to proceed. We are just waiting for the child's mother, Julia Niemann."

"Well, Ms Thompson, I'm assuming Mrs Niemann was duly notified of this hearing?"

"Yes, Your Honour, but there has been some confusion about Mrs Niemann's whereabouts......and......"

At this point, Julia entered the courtroom accompanied by Ms Thompson's colleague. They both sat down in the front row behind her.

Judge Wilson frowned. "Mrs Niemann, I would like to point out that you are 20 minutes late for this hearing. Are you now ready to proceed?"

"Yes, yes, I am" from Julia.

"Very well. Then you must be aware that the Department of Social Services is applying for custody of your child, Regina Niemann, who is deemed to need a secure home."

Julia sat mute.

"Are you aware, Mrs Niemann?" the judge repeated.

"Yes, sir", Julia whispered.

"Then we will begin. Proceed, Ms Thompson". At this point, Ms Thompson recited the previous history regarding Gina ---in care of grandparents, mother hospitalized, continued domestic difficulties of Mrs Niemann. Finally, abandoned in February and placed in interim custody at the February hearing, pending further investigation.

Ms Thompson concluded with: "Although Mrs Niemann has returned to Sandy Bay and is requesting the return of Regina, Social Services considers that her present circumstances and living conditions are neither satisfactory nor stable. We are therefore applying for an order of temporary custody so that Regina's needs can be properly addressed."

The judge remarked, "I note that Mrs Niemann is here alone.", and to Julia, "Mrs Niemann, do you have anyone here to represent you in this hearing."

"I will be representing myself" Julia replied.

"Very well, Mrs. Niemann, do you have any witnesses to testify on your behalf?"

"No". Then, after a short silence, Julia said, "I will be a witness for myself."

"Well, then, Mrs Niemann, kindly come to the witness stand and be sworn in.

Julia rose slowly and began making her way to the witness box. While this was happening, I spoke briefly to Ms Thompson who told me that when her colleague had gone to the motel to pick Julia up for the hearing, she wasn't there. But the two little ones were there alone! It seems that the door had been left unlocked and the beach was right across from the cottage. When questioned, the manager of the motel said that she had seen Julia walking along the road going in a northerly direction. After making sure Scott and Lucy were being supervised, Ms Thompson drove north where she found Julia walking along the side of the road carrying a bag of groceries. Julia said that she had decided to go to the nearby supermarket for supplies and had simply set off without considering how long it would take. Hence the delay.

"Now, Mrs Niemann", continued the judge, "Ms Thompson here has stated that you abandoned Regina. I understand you weren't at home when she returned after school on the 12th of March. Is that correct?"

"Oh, no, I never abandoned Gina," stated Julia.

"Well, then, Mrs Niemann, where were you when she came home from school?"

"I didn't abandon her," Julia insisted, "I just left without telling her I was going."

"I see". Judge Wilson sounded perplexed. "Where did you go?"

"I went to Winnipeg, Scott and Lucy and I got on the bus to Winnipeg".

"Winnipeg! Why were you going to Winnipeg, Mrs. Niemann?" Silence. "Why did you leave so suddenly?"

"Well, your Honour, I have always felt really happy in Winnipeg. So I decided we should go there."

The judge glanced at his papers, then asked:

"But according to Ms Thompson's report that I have here, you didn't go to Winnipeg, did you? This report says you went to Calgary. Is that right?"

"We were going to Winnipeg. But then we got off the bus in Calgary"

"Why did you get off the bus there?"

"Well, I met this really nice man on the bus, and he said we would be much happier in Calgary, so we got off the bus there."

Judge Wilson frowned. "But I thought you said that you were always happiest in Winnipeg?"

"Well, he seemed to feel that we would be much happier in Calgary, so we got off the bus and stayed with him."

"Ms Thompson's report says that you were at the Women's Shelter in Calgary and they arranged to return you and your two youngest children to British Columbia. Is that true?"

"We had a disagreement with Al, the man we met, and we had to leave his place; so we all went to the Women's Shelter."

"And they arranged to transport you and your infant children back to British Columbia?"

"Yes, that's right".

And where are you living now?'

"I stayed with some friends out at Felton when I arrived and then Social Services arranged for me to live at Hobbit Court again."

"Are you working?"

"No. I'm a full-time mother."

"And now that you have returned, you want Regina to return to live with you?"

"Yes. We love her. Scott and Lucy miss her. She is part of our family."

"But you didn't want to bring her to Winnipeg with you, did you?"

No reply.

"Mrs Niemann, is there anyone who might be able to testify on your behalf, who might support you in your desire to have Regina returned to you."

After a long pause: "Scott and Lucy can testify".

"I'm afraid that's not really what we need here, Mrs Niemann. You can return to your seat now, thank you."

Judge Wilson nodded to Ms Thompson: "There will be a short recess while I review the evidence."

As the judge disappeared into Chambers, Julia went over to Ms Thompson and I could hear her discussing a time to pick up Gina. About fifteen minutes later, Judge Wilson reappeared, and Court was called to order.

"I have reviewed all the evidence carefully, bearing in mind that this application relates to the care and wellbeing of Regina. While I am not unsympathetic to Mrs Niemann's desire to have Regina returned to the family, in my view, more time is needed to assist

Mrs Niemann to take on the additional responsibility of caring for another child. I, therefore, order that Regina remain in the temporary care of the Ministry for Children and Families and that the matter be reviewed at such time as the Ministry deems it appropriate to reconsider the matter of care.'

With that, Court was adjourned.

I was shocked and dismayed. Of course, from what Gina had told me so far, I had realized Julia had some psychological difficulties, but it seems those difficulties were a great deal more serious than I had imagined. I felt relieved that Gina would be remaining with us – at least I assumed that much, but at the same time, I was concerned about the two children remaining with Julia. I began to understand why Gina worried about them also.

When we left the courtroom, Ms Thompson took Gina and me into a small conference room where she explained things to Gina and reassured her that she would be remaining with us and that she would be able to visit with her mom and Scott and Lucy before we returned to the mainland.

As we drove away, both Gina and I were in a happy mood. We were relieved! Later that afternoon, Julia and some of her friends from Felton, picked Gina up and took her for a visit at Hobbit Court where, Gina reported, "We all had pizza!"

Tomorrow Gina and I would return home and settle down to 'normal' life.

PART V

Plain Gailing

Chapter Twelve

Gina settled back happily into a member of the Kerry family. Mrs Mercer told us that we would soon be officially approved as a foster family for Gina. The children were busy at school, Steve and I enjoyed our work and lots of happy family times. Life was normal. Life was peaceful. Life was good.

June arrived. All three children did well in their year-end tests, especially Gina. Since returning from the hearing at the end of May, there had been no communication from Julia. Gina made no mention of her mother to me, and I decided to leave the entire subject alone. Both Gina and I need a rest, I thought.

By the end of June, we were all happy to be back at Sandy Bay once again. The sand seemed sandier, the trees seemed leafier, the cottage seemed even more comfortable than before, or was it just our imagination? Gina told me that she had dropped in to see Henry and Lillian and they were both well. When I was in the drugstore, I had a chat with Lillian. She was pleased that Gina was so happy and doing well at school. She also told me that Julia was no longer living at Sandy Bay. She had met a man who lived at Tofino, some distance away on the west coast of the Island. Julia and the children were living with him. Lillian said she hoped that it would be a long-term relationship, that he had a job in forestry and seemed to be a reliable person. I said I hoped so, too.

The weather in August was just about perfect for the beach. We bought a dinghy which the kids enjoyed rowing up and down while Tessa romped along on the shore barking and trying to keep up with them. I enjoyed my time sunbathing, reading or just sitting staring down the miles of the beach and enjoying all the beauty around me. There were some houses bordering the beach at our end, but most of the time, we were quite alone. One afternoon, Gina appeared with a girl in a blue swimsuit.

"Hi mom, this is Kelsey" – Gina introduced her.

Kelsey was a lively little girl with curly dark flyaway hair, a turned-up nose and rosy cheeks.

"Hi Kelsey", I said, "do you live around here?"

"No, mom. Kelsey lives way up north at Seal Bay," Gina replied.

"Seal Bay – that's quite far. Are you on holiday?" I asked Kelsey.

Gina answered again, "Kelsey used to live here in Sandy Bay. She was my friend when I was going to school here."

"Oh, so you are old friends then?...

"Yes," said Kelsey. My dad's from Sandy Bay and my grandma lives here too. We're down here for a few days to visit my grandma."

"I guess you were surprised to see Gina?"

"I sure was," said Kelsey, "but Gina's grandma told us Gina had gone to live on the Mainland"

"She did?", I asked.

"Yes, my grandma knows Gina's grandma."

"Well, Kelsey," I said, "pleased to meet you. I can see Gina's glad you're here."

"We're going to walk out to the point," said Gina, "is that okay?"

"Yes, it's okay," I said, "but come back up to the house right after that for supper. Maybe Kelsey would be able to come for supper, too? She can call her mom from the house."

Kelsey came for supper and the two girls had a good time together. Before returning home, Kelsey asked if maybe we could all come up to Seal Bay. It's a remote place, but I decided it might be fun, so about a week after that, we packed some overnight things, gassed up the car and, to Gina's delight, set off for Seal Bay.

Before we left, Val Jackson, Kelsey's mom, called and asked me if we could stop at the u-pick at Bar Creek (a fruit farming area on our way) and bring her a bunch of raspberries for jam. So, on our way, we stopped there and all of us spent most of the afternoon picking a great many boxes of raspberries which we loaded carefully into the trunk of my car. That evening, we stopped about 5 minutes' drive from Seal Bay at the Trout River Court, a rather rustic motel

56

with 'outhouses' which caused a great deal of hilarity among my three energetic passengers. I checked us in for two nights, allowing for a whole day visiting Kelsey and her family, and returning to Sandy Bay on Sunday. For supper, we dined at a hamburger stand conveniently located about a block away. The plan was to get up early and drive to Kelsey's house. As it turned out, we didn't leave Trout River Court until after 11:00 a.m. because my three raspberry-eating u-pick enthusiasts had consumed almost as many raspberries as they had picked, resulting in a rush on the 'outhouses' all of which took some time. A lot of nose-holding and hilarity resulted!

The Jacksons, Kelsey, Val and Greg her parents, and Tod, her 15-year-old brother lived in a large log house on a forested side road near the only gas station in Seal Bay. Bosco, 2 hours south by car, was the nearest town for shopping or just about anything. Apart from the gas station, Seal Bay boasted a liquor store and a Seven-Eleven Supermarket. The area itself was wild and beautiful, fishing and forestry being the main source of employment. We all loved the freedom of it.

Val Jackson resembled her daughter, except that her dark hair was short and swept back from her face, and her nose wasn't quite so turned up. She had a warm relaxed manner that put me at ease, and she was delighted with the raspberries. Val suggested we should all go to the picnic ground beside the beach for lunch. She had even made sandwiches and put drinks in the cooler, so we followed her car and were soon enjoying lunch at a picnic table in a grassy spot under a willow tree. After lunch, when the kids set off with Kelsey to explore the beach, Val and I relaxed over coffee.

"It's good to see Gina getting along so well," Val remarked.

"Yes, she's doing just fine", I said. "Kelsey tells us that she and Gina got to be friends at school when Gina came to Sandy Bay"

"Yes, my husband, Greg is from Sandy Bay. For a while, we lived in Sandy Bay while Greg spent time working at camps on the west coast. Then this job at Seal Bay came up, and we moved. Greg wants to spend more time with the kids. Tod is fifteen and Greg feels it's important to be around with him as he grows older."

"Kelsey told me that Greg's mom knows Mrs Spencer?" I asked.

"Yes," Val said, "It's more or less through her that I got to know quite a bit about Gina. And I must say that I think it was a great piece of luck for the Spencers when they found you as foster parents. Have you been doing this kind of thing for long?"

I couldn't help showing my surprise, "They found us? I'm a bit confused, Val. It didn't happen that way at all."

"You mean you aren't in the foster parenting program?", Val asked.

"No. No, we're not. I didn't know there was such a thing! We never planned to be foster parents at all. But it looks now like we are going to be...."

"Well, then, how did the Spencers find you?" Now Val was really puzzled.

"Val," I explained, "We live in West Vancouver, but about 3 years ago, we bought a summer place just along the road from the Spencers' house. When we met Gina, we didn't know anyone there, except for our close neighbours."

"Then how did you meet Gina?"

"Well, when we arrived for the summer (we always come over to the cottage in June) in 1973, Gina turned up in the garden one morning. I guess she was walking along Manders Road and happened to see Amy and Ben. We have a big garden and it's easy to open our little gate and come in. Anyway, Gina began coming almost every day and by the end of the summer, she was just like one of the family."

"And you didn't even know the Spencers?"

"No. We didn't know them at all. We knew that Gina was staying with her grandparents. Later on, she told us her mother was in hospital in Winnipeg and she had a little brother and sister who were with her mother. We just assumed that her mother would return to Sandy Bay and she would go back to family life."

"Oh, my," said Val, "you had no idea at all about the Spencer family, did you?"

"None, I guess" was all I could say.

'This is amazing," exclaimed Val, "do go on...."

"Well, when we returned the next summer, we expected to see Gina, but there was no sign of her. Ben and Amy missed her. Then when I was in the drugstore in the middle of August, I happened to remark to Mrs Spencer that we missed Gina and how was she, and Mrs Spencer said that they had sent her to her father and hoped that he would keep her because they were having company and no longer had room for her."

"They didn't. They really said that!". Val seemed quite shocked.

"Yes, Val, they did. And I was so upset when they said that they didn't have room for her any longer. I just kept asking myself what would happen if her father didn't want her and then, quite honestly, I got annoyed. I mean, really, Gina is a lovely kid, not a can of beans!"

"I can understand that", agreed Val.

"So in the end, after stewing over it at the beach for a couple of days, I got this crazy idea of going to the Spencers and telling them that we really cared about Gina and if her dad couldn't keep her and they hadn't room for her, then we would be glad to have her."

"My God!" from Val.

"Of course, I talked to Steve first, and he was okay with the idea, so I walked over to the Spencers' house the next evening and made my little speech to Lillian, and then Henry came into the kitchen and they said they thought it was a great idea and could they call me back after they had spoken to Max, Gina's dad".

"I don't believe it", Val's eyebrows shot up.

"Anyway, as it turned out, Max said he couldn't keep Gina, so the Spencers came over to see me two days later. We talked. and they filled me in a bit about why Gina was living with them. She had only been with them a short while when she turned up at our place and began playing with Ben and Amy."

So that's what happened," Val leaned over and lowered her voice, "You know, I didn't grow up at Sandy Bay, but Greg did and, between you and me, the Spencers aren't exactly the most popular people in the place."

"They're not?"

Val continued, "Maura, you know what small places are like. To begin with, Henry Spencer has always kind of acted like he thinks he's kinda superior to mostly everyone. He's English, and I hear he came to Canada when he was in his early thirties. The Spencers make a big thing out of how important they are, Henry being the principal of the private boys' college and so on. It seems that Henry's brother married into the English nobility, Lady Margo Harrison-Copps or something like that. That's who was coming to visit, you know. Henry wouldn't have been too keen to have his sister-in-law start asking questions about why he was looking after his granddaughter. They came in September, just after Gina moved in with you. No wonder they were so quick to take you up on your offer!"

"They never told me much about the company that was coming," I said, "Anyway, after they came over and told me all about what had happened to Julia, we got very busy, packing up, returning to the mainland, school starting etc."

"Oh yes, the Spencers have always pretty much swept the whole Julia thing under the rug. But everyone in Sandy Bay knows all about Julia. She certainly is a looker, you know, takes after Lillian that way. She was Miss Sandy Bay of 1960 and boy, did she know it. The original party girl; parties, drinking and every other kind of 'kick' in the book. And plenty of guys; she wasn't particular how many or who. All the guys around Sandy Bay knew what she was like, but poor Max Niemann didn't. He came over with a couple of college friends one summer, met 'our Julia" at a beach party, and before the poor sap knew what was happening to him, he was engaged to her. I think she saw Max as her ticket out of Sandy Bay. He was studying hospital administration and get a really good job just before they got married, so I was told."

"Yes, I've met Max," I said, "he's a nice guy. I like him and Gina enjoys visiting him."

"Well, that's good. From what I have heard, the kid has had a pretty rugged existence since the divorce. It's about time she got a break....................."

The four children suddenly raced up breathlessly from the beach, "Hey, Mom' gasped Ben, "you've gotta come down to the water. There's an actual seal on a rock out there, but you have to get closer to see it....... hurry".

They were right --- a large black seal was sleeping on a rock about 50 yards from the shore, which as I remarked "after all makes sense, at a place called Seal Bay". There were groans and comments like "oh, mom", while we packed up all the picnic stuff and headed back to the Jacksons' house.

When Greg Jackson arrived home from work that evening, he insisted that we stay for barbecued fresh salmon, salad and all the trimmings. It was a warm summer evening and the heat from the barbecue kept the mosquitoes at bay. Greg, Ben and Tod got into a big discussion on fishing and hunting, and Gina and Amy went on a tour of the house with Kelsey, leaving Val and myself to tidy up the kitchen. It was a relaxed, happy evening. I had planned to pack up first thing next morning and head back to Sandy Bay, but Tod and Ben insisted that on our way out of town, we absolutely must go to the Seal Bay Garbage Dump where we would be able to see 'multitudes of bears'. I wasn't all that enthusiastic, but the kids outvoted me.

In the morning, we checked out of our luxurious cabin at Trout River Court and drove to the Jacksons house where we picked up Tod and Kelsey. Val, who was busy cooking up a large batch of raspberry jam, opted out of the trip, so I led the 'expedition'. What can I say? Before the Seal Bay Garbage Dump experience, I had seen a couple of bears in the wild; large, hairy black bears which appeared rather attractive .... from a considerable distance! The bear population at the Seal Bay Garbage Dump were definitely of a different 'tribe'. To put it kindly, they were short-haired, fat, brown bears with the ugliest faces I have ever seen. Seriously! As soon as we drove up and parked, they headed en masse, for our car -- in anticipation, I suppose, of receiving a bag or two of McDonald's leftovers or similar? To my relief, the kids found them to be equally repugnant. Ben took a few photographs, but nobody wanted to get out of the car, and after two of the urgly bunch pressed their noses against the rear windows, leaving steamy streaks on the glass, by unanimous consent, we drove out of there without even looking back. As Amy later joked, 'the whole experience was unbearable'! Of course, the expedition was a favourite family discussion topic for several weeks thereafter and the photographs of the Seal Bay Bears were widely circulated and commented upon.

We dropped Tod and Kelsey back at the Jacksons, the girls exchanged telephone numbers, we thanked the Jacksons, and Val told me we were welcome back any time. After that. We drove south, to Sandy Bay.

PART VI

Obstacle Course

Chapter Thirteen

The last days of our summer holidays passed quickly. Gina made a short trip over to say goodbye to Lillian and Henry before returning to the mainland. She told me that she had talked to her mom and Scott and Lucy on the phone, long-distance, and they were all well and liked living at Tofino. It seemed her mother's life was more settled. Gina was happy about it all. I was relieved.

After the usual day trip to Nanaimo for school supplies and necessary clothing items, we dismantled the ping pong table and moved it into the basement along with the patio furniture. We tidied away the games, puzzles, books and other rainy day amusement materials and after our final evening swim at the beach, departed for the mainland in a car stuffed with children, cat, dog, guinea pigs, duffle bags and miscellaneous summer 'memorabilia'!

Compared to the struggles of the previous year when Gina first joined the family, this year 'back to school' and the usual family routine went without a hitch. They were all happy to reunite with their school friends and begin classes. Somewhere along the way, the topic of visiting Disneyland was discussed and we all agreed that it would be great to go. There was more discussion. All agreed we needed some money! We would have to buy air tickets, stay at a hotel and have spending money. We made a plan together. Mom would help save for the air tickets and hotel, Ben and Gina would both get evening paper routes, Amy would receive an extra allowance for helping with household chores. If we all did our part, we would be able to go next March, during spring break. It was a good team plan.

Family life was much more relaxed. Steve and I even managed to go to a few movies and concerts. Grandma Dorrie came over for dinner most Sundays when we all went to the pitch and putt and had great fun together. I was busy at work, Steve's practise was doing well, Amy was turning into quite a little housekeeping assistant, and their paper routes kept Gina and Ben busy after school.

Suddenly it was Thanksgiving. Dorrie came over to help me with Thanksgiving dinner which was quickly eaten amid 'yums' and 'pass more of that please'. After dinner, Steve and the kids went down to the family room, while Dorrie and I finished up in the kitchen. Suddenly, the phone rang. Dorrie answered, said "Yes," and passed the phone to me, mouthing 'it's for you'.

"Hello," I said.

"Oh, hi, is that Mrs Kerry?"

"Yes".

"This is Julia Niemann, Gina's mother,"

"Yes – Julia?......." I was surprised. "how are you?"

"Fine. I, we, well Scott and Lucy and I, we wanted to talk to Gina – wish her a Happy Thanksgiving......"

"Oh, I see. Can you hang on a minute and I'll get Gina to come to the phone," was all I could think of saying. I turned to Dorrie and whispered, 'can you go downstairs and ask Gina to come up". Dorrie went off down the corridor and I continued on the phone,

"Gina will be surprised. She told me that you are enjoying living at Tofino," I continued.

"It was okay there," Julia said, "but we're not there anymore."

"Oh......"

"No. I've moved to the mainland now. We're living on the East Side of Vancouver..."

They've moved to the east side of Vancouver! Gina arrived in the kitchen.

"Hello, Julia, I'm putting Gina on the phone now..."

Gina spoke to Julia for a couple of minutes, mostly yes's and no's at my end, followed by several animated minutes when her face lit up. It was obvious she was talking to Scott and Lucy. Then "bye" and she returned the phone to me and went back to the family room.

"I think Gina enjoyed talking to you and Scott and Lucy," I said.

"Yes. Yes," replied Julia, "they really miss her, you know. They want her to come back home. They want to see her. It's been a long time..."

"Yes, it has," I agreed, "I think that you would need to contact your Social Worker about that".

"I'm certainly going to do that, you know," said Julia, and then she hung up abruptly.

Finding myself alone in the kitchen, I pulled out one of the chairs in the nook and sat down with a thump. I felt deflated – flattened. Was this "I want my daughter back" thing going to happen all over again?

Dorrie reappeared in the kitchen and, of course, asked me what it had all been about. Her feeling was that I shouldn't overreact. It looked like Julia's new relationship at Tofino hadn't worked out, but considering what we knew of her past, we shouldn't be surprised, should we? She had most likely moved to Vancouver to get a job. After all, the little ones were getting bigger. She would probably want to see Gina occasionally, but maybe not. After all, since the hearing, she hadn't made any attempt at all to contact Gina. Best to do nothing....wait and see. My mother always made a lot of sense, so I calmed down and enjoyed the rest of the evening.

Chapter Fourteen

Mrs Mercer telephoned two evenings later, on Wednesday. She had received a call from Doris Parks, Julia's social worker, telling her that Julia was now living in East Vancouver and she and Scott and Lucy wanted to have a visit with Gina. She wanted to know if Gina was free on the coming Saturday. Either Mrs Mercer could pick up and deliver Gina to Julia, or if it was convenient, I could do it. We agreed I would speak with Gina and call her back.

It was clear that Julia intended to re-establish contact with Gina and I was a bit apprehensive about how that would play out. When I went into Gina's room for our usual bedtime chat, I told her about Mrs Mercer's call. As I had expected, Gina was enthusiastic about seeing Scott and Lucy but a little hesitant about spending a lot of time with her mother. Gina wanted me to do the delivery and pick-up part, and we both agreed that I would ask Mrs Mercer if the visit could be just for lunch and early afternoon so that she could be home in time for supper and spending time with Ben and Amy watching television or whatever! Between Mrs Mercer and Miss Parks, the visit was scheduled between 11:00 a.m. and 3:30 p.m. on Saturday. And Ben, very obligingly, agreed to do Gina's paper route that afternoon. After all, Disneyland was a top priority!

Saturday morning arrived. Gina climbed into the car with a bag full of apples, bananas, and oranges. In the beginning, she had thought of bringing some little storybooks for Scott and Lucy but in the end, decided that her mother wouldn't like that.

It was a forty-minute drive from our house on the north shore over to the East Side of Vancouver. It was a sunny Saturday morning, so traffic was busy. Julia Niemann was living in an old frame house with a big verandah, one of many such relics built on the East Side in the 1940s. There was a postage stamp patch of grass on either side of the front path which led to a large, wide flight of steps up to the front door. I rang the bell, there was some thumping, and the door was opened by a bushy-haired chap, with bare feet, wearing an enormous green sweater and jeans.

"Hi?" he asked.

"I'm looking for Julia Niemann," I replied.

"Oh, Julia. She must be the new gal upstairs". As he turned and motioned to another door, I noticed that at some point the house had been converted into separate apartments, by building two more doorways inside the main door – one door leading to the downstairs apartment, and the other leading to the upstairs apartment. He had heard the doorbell first.

"Just bang on her door," he said cheerfully, "if the kids are making a noise, you'll need to make it loud." He disappeared back through the downstairs apartment door.

Gina gave the other door a few loud bangs. We heard a child laughing and then Julia called, "Hi, is that you Gina? The door's open. Come on up."

Gina pulled the creaky door open and we both gazed up a dark wooden staircase. Still no sign of Julia. Gina looked at me questioningly.

"Okay," I said, "it sounds like your mom is busy. Just go on up. I'll be here to pick you up at 3:30. If there's any problem, you can call me at home. Okay?"

"Great, mum, see you at 3:30," and she started up the stairs clutching the bag of fruit.

When I returned, I found Gina sitting at the foot of the front steps. Still no sign of Julia. I debated whether I should knock on the door and go upstairs, but Gina said, "No, mom, my mum's getting supper and she's busy. Let's go home."

We had a chat in the car on the way home. How did it go? "It was great to see Scott and Lucy again, mum. I've really missed them and have they ever grown!". How did the gift of fruit turn out? "Best idea, ever, mum. My mum said they would have the bananas for dessert." Did you have a good talk with your mom? "Oh, just a bit."

And then, "What's for supper?" When I suggested she was hoping for steak, we both laughed!

After supper, while the kids tidied up and loaded the dishwasher, I joined Steve who was hidden behind his evening paper in the living room. I sank into my comfy chair, feeling both relieved and relaxed. The visit had gone well. Admittedly, I didn't have an opportunity to communicate with Julia at all, but that seemed to be the way she was. Gina had returned home happy, although I was a bit surprised that Julia hadn't talked very much to her. Maybe that was because it had been such a long time since they had been together.

On the Monday following the visit, I called Mrs Mercer and told her how it had all gone. Our family life continued as usual until Wednesday evening at around 10:00 when I was finishing packing the kids' school lunches, when the telephone rang. I had been expecting a call from my mother, but it was Julia once more. "Can we speak to Gina?". This time, there was no 'hello Mrs Kerry', no 'this is Julia', and certainly no apology for calling at 10 p.m.

"I'm sorry, Julia, but it's quite late and Gina has gone to bed."

"Can you get her to the phone. We want to speak to her. Scott and Lucy are here. They miss her. They want to speak to her.". I could hear one or both of the children crying.

"I'm sorry, Julia, but Gina has to be up early in the morning. Can you give me your phone number and I'll have her call you tomorrow?" I said.

No response from Julia, just silence. I waited for almost a minute. Still nothing. So I hung up.

I felt stressed. This was not a good situation. I was tired. I was concerned that these telephone calls were starting to become a pattern. Maybe the time had come to ask Mrs Mercer to take action to prevent this behaviour. I needed to talk with someone about this but everyone in the house had gone to bed. I decided to call my mother but when I picked up the phone there was no dial tone. I couldn't understand it. At first, I thought that something was wrong with the phone, but it wasn't. Finally, I realized that Julia hadn't hung up the phone at her end leaving the line open. I would have to go over to the neighbours and call the operator for assistance, but it was much too late to do that now. It would have to wait until the morning. I went to bed and it took me a long time to fall asleep.

When I checked the next morning, to my relief the dial tone had been restored. We were all in a rush to get out of the house, so I didn't call my mother after all. Maybe Julia hadn't intentionally failed to hang up. At work, we had a big case coming to court on the coming Monday and I had more pressing things to think about. On Friday afternoon, Gordon, my boss, asked me if I could stay until 5 p.m. instead of leaving around 3, to help him organize documents. I thought, okay. Friday night was 'do your own thing' night at home .I generally shopped on Thursdays, so there was always lots of food in the house, and everyone got their own 'supper' and ate it wherever. All I had to do was call home and let them know. The kids usually arrived home around 3:30 or 3:45 but the line was busy when I rang. I waited a while and tried again, Still busy. Were they hogging the phone to talk to friends or what? After the fifth try, I gave up. I tried Steve's office but he had left for home by that time. They would just have to wonder where I was.

"Mom, where have you been?" was Amy's greeting when I stepped into the hall at around 6 p.m.

"Yeah, we thought you had an accident or something," added Ben.

"I had to work a bit late getting ready.................", I started.

"Well, you could have at least called!" Steve called from the kitchen.

"But I did call! In fact, I must have called at least five times," I defended myself, "but the line was always busy. Which of you was on the phone all that time?"

"Not me, said Ben.

"Not me", from Amy.

"It was me," said Gina as she came upstairs from the family room.

"You? You must have been on the line for a long time. Who did you call?"

"I didn't call anyone," said Gina, "it was my mum. She called me."

"Your mum?" I exclaimed.

"Yes," Gina continued, "she wanted me to talk to Scott and Lucy again and she said that when she called you the other day, you wouldn't let me come to the phone. She was really upset. Anyway, we talked and I said goodbye and hung up. So the line was free after that."

Steve had come into the room during the conversation. "Well," he said, "I've just picked up the phone and the line is blocked."

Now I understood, "I think your mother didn't hang up at her end, Gina, and when that happens the line is still busy. I'll have to go over to the Lowens to call the operator and have the line cleared. I'm sorry, everyone!"

I made myself a hot dog while Steve went over to the Lowens next door. He had heated up a pizza and we sat together at the dining table to eat.

"We can't have this kind of thing going on," he said. He was understandably concerned. We needed to be able to contact each other without this kind of difficulty. Next time, there might be a real emergency. He was right. I agreed to contact Mrs Mercer to ask that something be done. I had no idea whether or not Julia was intentionally blocking the line or whether she was simply emotionally distressed. Whatever the reason, it had to stop. In the meantime, we asked the children to call either Steve or me after they arrived home from school so that we knew everything was okay at home.

Getting assistance from Mrs Mercer proved to be complicated. She was sympathetic to the problem but first, she had to chat with Gina to make sure of the facts, and after that, she had to contact Julia's social worker, who then had to chat with Julia and then report back to Mrs Mercer. So we waited, and while we waited the phone calls continued, sometimes waking me at 4 in the morning (silence at the other end), sometimes just before I left for work or when my mother was there and picked up the phone. Always, the line was blocked. My mother was pretty good about it, but as time went by without any response from Mrs Mercer, Steve grew angry. I knew that Gina felt bad about it. Apart from "sorry mom", she didn't say a lot, but her usual bright, happy disposition began to fade.

In November, Gina spent a weekend with Max and Laura and returned home in a much happier frame of mind. Their baby was due towards the end of January and she was helping Laura decorate the nursery. Then, in the last week of November, Mrs Mercer called and arranged for me to visit her office for a chat. She had spoken at length with Julia's social worker, Miss Jackson. Julia was still struggling with managing Scott and Lucy. Miss Jackson was trying to make arrangements for Scott, now 6, to begin school, which would leave Julia with just one child to cope with. The consensus was that Julia was still dealing with trauma and depression so they were arranging for counselling. They felt that Julia was suffering from stress because of losing Gina, she continually talked about Gina and about when they would all be together again, Miss Jackson was also arranging for a financial worker to help Julia with budgeting and improving the family's eating habits. Everything possible was being done to help Julia rehabilitate herself.

But when I asked Mrs Mercer, what was being done to deal with the constant telephone call problem, and what remedy was proposed to eliminate the pressure on Gina caused by Julia's constant references to 'when Gina comes home', she offered no tangible solution, other than to tell me how important it was to be patient and to "be tolerant of Julia's situation".

I left Mrs Mercer's office feeling frustrated and annoyed. It was all very well, I thought, to try to help Julia, if only for the sake of Scott and Lucy, but what about Gina? What about us, the (now official) foster parents? As far as I could tell, we weren't in the picture at all.

November came to an end. Christmas loomed on the horizon. Max called to invite Gina to spend an overnight with him and Laura. We talked about a gift for Gina and of course the subject of Julia and her return to Vancouver. I told Max about the telephone call problem. He was sympathetic but made it clear that he wanted to avoid any contact or involvement with Julia because of past experience. He asked if I had any suggestions for a Christmas gift for Gina. That was easy. A bicycle would be great! Since she joined us, Gina had been borrowing Ben's bike. Max was delighted with my suggestion. He would drop it off at our house just before Christmas. I would keep it hidden until Christmas Day, and we agreed that Gina would visit Max and Laura over the New Year weekend.

Soon we were in December with its flurry of increasing activities. Tests at school, who would buy tickets to the school concert, whispering about what to get for who, bundling up well for the paper routes, checking bank balances. Lots going on. I signed Ben up for ski lessons, then discovered that they took place at 'paper route time', so Amy and I subbed, toiling up and down steep, sometimes slippery driveways. "All in a good cause," said Ben!

Inevitably, Gina received a call from Julia. "Scott and Lucy are making Christmas presents for you," she said, "and I am going to make a special Christmas dinner." Julia was expecting Gina to spend Christmas with her. That was clear. While for me it was an irritant, it was certainly understandable. But what about the Kerrys' Christmas? It was logistically difficult.

I decided to call and speak to Julia about it and we agreed that I would bring Gina to her during the afternoon of Christmas Eve, she would stay overnight, enjoy all Christmas Day with Julia, Scott and Lucy, and I would drive over in the late evening of Christmas Day to bring her back to us.

But before I could confirm this arrangement, I would need to speak with Mrs Mercer, and she would hear back after that. Julia seemed happy with this. Mrs Mercer was also happy with it. However, Steve was not. It meant a lot of driving in heavy traffic on Christmas Eve and also taking me away from our family on Christmas evening. He was right, of course, but because it was a statutory holiday, the Social Workers wouldn't be available. I confided to Steve that I was hoping this helpful gesture would improve Julia's attitude and permanently halt the irritating telephone calls. He still wasn't happy. "I hope you're right," was all he said.

In due course, we all went shopping for a Christmas tree and after looking at what seemed like every tree on the lot, and arguing over which was best, we did what we always did and purchased the very first tree we had picked, loaded it on the roof of the car, and took it home. For us, it was a familiar ritual, but for Gina, it was all completely new and exciting. He eyes shone like stars, her cheeks were flushed, she was filled with happy animation. Out came the decorations and we all got to work. It was great to see all three of the children sharing the excitement and expectation of Christmas to come.

Christmas Eve arrived and Gina disappeared into her room with tape, ribbon and fancy paper and began wrapping presents. From her paper route money, she bought a cute baby doll for Lucy. For Scott two toy racing cars (she said he liked them), and for her mom, a pretty scarf made of soft rose-coloured wool. Gina and I had discussed it beforehand, and we both felt that her mom would be okay with a warm scarf.

Just after 4 o'clock, Gina got ready to go, her gifts and overnight things stuffed in her duffle bag. She had brushed her blonde hair back and pinned it on the sides, and wore her new red sweater and her regular jeans. She looked lovely.

It was dark when we arrived at Julia's apartment. I decided to see Gina to her mother's door, so I parked the car outside and we scaled the long flight of steps to the main door which was slightly ajar, allowing us to step inside out of the cold. I knocked on Julia's door and we waited. As we stood there, the man who had spoken to me on the previous occasion opened his door and peered out at us. I said "Hi". He smiled. "Julia's in," he said, "just open the door and go on up." His head disappeared and his door closed.

Gina tried Julia's door which wasn't locked. We could hear Lucy laughing. "Okay, go on up," I said. I'll be back at about this time tomorrow."

I waited until Gina reached the top of the dark staircase, then returned to my car and drove home.

Christmas Day seemed a bit odd, I suppose because it was confined to just our family – Steve, Ben, Amy, my mother and myself. I decided it felt odd because we hadn't been just "us" for quite a few months now. I began to realize how much things had changed. Adding another child hadn't seemed so significant at the time but it had set in motion a chain of events that none of us had contemplated. Some good. Some not so good. But we were now a new kind of family and we were functioning well, despite all the challenges.

Dorrie helped me tidy up after dinner. Like Steve, she wasn't happy that the Social Workers seemed so unconcerned with the difficulties and extra work that Julia was causing. I wasn't happy either, but I hoped that by working with them and being reasonable, they would begin to spend at least some time determining what was best for Gina. I had resolved to persevere.

Chapter Fifteen

At around 4:30 p.m., I arrived at Julia's apartment to pick Gina up. It was dark outside, the old house was also in darkness, and I had to use my flashlight to navigate the mighty flight of front steps. However, the small inner hall was dimly lit with one lonely light bulb in the centre of the ceiling. I knocked on Julia's door. After a few seconds, I heard steps, the door opened and Gina was there. "Can you hang on a minute, mum," she said, "I'm not quite ready."

"Fine, I'll just wait here," I replied.

Gina disappeared, shutting the door behind her. I waited. Five minutes went by, but no sign of Gina. Another five minutes passed. Still no sign. Then, just as I was about to open the door and go up the stairs, Gina popped out, wearing her ski jacket, carrying her duffle bag.

In the car, I asked, "How did it go?".

"Okay,"

"Like, HOW DID IT GO," I repeated. "Did your mom like her present. What about Scott and Lucy?"

"Oh, yes", they really liked their presents. "And my mom liked the scarf. I'll show you their presents when we get home."

"And what did you do on Christmas Eve, and today?" I continued.

"Well.......... (a long pause).... well, when I got there yesterday, my mom gave me and Scott and Lucy some sandwiches and pop......."

"And then what did you do?" I asked.

"Well...................... those guys --- you know there are those guys who live downstairs, they were having some kind of party, I think. Anyway, after the sandwiches, my mom told me to stay with Scott and Lucy and she went downstairs to their party."

"So what did you do?"

"Well, Scott and Lucy wanted to open their presents right away, so they did that and then I played with them until they wanted to go to sleep."

"Did your mom come back to put them to bed?", I asked.

"No, mom, you see it's not like at our house, my mom never does bedtime. You just have to go to bed or lie down somewhere and sleep when you are tired."

"I see. So Scott and Lucy got tired and went to sleep?"

"Well, I put them in the bed, and I lay down beside them and I guess we all went to sleep eventually".

"Well, when did your mom come back?"

"I don't know. I think she must have come home when I was asleep. She was there asleep on the couch when I woke up this morning."

'So what did you do today?"

"Well, my mom was tired, so I took Scott and Lucy out for a walk to the park. They like to play on the swings and the round-about, and we played there until we got hungry. Then we went back home".

"I guess you were all ready for lunch,"

"We sure were."

"Did you have a big piece of the cake your mom made?".

"Well, actually, she didn't make the cake because she couldn't find her recipe book."

"So what did you have?"

"My mom was tired. So I opened up a can of pork and beans and I made that with toast. There was some cheese and crackers. And I found some chocolate cookies for dessert."

"I think you've been holding out on me, Gina, You never told me you could get lunch. Maybe you can make it for us someday soon?"

Gina grinned. "Okay. If you like. I've done it lots of times. I used to get it when I stayed home from school to look after Scott and Lucy when we were in Winnipeg."

"Yes, you've jogged my memory. So you all had a meal. Is your mom okay?"

"Yes, I think she's okay. Maybe she stayed up very late and needs extra sleep today. That's why I had to make you wait, my mom was asleep and I had to wake her up to look after Scott and Lucy. I didn't want them to be alone there when my mom was asleep."

"And did she wake up?"

"Oh, yes. She's awake. She sleeps a lot. I'm kinda used to that. But, mom, I'm a bit worried about Scott and Lucy....."

"Why? What are you worried about," Gina really did look worried.

"Well, Scott is almost six now, and we have some good chats, and he told me that sometimes my mom gets kind of mad, and a few nights ago she took the scissors and stuck them into the bedroom wall. He was a bit afraid."

"Is it like when you were in Winnipeg, maybe," I asked?

"I really don't know, but Scott isn't making up a story, and he and Lucy are too little to be there when she does that kind of thing."

"Yes, Gina, they are. I know you don't like me talking to Mrs Mercer, but I think if this is happening, I really must talk to her because we have to make sure Scott and Lucy are safe."

"I know," said Gina, "but I don't want my mom to know I told Mrs Mercer."

"I'll explain things to Mrs Mercer. She will understand," was all I could promise.

By then, I had turned the car up our steep driveway. "Well, Gina, Merry Christmas. Your presents are waiting under the tree and there is a big one that I have to bring in from the shed."

"From the shed?!"

Gina loved all her presents, but the bike from her dad was by far the hit of the season! She bounded around the house in an explosion of joy and we managed to bring the bike into her bedroom so that she could look at it as she was falling asleep.

I went into the living room and sat down beside the fire. The house was peaceful and quiet, My mind was quite the opposite. After Boxing Day, I would have to contact Mrs Mercer. Julia Niemann and her little children were definitely in need of attention. I just hoped that nothing serious happened in the meantime.

Chapter Sixteen

Steve and I brought in the New Year at the home of Bette and Jorg Vogt who lived in nearby North Vancouver. We organized our long time babysitter, Lori, to keep an eye on the kids and to order in pizza, which was a favourite.

Bette and Jorg had invited us for dinner. Jorg was one of Steve's clients. He had a small but successful civil engineering company and, over the years, he and Steve had become good friends. His wife Bette and I shared many interests. Jorg and Bette had come to Canada from the Netherlands soon after their marriage. They had a son and two daughters, the older two have finished their schooling and left home, and Darlene, their youngest was in her last year of high school.

It was always good to visit Jorg and Bette. Bette was a great cook and Jorg made sure that the wine glasses were never empty. For Steve and myself, It was perhaps the first real social outing we had enjoyed in quite a long time. After dinner, Jorg and Steve disappeared into Jorg's den to look at some designs for a proposed new building, leaving Bette and me to relax and catch up on recent events. Bette and I often chatted on the phone, so she knew about Gina and some of the challenges we had been dealing with over the past months. However, we hadn't spoken recently because the Vogts had been on holiday in Hawaii.

I found myself sharing all our recent struggles with Bette: The phone calls, Gina's visits to her mother, the fact that I had never yet had a decent conversation with Julia, the constant pressure on Gina by her mother, the lack of response from Mrs Mercer, Gina's fear of confiding in Mrs Mercer, the abysmal Christmas visit and, finally, Scott's remarks about Julia's violent behaviour. Bette was shocked.

"But this is altogether too much!", she exclaimed, "Mrs Mercer needs to do something to protect Gina from all this pressure. I'm no expert, but it seems to me that Julia needs help, and the two little ones are not safe at all."

"I agree," I responded, "I feel quite helpless. I speak to Mrs Mercer and tell her what is going on, but all she ever says is that she will talk to Miss **Parks**, and then she goes on to tell me at length about all the things that are being done to help Julia."

"Has Mrs Mercer spoken to Gina?" Bette asked.

"No. That's just it. I've never been a foster parent before, but my understanding is that Mrs Mercer is the Social Worker for Gina and Gina's family. So I don't understand why she doesn't see Gina and come to understand how Gina is feeling. Gina needs to feel safe and secure and settled." I realized I must sound pretty emotional.

"You're right," Bette agreed, reaching over and squeezing my hand.

"I know I'm a bit worked up," I said, "but this situation doesn't just affect me. It is worrisome to Steve, it upsets my mom to see me upset, and to top it off, Gina is really happy, she has settled into her school work, has made new friends, is doing a paper route. No more arguments over family rules or anything like that. But this situation with her mother is unsettling to all of us."

"Have you thought what you can do about it," asked Bette.

"As I see it, after this Christmas fiasco, I will ONCE AGAIN call Mrs Mercer and suggest that she have a chat with Gina as well as report what happened to Miss **Parks**. I don't want Gina to visit again until something has been done."

"Well, that sounds reasonable to me, Maura. But there's something I would like to mention to you. I went to high school with a guy called James Foster. We were pretty good friends, and as it happens, James Foster is now the Superintendent of Child Welfare. I see him occasionally when Jorg goes over to Victoria on golf weekends."

Bette could see that I was surprised. She continued: "Maura, we have been friends for quite a time and I know you aren't some kind of 'nut' ... and I don't like to see you encountering what seems like unnecessary stress in doing a good thing for a little girl,,, so I want you to know that I'm quite prepared to call James, tell him about the situation, and ask him to take action to resolve the matter...."

"God, Bette, I had no idea..."

"Maura, I'm serious. It's no problem for me to call James and I'd be glad to do it if it will help you and Steve and, of course, Gina."

"Bette, this is so good of you," I said, "and we do need help...... but I'd like to give it one more try at doing it 'by the book'."

"Okay, it's up to you," smiled Bette, "but my offer is good – any time."

"I won't forget," I said. "I'm going to call Mrs Mercer just as soon as she's back in her office.....

Just then Steve and Jorg emerged from the den, the New Year toasts were poured, the New Year festivities on CTV were turned on, and we awaited the countdown to midnight. Roll on 1976 and, hopefully, a year of smooth sailing for the Vogts, the Kerrys and Gina!.

Chapter Seventeen

Gina enjoyed her visit with Max and Laura over New Year. She was thrilled with her new bike and it was clear that she enjoyed being included in the excitement of preparing for the arrival of the baby. Before the kids returned to school, all of us, including my mother, went to see The Nutcracker at the Q.E. Theatre. It was the first time Gina had seen a live ballet and she was captivated. All things considered, Christmas and New Year had gone very well for each of us. Ben had even been able to go skiing with some of his school buddies.

In the new year, not wanting to pounce on her on the very first day after her office reopened, I called Mrs Mercer on day two. She was pleased to hear that Gina had enjoyed her holiday visits. I told her what Gina had said about her mother's behaviour and about Scott telling her that her mother had struck the wall with scissors. Once again, Mrs Mercer said that she would contact Miss Parks regarding Julia's situation. Once again, she repeated that everything possible was being done to assist Julia with the children. And once again, I felt frustrated that the effect of all of this on Gina wasn't receiving very much attention at all. Maybe this time, Miss Parks will look into Julia's state of mind and if she doesn't believe what Gina has told me, then she is certainly in a position to check the walls in Julia's apartment for scissor marks, I thought!

In the meantime, the Kerry family had a busy life. Christmas was over. It was rainy, cold January and, as I pointed out to the kids, work and school and chores went on forever!

On the plus side, the worrisome calls from Julia had stopped, which was a great relief.

On January 12th, Gina celebrated her 14th birthday – her first birthday as part of the Kerry family. We let her choose what she wanted to do, and she chose to invite her two closest friends over for supper and a video sleepover. It was a big success. Gina made a cake, we both frosted it and Gina put all the candles on it. Burgers and other 'delicacies' were served, and after supper, we all gathered around in the living room while Gina opened her gifts. Don't ask me what they all were because I really can't remember. What I do remember is how Gina looked – the joy in her expression, the sparkle in her violet eyes, her happy laughter, and a lot of good-natured teasing by Carla and JoAnn, her friends. Afterwards, Gina, Ben, Amy and Gina's friends went down to the family room where they laughed, giggled, watched videos and munched on snacks until Steve finally told them it was time to 'cool it' and get some sleep!

In the third week of January, Julia called with the usual request: Scott and Lucy wanted to see their sister. Could Gina come for a visit? This time Julia spoke to me and we agreed that I would discuss it with Gina and call her back.

After the Christmas visit, I wondered how Gina would feel about seeing them so soon again. It was no longer the holidays, so it would have to be a day visit. Gina was conflicted. She said she wanted to see Scott and Lucy but she wasn't very keen to spend time with her mother. In the end, we agreed I would take her over for the afternoon on the coming Saturday. I called Julia and we arranged that I would drop Gina off on Saturday around 1 pm and return to pick her up at 7 pm so that she could have supper there. Julia had sounded a lot better. Maybe Miss Parks had been to see her, I hoped. Perhaps Julia's coping skills were improving. Gina was quite relieved when I told her that her mother seemed okay.

When we arrived at Julia's apartment that Saturday afternoon, I decided to walk Gina to Julie's door, to make sure Julia was up and awake if nothing else. We entered the small downstairs hallway and Gina knocked No 2 (her mother's door). Just then the door to No. 1 was opened by the bushy-haired fellow who had spoken to us at Christmas. This time he was wearing a leather jacket, denim shirt and jeans.

"Julia's in, I think," he pronounced. Then, seeing Gina, "Hi there Gina, cutie!".

Gina smiled. Then Julia's voice rang out. "The door's open.... is that you Gina? Come on up."

Gina opened the door to No 2, I hugged her. "I'll be back around 7 pm and look for you on the steps."

"Okay, mum," and she was gone, leaping up the stairs out of sight.

It was dark that evening as I drove back over to Garden Street and it was five past seven when I parked at the front path of No. 10. There was no sign of Gina at the front steps. I waited for about ten minutes and when she still hadn't appeared, I decided she must have lost track of the time. I got out of the car, climbed the steps into the hallway and knocked on Julia's door. It was very quiet in the hallway. I knocked again. Still quiet. Then I heard Julia's voice. "Who is it?".

"Hi, Julia, it's Maura Kerry, I'm here to pick up Gina. Is she ready?"

After a pause, "Oh, Gina's gone out for a ride. She'll be back soon, I think. Do you want to come up and wait....."

A ride? With whom, I wondered. I decided to stay outside where I could see the road.

"Thanks, Julia," I shouted up the stairs, "I'll just wait out here."

As I turned to go back down the steps, a loud noise like a motorcycle broke the silence.

Then followed thumping noises outside the door, the sound of voices, and Gina appeared in the company of the bushy-haired guy in the leather jacket. He was carrying a motorcycle helmet.

"Oh, hi," he said. "We're a bit late, I guess. All my fault. I took Gina out for a spin and we went a bit further than planned,.,,"

Gina smiled sheepishly, "Sorry, mum. This is Ron. He has this great motorcycle and I've never been on one, so he took me for a spin. It was great."

"Yeah, Miss Cutie here really enjoyed herself," Ron turned and gave Gina a hug.

"Miss Cutie"! "Miss Cutie"! I didn't like it. Wasn't this one of the guys who had the Christmas party? I didn't like it. And I didn't like the way "Ron" was looking at Gina.

But all I said was, "I expect she did enjoy herself, Ron." Then to Gina, "Okay, Gina, it's getting late, time to go. Goodbye, Ron".

"Bye, Ron, and thanks," from Gina.

We went back to the car and drove home in silence, without our usual conversation about how it all went. We didn't talk because I was upset. I hadn't been prepared for Julia letting Gina go off with anyone, or even by herself. In my mind, this was a visit for Gina with her mother and siblings. It just didn't fit. As I drove, I began to realize why I was so disturbed. Even at 14, Gina was well on her way from girlhood to becoming a young woman. Since our first meeting, she had grown several inches taller. More pointedly, her figure was changing, her periods had started, her breasts were developing, and dressed as she now was in a t-shirt and jeans, her wavy blonde hair all tousled, and her violet eyes dancing with excitement, she was a very attractive young woman. If I could see it, so could "Ron". But what about Julia and what happens when the daughter becomes even more attractive than the mother? The more I thought about it, the more concerned I felt.

It was finally beginning to dawn on me that the combined efforts of Mrs Mercer and Miss Parks were entirely focused on the idea of returning Gina to her mother. While this is certainly a noble goal and the most satisfactory outcome to be achieved, I was beginning to learn that real life doesn't always work out like that and that it can be entirely possible that such an outcome doesn't work in the best interests of the child. Here with me, in my car, was a child who needed to live a peaceful, happy family life that was, over and above all else, secure. Gina needed to know where she would be living and who her friends and family would be, so that she could grow up with the same advantages as her friends, at the very least. In four years, she would be 18 years old and deemed ready to be independent, so at least to me, it was critically important that for the next four years, Gina be given this long-overdue secure foundation for her life.

Time, I decided, to give Mrs Mercer another call, and this time insist on sorting out Gina's future, with attention to Gina's needs.

Chapter Eighteen

As soon as I arrived at work on Monday morning, I made a call to Mrs Mercer's office. Mrs Mercer was in a meeting, so I left a message to call me at my office. The morning passed without a response. At lunch time, I called again. Mrs Mercer had an appointment in another location. I left another message, this time to call me at home. Finally, about five minutes after I arrived home, she called back. I was not in a good mood. "Hello," I said tersely.

"Hello, Mrs Kerry," Mrs Mercer's voice sounded calm and unhurried, "I'm sorry about the delay. I've had a busy day." So have I, I thought. "What can I do for you?" she asked.

"It's about Gina's visits," I began,

"Oh yes, Mrs Kerry, you've been having some ongoing difficulties with communications, as I recall....."

"I wouldn't say that there are ongoing difficulties," I retorted, "it's more like we continue having communications without any resolution of the problems, Mrs Mercer."

"Well, Mrs Kerry, as I have repeatedly reassured you. Miss Parks is working with Julia to help her deal more effectively with Gina's brother and sister, and a Financial Worker has now been added to the team......."

I interrupted, "I think that's great, Mrs Mercer. I'm all in favour of helping Julia to overcome her problems, but I don't entirely see how that helps Gina. What I would like to know is what is going to be done to improve Gina's ongoing problems with her mother."

"What exactly do you mean, Mrs Kerry?". Mrs Mercer's tone was sharp.

"Mrs Mercer, at this point I'm really confused. From the beginning, it was my understanding that you are Gina's social worker ---

the person who she can talk to about any problems she has, either with our family or with her visits to her mother. And Miss Parks is Julia Niemann's social worker who deals with Julia and her problems. Obviously it makes a lot of sense that you and Miss Parks should work together in this situation......"

"And we are, we are......," Mrs Mercer interrupted.

"But Mrs Mercer, I don't understand why you don't discuss Gina's feelings about things with Gina herself. At least to the best of my knowledge, you haven't discussed any of the visits she has made to her mother or her feelings about those visits."

"Mrs Kerry, I have constantly made it clear to you that Miss Parks and I are working together towards reuniting this family..............."

"But that's just it, Mrs Mercer," Somehow, I just had to get through to her that Gina needed to be consulted, at the very least, "how do you know that Gina even wants to return to live with her mother. Gina has now been part of my family for almost three years. We didn't go to Social Services and ask for her. We never even contemplated becoming foster parents. All we knew was that, apparently, no one in her immediate family actually wanted her (or so we were informed). She came to us because we asked for the opportunity to have her join our family where she was wanted and loved. We didn't plan for this to happen. It just happened."

"Now, Mrs Kerry, there is no cause for concern. I am quite satisfied that Gina is being well looked after in your home," All of this was spoken in Mercer's 'soothing and reassuring' voice (my interpretation).

I took the bull by the horns !"Mrs Mercer, the problem isn't with my house. The problem is with the entire setup at Julia Niemann's house....." and I proceeded to launch into a detailed description of our arrival in the hall, the unlocked door to Julia's apartment, the overly familiar attitude and manner of "Ron" in No. 1, Gina's unsupervised motorcycle ride to God-knows-where" with Ron, her late return and Ron's behaviour towards her, and of course Ron's 'familiar' attitude. On top of which, I had yet to meet Julia Niemann in person and I was beginning to feel that these so-called visits were more harmful than beneficial. I finally unloaded all the concerns that had been building up in my mind for months. I was very worked up and it didn't go down very well, especially when I concluded with "and I fail to see how any of these visits to her mother are in Gina's best interests. The only person whose best interests seem to be first and foremost is Julia Niemann."

There was a long silence on the line when I finished speaking. Finally, Mrs Mercer remarked: "Well, Mrs Kerry, it is clear to me that you are really upset. Perhaps, Mrs Kerry, if you are the kind of person who becomes so easily upset, you aren't the kind of person suited to be a foster parent for Gina?"

I was shocked, shocked. I was incredulous! I just couldn't believe my ears. But I certainly wasn't going to listen in silence to this kind of reproof. I took a few seconds, which seemed like minutes, to clear my mind! Then I shot back: "Mrs Mercer, Gina has been with the Kerry family for almost three years. She is a part of our family. We care about her. We love her. We want the very best for her and we are prepared to do whatever it takes to ensure the best possible life for her. Right now, Gina is entering puberty. She needs to feel secure, she needs guidance, she needs friends, she needs a happy, stable home. If anything should happen to interfere with the right of ANY member of my family to all those things, whether it is Ben or Amy or Gina, I would be upset. Right now, Gina is a member of my family. If she is upset, we are upset."

I paused, I knew that I was emotional. I had never spoken in this way to Mrs Mercer before, but a point had been reached where I was determined to be heard and where Gina's needs had to be considered as part of the entire equation.

I continued " We're a pretty normal family. I'm a pretty normal mother. That's what happens in a normal situation. Rather than making me unfit to be a mother, I believe it makes me extremely fit to be a mother, anybody's mother."

Another long silence followed. Then, "Mrs Kerry, this is a very typical foster home situation and it will be taken care of. I think you are over-reacting and need to relax. Gina is doing well and there is no need to worry. I'll make a note of your concerns." And she hung up.

I dropped the phone onto the receiver and sat down with my head in my hands. There was no good reason for it, but I felt completely crushed. NOT FIT! The words burned a hole in my heart. I might have started to cry, but just then I looked up and through the living room window I saw Gina coming up the driveway with her friend, April. Two happy young girls, giggling, arm in arm, laughing, enjoying each other's company after school.

I thought: So what, I love that happy girl with the fair hair and violet eyes. What if I'm not her 'real' mother. Who was I? Did that matter? What mattered to me was that I was the person who was there for her, in whatever role, and she was as much mine as any child can belong to any mother. Just like Ben and Amy, Gina would be mine for just a little while, until like any baby bird, she flapped her wings and flew up, up, up and away in the big sky of life.

In the meantime, this mother bird would do whatever it took to make the future of this little lost chick as bright as possible and to make sure her wings were ready when the time came to fly up up up into that sky.

On Tuesday evening, I called Bette Vogt.

Bette listened patiently as I gave her a rather colourful description of the recent drama, Gina's last visit with Julia, the motorcycle trip with Ron, and finally my discussion with Mrs Mercer including Mrs Mercer's comments regarding my suitability as a foster mother.

"Of course, you were upset," she sympathized.

"Bette," I continued, "it's not so much that Mrs Mercer is so perfunctory with me, what bothers me much more is the fact that she shows so little interest in the effect these visits are having on Gina. I realize that when children are in foster care, it's because there's a problem at home but even if the problem at home is solved, does that mean that the child is going to automatically okay when he or she is returned to the home, especially when the child hasn't been living at home for quite a long time? I just don't get it."

"I tend to agree," said Bette, "but it looks like Social Services has a different idea about all of this."

"Well, Bette, as you know I have been doing my best to work with Social Services cooperatively, but this attitude of theirs has been going on for months and months now, and it's starting to get to me. I have to find a way to put an end to it. That's why I'm calling you --- to take you up on your offer to call James Foster in Victoria."

"Yes, of course, I can call James," she replied.

"But, Bette, I would like you to be clear that although I'm a friend of yours and you are close to the situation, I'm not asking that he take action just because of that. All I want you to ask him to do is to request Gina's file and read it over, and then take whatever action he considers best. Never mind that we're friends. Just do what he thinks best."

"I'll make sure make that's clear when I talk to him," agreed Bette.

"Oh, Bette, I'm so grateful. Thanks a million – for me and Gina --- I feel so relieved."

"Glad to do it, Maura. I'll get back to you after I've spoken to him, and in the meantime, try to relax."

'I will. It's spring break in a couple of weeks, and we'll be off on our trip to Disneyland. That should help".

"Great timing. Are you all going?"

"Not all of us," I replied, "Steve is too busy to take time off, so my mom is coming along to keep me company and help organize the kids, etc."

"Sounds great. I'll be back to you before then," and Bette hung up,

I honestly felt as if a great weight had been lifted. I believed I had always been more than reasonable with the local Social Services office about the situation. I had never intended to go over Mrs Mercer's head, but when you have been 'spinning your wheels' for quite a while, there comes a point where you have to exercise your options.

Two days later, Bette called to advise me that she had spoken to James. He had requested the file, and we would hear something as soon as he had reviewed it.

In the meantime, we were going to Disneyland! It would be a really good spring break for all of us.

PART VII

Escape to Disneyland

Chapter Nineteen

The idea of a visit to Disneyland had been enthusiastically received and planned for by Ben, Amy and Gina for over a year now. At the end of each month, both Ben and Gina had tallied up their paper route money, kept some cash on hand for 'expenses', and then we made a pilgrimage to the bank where Disneyland funds were deposited to savings. Amy did very well in her housekeeping assistant role, and she generally came along with us and built up her own Disneyland nest egg. Once the agreed savings program had begun and the children began to see their savings grow, a friendly contest began between them, as to who could save the most. When the third week of March arrived, each of them had amassed a tidy sum of spending money and they were ready for the trip and as enthusiastic about spending it as they had been about saving it! It was agreed that I would be the 'banker' for the trip. I would make a note of the amount of money each of them had, and I would issue funds to them and keep a tally of the remaining balance. It seemed like a sensible plan.

My mother packed and came over to stay at our house the night before our departure, the idea being that all five of us would take a taxi to the airport, arriving at around 10:00 a.m. Our charter flight left at Noon and included lunch and we arrived at San Diego about 3 hours later. The plan was fairly straightforward. However, as with most plans involving three excited children aged 14, 11 and almost 9, it proved to be somewhat chaotic in practice.

We were all ready for a complete break, so we made the most of Disneyland, beginning with breakfast at the Disneyland Hotel on our first morning, served to an unbelievable hoard of parents and children. For Gina, who had missed our trip to Hawaii, it was perhaps her first experience of a family fun holiday. She was flushed and excited and determined not to miss anything. I was glad to have my mother along to keep track of all three children and, after the stresses of the last few months, it was good to lighten up and just enjoy our time together. Breakfast at the Disneyland Hotel was quickly followed up with Pirates of the Caribbean when we all shed our inhibitions, laughing and screaming like a bunch of idiots. We enjoyed everything, including a day at the San Diego Zoo where we agreed that the most interesting animal was the aardvark, which none of us had ever seen before. We even learned how to spell "aardvark"!

On another day, we took a stretch bus to an enormous shopping centre at Newport Beach where the girls purchased gauchos, which were the 'in' fashion at the time. Keeping track of three children in a large shopping centre proved to be quite a chaotic experience, which Dorrie and I barely survived. The highlight of the trip, as far as Ben was concerned, was when he found a crumpled up twenty dollar bill in a bush outside a drugstore. When we took it to the cashier, we were informed that the store policy was to hold any 'found' money for two days and if it had not been claimed by then, the money would be given to the finder. Ben was in luck! After waiting patiently for two days, it wasn't claimed, and he became $20 richer. Feeding five people for over a week wasn't without its budgetary challenges. We finally discovered a chain of restaurants where they charged by the inch of height of each child. Since Amy was relatively short for her age, this worked very much to our advantage!

For my mother and me the most shattering experience was our ride down the Matterhorn. We made the mistake of buying ice creams just before we climbed into our seats. By the time we arrived at the foot of the 'mountain', the ice creams were as shattered as we were! The children thought it was hilarious.

Perhaps the biggest challenge was in establishing the order of progression in getting everyone off to sleep each night. Our problem was established on the first night. After the long trip, we were all very tired and, as it transpired, Dorrie and I fell asleep first. That wouldn't have been a problem, except for the fact that, according to all three children, both Dorrie and I snored VERY LOUDLY, preventing them from getting to sleep "for ages", as Ben said. After that, we timed it so that Dorrie and I would sit outside beside the hot tub and enjoy a glass of California wine, returning when everyone was asleep, or almost asleep so that the two of us would be the last ones to hit the sack. That worked, thank God. It also gave Dorrie and me some time together and I realized from our chats that spending time with the children on the trip had given Dorrie a better understanding of Gina. The two of them had sat together on the bus ride to the shopping centre and Dorrie told me that Gina had told her all about how hard she had worked to catch up on her reading and how much better it was going now.

Dorrie said, "Gina told me that she didn't begin learning to read until she was 8 years old!".

"Yes," I said, "Gina's mom kept her at home most of the time to help with the little ones, so she didn't start school properly until she was almost eight. Luckily, one of her teachers stayed late and gave her a lot of help."

"Gina's hasn't had it so easy then....." Dorrie remarked.

"Yes, mum, **it's** a lot. For a child her age, she's had many things to deal with," I replied.

Dorrie nodded, "I can see that now". I felt that Dorrie was realizing a lot about Gina.

Like all holidays, both the time and the money went too quickly. It was time to go home. The dirty socks, little gifts and new t-shirts were quickly stuffed into the suitcases, and we tumbled into the cab for the airport. A few hours later, we found ourselves back on the North Shore at the top of our drive, unloading our luggage in a sea of confusion with an excited Tessa jumping and barking all around. We were home!

PART VIII

Permanent Custody

Chapter Twenty

Spring Break was over. The kids went back to school, I returned to work, and Dorrie went home to her apartment. Tessa was certainly glad we had returned. There is nothing quite like a friendly dog to make you feel appreciated. Steve was glad to see us, too, but he confessed to me that the peace and quiet of having the house to himself without the phone calls and stresses from the Gina situation, did him a lot of good. He looked and sounded more relaxed and I realized that the trip had done a lot to de-stress me as well.

Of course, it wasn't long before 'real life' began again, heralded on Monday morning by a phone call from Julia Niemann, asking if Gina could visit on the coming Saturday afternoon. After a two week break, it was a reasonable request, so I made arrangements to bring Gina over for lunch on Saturday and pick her up later that afternoon and bring her back home to us for supper. Gina was okay with that. She had bought some little souvenir gifts for Scott and Lucy. Like all of us, she was much more relaxed.

Just before supper time on Wednesday, I received a phone call from Mrs Mercer. I hadn't expected to hear from her so soon after our return. However, the reason quickly became clear.

"Hello, Mrs Kerry, how was the trip to Disneyland?", she began.

"Just great, thanks," I replied, "we had a good time".

"That's good," she commented, "everyone benefits from a break. I imagine the children are all back at school, now......."

"Yes. It's back to the usual stuff. What can I do for you, Mrs Mercer?" I asked.

"Well, Mrs Kerry, I'm just calling to let you know that we have been advised by the office of the Superintendent of Child Welfare that the Superintendent will be making an application for permanent custody of Gina."

"Permanent custody.......", I echoed.

"Yes. The Superintendent's office has been reviewing Gina's file and a decision has been made that it's in Gina's best interests to remove custody from her mother."

I thought it best not to comment, so I simply asked, "What will happen now?"

"We are waiting for more instructions from the Superintendent's office," Mrs Mercer continued, "but there will be a hearing in Family Court."

"When will that be?" I asked.

"Well, first of all, because Gina is over 12 years of age, she is entitled to representation, so a lawyer will be appointed to represent her and, as her foster mother, you'll be contacted about that. Also, a lawyer will be representing the Superintendent and Gina's mother will also be entitled to legal representation."

"I see," I commented, "so it looks to me like it will be a while before a hearing takes place."

"Yes, Mrs Kerry, there's a lot of preparation involved. All that we require is, of course, that you co-operate with us in the entire matter of the hearing. The hearing itself won't likely take place until the Fall or later."

"Of course I'll help. So, do you want me to tell Gina about it, "I asked, "she's going to visit her mother this Saturday? And can you tell me if her mother knows yet? It would be helpful if we knew this before Gina's visit" I continued.

"I think Julia has been informed, but I'll see if I can reach Miss Parks before the end of the week so that I can get back to you before Saturday," Mrs Mercer replied.

"That would be a big help," I said, "I'm a bit concerned about how Julia may react to the news."

"Yes, I think we all are" replied Mrs Mercer. "I'll get back to you as soon as possible."

"Thanks," I said, and hung up the phone.

I sat down and caught my breath! All I could think was, IT'S ACTUALLY GOING TO HAPPEN! Bette Vogt had called James Foster and her call had borne fruit. Yes, I had done an 'end run' around the system, but what counted most, in the end, was that James Foster had read the file and he had decided Gina needed a break! It wasn't going to be easy! A lot of people were going to be involved. But all the facts would be aired in court and Gina would have a chance for a better future. I felt an overwhelming surge of relief. But first I would need to talk to Gina about it.

It was a busy first week back at home, but I finally got a chance to tell Gina on Thursday evening. She appeared in the kitchen right after supper, wondering where she could find some wrapping paper. At Disneyland, she had bought a little Tinker Bell doll for Lucy and a kind of space car for Scott, as well as a pretty star-shaped dish with 'When you Wish Upon A Star" painted on it, for her mother. I brought the paper to her bedroom and we chatted as she began wrapping them.

"How did my mom sound, when she called?" Gina wanted to know.

"Just fine, Gina, she sounded just fine."

"Well, I hope she's a bit easier to get along with now than before we left." The two of us were remembering all the blocked phone calls and hoping that such things were now in the past. I decided to seize the opportunity to discuss Mrs Mercer's call.

"Gina," I began, "when Mrs Mercer called the other day, she gave me some news that I think you should know before you see your mum".

"What kind of news? They're not sick or anything, are they?"

"No. They're just fine. But Mrs Mercer told me that while we were away, she received a letter from the office of the Superintendent of Child Welfare – that's in Victoria --- and it has been decided to apply to the court to change custody from your mother to his office."

"Change custody! What does that mean, mum? Will I have to move and live somewhere else?" Gina sounded anxious.

"No, Gina. What it means is that the Superintendent thinks that it would be better if you were in the care of his office, rather than continuing in your mother's care. I mean, as you know, your mother hasn't been well, and she is still struggling to take care of just herself and Scott and Lucy. So the Superintendent's office feels that it would be better for both of you if his office took over the responsibility of looking after you."

"But I don't know the Superintendent....."

"No, of course not, although I can tell you that he is okay and his name is James Foster. So if custody is given to the Superintendent, his office will be in charge of where you live and you will continue to live with us."

"And what about my mom?"

"You would still be able to see your mum and visit her, just like now. But you wouldn't go back to live permanently with her unless that was agreed with the Superintendent."

"So the Superintendent would be the boss of me, and not my mom anymore?"

"Yes. I believe everything would pretty much stay as it is. Mrs Mercer would be your social worker and you would continue to live with us. At least, that would be until you were 18 years of age."

"What happens then?"

"When you reach 18, you are considered to be an adult and nobody would have custody any longer. You would be grown up and free to do as you wish."

"Wow........!" Gina exclaimed, "I hadn't thought much about that before ... but I'm soon going to be 18, aren't I?"

"Yes, Gina, you are growing up fast."

"So when will all of this change be done?" Gina wanted to know.

"Well, Gina, it's not as simple as it sounds. That's why I thought I should talk to you about it now before you see your mother again. You see, before any of this can happen, there has to be a hearing in the Family Court."

"Why?".

"Well, now that you are over 12 years of age, the law says that you have to have a lawyer to represent you. The lawyer will talk to you to make sure that you are happy with making the change."

"Really?"

"Yes, really. Also, your mother will have a lawyer to represent her because the Superintendent is asking that you be placed in his care – which is actually the care of the Government."

"But what happens if my mother doesn't agree? You know how difficult she can be. And she gets upset easily….."

"Yes, Gina, I know, and that's why your mother will have a lawyer. She will also have Miss Parks to work with her. I think the Superintendent is hoping that your mother will see how much better it will be for her not to have to worry about how you are doing."

"But we don't know how my mother will feel, do we?"

"No, Gina, we don't."

"And, lastly, the Superintendent will have a lawyer who will work with Mrs Mercer and tell the court all the reasons why the Superintendent feels you should be in his custody."

"And when will it all happen?" Gina asked again.

"Mrs Mercer says that it will likely happen in the Family Court in the fall……."

"After we get back from Sandy Bay?"

"Yes, after we get back from Sandy Bay".

"Oh, what a relief, mum, I don't think I can get my mind around all of this for a while. And I'm wondering if my mom knows about it. Have they told her yet?"

"That's exactly what I thought, too, when Mrs Mercer told me," I said, "Mrs Mercer is going to check with Miss Parks and she has promised to let me know by tomorrow, so you will know what the situation is when you are visiting. But when your mum called me to arrange the visit, she didn't sound much different, so I don't think she knew then."

"Just so long as I don't have to leave home ---- like, I can still be here with you………

"Of course you will still be here with us! I'm sorry to have dumped this on you all at once," I apologized, "but I felt you needed to know before you see your mother."

"That's okay, mom" .She smiled.

"And, Gina, I realize you will need to take a bit of time to think all of this over. It's important for you to understand what the

Superintendent wants to do, and it's also important that you are happy with the whole idea. That's why you will have a lawyer of your very own because nobody, including all of our family, wants you to have to do anything that makes you very unhappy. I know that you may sometimes feel a bit guilty about not being around to help your mother with Scott and Lucy ---- but you must realize that while you are their big sister and have been very kind to them, especially in Winnipeg, it is your mother's job to take care of them......."

Gina leaned over and hugged me. "I know, mom. Now, what do you think, have I done a good job with the gift wrap?." She had topped the parcels with curly bows. They looked lovely and I told her so. Then it was time for homework. And tomorrow I would hear from Mrs Mercer.

Chapter Twenty-One

"They look really good, don't they, mum?" It was Saturday morning and time to drive across the city to Julia's place. Gina was asking for my approval. She was wearing the dark blue gauchos she had bought on our shopping trip to Newport Beach together with a matching blue gingham shirt and summer sandals. Her hair was tied back into a ponytail. She looked great and I told her so. Holding her bag of gifts, she hopped into the passenger seat, we fastened our seat belts and were soon on the highway.

Both of us were feeling a bit apprehensive. Mrs Mercer had called on Friday to tell me that she hadn't been able to reach Miss Parks, so she didn't know whether or not Julia had been advised of the Superintendent's decision, etc. I had a talk about it with Gina on Friday evening and we decided we would wait until we knew for sure that Miss Parks had told Julia before Gina mentioned it. Even so, we both felt nervous.

We pulled up in front of Julia's house in good time – just before noon. I wondered if I would have an opportunity to finally speak to Julia this time and meet Scott and Lucy as well. When we arrived, there was no one around except for a guy in a T-shirt and jeans who appeared to be tinkering with a very old blue Ford that was up on jacks and parked in the lane that ran along the far side of the front yard. As we started up the path, he scrambled out from under the car and walked towards us.

"Hi, there," he said, "I guess you must be Gina," and to me "you are the foster mum."

"Yes, I'm Gina. Who are you?", she asked.

"Oh, I'm Dave. I've moved in with Ron downstairs. He told me all about you."

Gina and I started up the long flight of stairs. We were almost at the top when the front door burst open and a little boy more or less tumbled out. It had to be Scott ---- he was about 2 feet tall with reddish hair that seemed to be sticking out in all directions, blue eyes, a wide mouth and a slightly over-size nose covered in freckles.

"Gina, Gina --- hi there Gina." Scott flung himself at her. "Hey Scott," Gina gave him a big hug, "good to see you!"

By this time, we had entered the downstairs hall where Ron was standing, and Julia was about halfway down the stairs, carrying a little fair-haired girl---- Lucy ----.

Julia said, "Thanks for bringing my Gina over."

"She's been looking forward to seeing you all," I said, "It's good to meet you, Julia. I hope you all have a great day".

"Oh, we will", said Ron. "We have big plans."

"Great," I said, "I'll be back around 7:30 to pick Gina up."

"'Fine. Bye now," said Julia as I turned and left.

That had all gone pretty well, I thought as I drove away. If Julia did know about the hearing etc., she hadn't shown it.

On the drive home, I thought about the entire situation. I had already called Bette Vogt to tell her the result of her call to James Foster. Bette was pleased. Like me, she believed that removal of custody from Julia would be in Gina's best interests She asked me to let her know how things were going as the matter progressed.

I had also talked the matter over with Steve and my mother. Steve had never been impressed by Julia's behaviour, but he wasn't so sure that putting Gina in the custody of the Superintendent of Child Welfare would work out well. My mother, who had never had to deal with anything other than her own "normal" family situation, was horrified at the idea that Gina would have a lawyer who would come to our house to see what kind of home Gina was living in. To my mother, this seemed a bit insulting. I did my best to explain to her that if you are going to remove a child from the care of his or her birth mother, it's important not to make the situation even worse by placing the child in a home that may not work out any better. Somewhat to my chagrin, I began to think about our home and ask myself how I was doing as a mother and "homemaker" – a question I had never even thought about before we added this 'new' child. Yes, I had a lot on my mind these days.

It was quiet when I returned to Garden Street to pick Gina up. The old blue Ford was no longer there, and Ron was sitting at the top of the front steps with a can of lager in his hand. "Hey there, Maura," he greeted me as I started up the stairs. It appeared that Gina had told him my name.

"Hi," I responded. "Where's the rest of the gang?".

"Oh, they've all gone off in the car with Dave. He finally got it going and has taken them to get ice cream."

"Then I might as well join you and wait," I said. "You didn't go along for an ice cream too?".

"Well, it's this way," he said, "Dave doesn't like sharing Julia. And anyway, I'm more of a beer fan," Ron smiled. "Would you like to join me?"

"Thanks for the offer, but I'm driving…" I began.

"Don't beat yourself up," Ron laughed, "one beer never hurt anyone".

"All the same," I said, "I think I'll pass."

"It's your loss." Ron smiled.

Just then, we heard the sound of an engine as the old Ford clunked its way down the street, turned into the lane and parked. As Dave and Julia emerged from the front seats, the back doors opened and Gina, Scott and Lucy tumbled out and ran across the grass to the foot of the steps. "Hi, everyone," I said. "Where's the ice cream?"

"Oh, it's all eaten up already," gasped Gina.

"It was good," said Lucy, "I had chocolate".

"And I had Neapolitan", added Scott.

"Then I guess it was a successful trip," I said.

"Yeah," they're a great bunch of kids, Dave commented."Julia has a great little family."

It was the first time I had seen Julia with the children and, for that matter, the first time I had heard her speak, "Scott and Lucy are wonderful kids and we're all so happy with Gina here because then we are a complete family."

I turned to Gina, "Gina, it's getting late. We should say 'bye' and head back." As I walked down the steps to the front path, Gina hugged Scott and Lucy and Julia. We arrived at my car and just as we turned to wave, Ron called, "Bye, Cutie, see you soon!" ... to Gina, I assumed. This, followed by Dave, who shouted, "Just remember, Gina is Julia's daughter and always will be."

This kind of farewell, coming from someone we had just met and who, as far as I knew, had only recently met Julia, struck me as rather odd. I turned to Gina as we fastened our seatbelts, "What was that all about?"

Gina looked at me with a frown, "She knows, mum, she knows",

"You mean your mum knows about the Superintendent and the custody hearing?"

"Oh, yes, she knows all about it", Gina continued, "She didn't say anything when I arrived there --- not at first. I gave Lucy and Scott their gifts and they really liked them. And my mother loved the little dish. Then she asked me all about the trip to Disneyland and I told her what a good time we all had, and then she said that she was glad that I was able to go there but that it had kind of spoiled things for her. So when I asked her what she meant, she said that she had planned on OUR family going together but it would be spoiled now because I had already been there."

"And then?" I intervened,

"I told her that it wouldn't make any difference because Disneyland is the kind of place where you could go every day for days and days and still not have seen everything, but she was kind of angry about it. Then I told her I was sorry about that, and anyway, there were lots of other things we could do as a family. That was when she got really angry. She said that she was fed up with the social workers and having to arrange visits with me and she wasn't going to put up with it much longer. She said she wasn't going to let the Superintendent break up her family and she was going to see to it that I came home to live with her and Scott and Lucy again."

"What did you say to that?" I asked.

"Well, I didn't say anything. When my mom gets mad, the best thing to do is to say nothing because she doesn't really listen."

"Didn't she ask you how you felt about the whole thing, and how you felt about coming back to live with her and the kids?"

"No. My mom never asks you how you feel about anything."

"Well, maybe Miss Parks and Mrs Mercer can arrange for you to sit down with your mom and talk things over."

Gina smiled wryly, "That would be good, but I don't think there's much chance of that ever happening."

"You don't?", I was surprised.

"No, I don't," Gina said firmly, "You see, this guy Dave is around my mom all the time. He kind of bosses her around, tells her what to do all the time."

"But he's just a downstairs neighbour, isn't he?" I asked.

"Oh, he is NOW," said Gina, "but my mom told me that she and Dave are going to move in together....."

"Well, there won't be much room for you if that happens......"
I began.

"But that's just it", Gina continued, "she says they are going to rent a house, and it will be big so that I will have my own room"

"But that would be pretty expensive, I think......" I commented.

"Yeah --- well that's the other part that I don't like," Gina's voice was emotional, "they're planning on having Ron move in with them to help with the rent."

"You don't like that?"

"No, I don't. I don't like Ron at all."

"Why not?" I probed.

"Well, when I'm there, he's always hanging around. And he calls me "cutie" --- Yuk! I don't like that. And he's always asking me if I would like to go out somewhere."

"Like, where", I asked.

"Well, this time, he kept asking me if I wouldn't like to go out for another ride on his motorcycle and we could go to a movie."

"Didn't you tell him 'no'?"

"I did tell him but he just kept asking me again and again. I didn't want to go out in the car with mum and Dave for ice cream, but in the end, I went with them just so I could get away from Ron".

"I see."

"He just embarrasses me," Gina looked stressed, "telling me that my hair looks cute, or he likes my gauchos."

"But your hair does look cute, and so do your gauchos," I pointed out.

"Oh, I know, but it's just something about the way he does it all the time. I just want him to leave me alone."

"Then we'll just have to see what we can do to stop all of this." I reached across the seat and squeezed her hand, "I'm glad you told me about it, Gina. I'll have to speak to Mrs Mercer about it. I wonder if Miss Parks knows anything about the plan to rent a house?"

"Probably not", was Gina's comment as we arrived at our front drive.

Once in the house, joking with Ben and Amy, and planning a trip to the pitch and putt on Sunday afternoon, it wasn't long before Gina was once again her usual sunny self.

From my point of view, it was beginning to look like a rocky uphill road lay ahead. My priority would be to discuss the fact that Julia was planning to oppose the Superintendent's application. And the second priority would be to determine if Miss Parks had any idea at all that Julia had a boyfriend and was making alternate plans about where she and her children would be living in the future.

Chapter Twenty-Two

I intentionally arrived at work early on Monday morning, giving myself time to call Mrs Mercer's office and set up an appointment to see her after work on Wednesday afternoon. About half an hour after I returned from lunch, I received a telephone call from Shelley Pope, secretary to Jeanette Munro of Harris & Harris, a well-known Vancouver firm, specializing in family law. Miss Pope advised me that Mrs Munro had been appointed to represent Gina, and she wanted to meet me as a first step in preparing for the eventual hearing. We made an appointment for 3:30 p.m. that Friday. I told Gina about the two appointments after supper that evening, and I could see that she was much reassured to know that we would be able to deal with the ongoing situation with her mother. Steve was happy that steps were underway to keep the situation under control because we were both somewhat apprehensive that Julia would once again begin the 'war' of blocked telephone calls etc. We had had enough!

My appointment with Mrs Mercer went very well. She hadn't heard from Miss Parks and, because of the information I gave her, would contact her immediately to find out what steps were needed. She wasn't happy to learn about the involvement of either Dave or Ron, whether with Julia's agreement or not, in her situation. And she was visibly unhappy when I told her about Ron's manner and behaviour towards Gina. She understood exactly where I was coming from in my concern about leaving Gina with her mother when there was little or no supervision. When I talked about our worry that Julia might again begin a barrage of blocked telephone calls, Mrs Mercer agreed that it would be best if Gina didn't visit with her mother again, until some progress had been made to deal with Dave and Ron.

That evening, Gina and I discussed my visit with Mrs Mercer, and I asked Gina how she felt about not seeing her mum or the kids for a while.

"Oh, that's okay with me," Gina smiled, "it's not forever. It's just a relief that I won't have to deal with Ron or Dave either. I hope your meeting with Mrs Munro turns out well." So did I.

Harris & Harris's offices were on the 16th floor of the TD Tower, with a **(deletion)** view over the harbour, which I admired as I sat in the reception area. Mrs Munro came out, introduced herself, and showed me into her office. She was a slightly built woman with short, brunette hair, lovely wide brown eyes, and a beautiful complexion, possibly in her mid-forties. She was good looking. Better still, she had what I considered a "kind" face. I liked her from the start. Since she knew I was a paralegal, we began with some 'shop' talk, followed by a summary of our families. It was good to know that she was the mother of two primary aged children also.

Then our conversation turned to Gina and how she had come to be a foster child. Mrs Munro had read the entire file and she told me how surprised she was when she learned how Gina had come to our family. Of course, I had always assumed that having an 'unplanned' foster child was different, but Mrs Munro – who represented children all the time – said it was very unusual and we talked at some length about the first summer when Gina had turned up on our doorstep and how she had returned to us again and again and, from my point of view at least, become a 'part' of us. Mrs Munro was intrigued by that.

As I sat and more or less narrated what had transpired from that first day until the present, Mrs Munro made notes (she also asked me if it was okay to record what I was saying --- which it was). When we finished, she explained that she needed to come to our house to meet Gina and be shown around. She wanted to meet Gina at home, rather than have Gina come to an office setting, where she would be less relaxed. It was important that Gina feels at ease with Mrs Munro because she was going to have to determine where Gina was at, from an emotional point of view, when it came to being taken into the care of the Superintendent; and Mrs Munro would be doing her best to explain to Gina what that meant and how it would work out as she continued to grow up.

We set up an appointment for Mrs Munro to visit our house and meet Gina on a Saturday afternoon two weeks' later. I felt very encouraged after the meeting. Mrs Munro was going to be good for Gina. That was what mattered most to me.

Chapter Twenty-Three

The following week was a busy one. I set up an appointment to see Mrs Mercer at her office on the following Wednesday afternoon. The time had come, I felt, to meet with Mrs Mercer in person and have a serious discussion about the situation during Gina's visits with her mother and the fact that it was bothering me so much that I was reluctant to be involved in any more visits, at least until the matter of Ron and Dave had been dealt with. Remembering Mrs Mercer's attitude when I was previously upset and disturbed, I was careful to remain calm and controlled.

Mrs Mercer was very pleasant and, as it turned out, she hadn't heard from Miss Parks and was completely unaware that Julia had been told about the Superintendent's application, etc. and intended to oppose it. For that matter, she knew nothing about Dave and Ron, or of Julia's plan to rent a house with Ron. I also mentioned that Gina had told me she was embarrassed by Ron's behaviour towards her, at which point Mrs Mercer's shoulders stiffened and she shook her head. "No! No! This kind of thing just won't do. Not when Gina is visiting. In fact, not at all. I'll speak to Miss Parks right away. As I'm sure you know, Julia doesn't have a very stable history when it comes to the opposite sex. These two fellows are definitely interfering. It must be nipped in the bud....."

"I'm glad you understand," I said. "Because I promised Gina that I would speak to you and ask you to help. Quite understandably, she doesn't want to do another visit with her mother if she has to cope with Dave and Ron also."

"I agree," Mrs Mercer nodded her head, "Until I have spoken with Miss Parks and we take steps to clear up this situation, I think it is best if Gina doesn't visit. If Julia contacts you, I suggest you make some kind of excuse.

"It's May now and, as you know, as soon as exams etc. are over, we'll begin packing up to go to Sandy Bay for the summer," I began.

"That's probably a good thing," said Mrs Mercer. "By the way, how is it going with Jeanette Munro?"

"I've already met with her," I said, "We got along very well. She's coming to the house to meet Gina and spend some time getting to know her next Saturday."

"Very good, very good!" Mrs Mercer continued, "It was wise of you to come to see me in person about all of this. It's quite serious. And of course, I'll let you know what action is being taken. Something needs to be done, not just regarding Gina, but also regarding the other children.

Gina was relieved when we talked about it that evening. Mrs Mercer understood how she felt and was going to help, and Gina wouldn't have to visit again until things had been straightened out. So if Julia called, all we had to do was make an excuse. We decided Gina would say she had to study for tests (which was true anyway).

Before we knew it, Saturday had arrived, and Gina would be meeting Mrs Munro after lunch. The two of us discussed it as we tidied up the breakfast dishes.

"Oh, mum, I'm nervous about it" Gina really did sound nervous! "How do you talk to a lawyer?"

"Well, you shouldn't be nervous," I reassured her, "I've met Mrs Munro, and I liked her. She's very nice and she has two primary aged kids of her own. She's about my age and I think you are going to become good friends."

"You think?"

"Yes, I think. Remember, her job is to help you.

"But what if she asks questions and I don't know the answer? Or what if she doesn't understand things --- like, you know, I explained a lot of things to you, but you are good at understanding.........."

"Well, Gina, one of the reasons she is coming here to see you is because she thinks it will be more comfortable for you to meet her in your own home. And she wants to see where you live and meet all of us and find out how you feel about things.

"Sounds good," Gina was a bit more enthusiastic now.

"Yes, it's good. And, Gina, Mrs Munro's job is to find out about you and learn what you want and what makes you feel happy. So it's very important that you are honest with her about how you feel. Don't tell her you are happy with something if you aren't happy."

"Even if it might make you upset?" Gina asked.

"Yes, even if it might upset me, or anyone else, for that matter," I said, "she needs to know how you feel. And I want you to be honest with her, even if it might not be exactly what makes me happy. Got it?"

"Yes, I've got it." Gina smiled. "But I'm sure there isn't anything that makes me happy that you wouldn't like, too!"

"Let's hope not!", I made a 'mad' face at her and we both laughed.

Chapter Twenty-Four

As arranged, Jeanette Munro arrived punctually at 2 o'clock that Saturday. She was dressed casually in jeans, a sports t-shirt, and a bomber jacket. As we made our way to the living room, she commented on the lovely view. She had parked her car and gone for a short hike around the block, to get an idea of our neighbourhood and we laughed when she commented on how challenging the hill to our house had been. I responded by pointing out that it was equally challenging when descended on a toboggan, which the Kerry family often enjoyed.

Gina was busy tidying her room, and I suggested to Mrs Munro that we might as well begin by going downstairs to meet Gina there. The introduction went well. Mrs Munro smiled and said 'hi' and Gina responded with a shy 'hi'. I must say Gina's room looked a lot more organized than it had in a long while. As for Gina herself, she was wearing her prized gauchos once again, her hair was down and looked a lot tidier than usual. Having done my little bit, I excused myself and suggested that they would most likely find me in the living room or kitchen when they were through.

I had a lot to do once I returned upstairs and it seemed no time before Mrs Munro and Gina appeared in the kitchen. They were laughing and appeared to be comfortable with each other. Just then, Steve, Ben and Amy arrived home from their shopping trip to the mall to buy new 'runners' for both kids. I made the introductions and they all chatted briefly until Mrs Munro excused herself. "That went very well, Maura, thanks a lot," she said as I saw her to the door, "I'll be giving you a call early this week as I think it would be a good idea if we could meet again soon. Several things came up during my conversation with Gina – and I'm hoping you can help clarify some of them."

"That's fine with me," I said, "just give me a call and we'll arrange a time."

With that, she was gone, and I returned to the living room where I found Gina by herself. Steve had gone downstairs to watch TV and Ben and Amy had gone to their rooms --to try on their new runners, I assumed.

Gina was standing at the window, watching Mrs Munro's car depart. "Well, how did it go?", I asked.

"Pretty good, I think," Gina turned to me, "You were right, mum, she's really nice. I liked her too."

"What did you like the most?". I was curious.

"That's easy," Gina smiled, "she told me it was okay to say how I felt. She said everything I said to her was a secret between the two of us. I like that best, mum because it means that I won't get into trouble if I say something my mom wouldn't like,"

"That's right, Gina, but don't forget it also includes everyone else --- me, your dad, and so on."

"Yes, I know" she replied.

"Which reminds me!", I exclaimed, "While you and Mrs Munro were busy downstairs, your dad called to ask if you would like to go over there for the day next Saturday."

"Yeah, sure," Gina sparkled.

"Okay, then. Why don't you give him a call and set it up?" I suggested. "And, by the way, I didn't tell him about the Superintendent's application and all that stuff. I thought maybe you would like to do that."

"Okay, but I don't know if I can explain it all exactly right," Gina frowned.

"Don't worry, he can always ask me".

"I'll call him now," she said. And off she went down the stairs to the phone.

I met with Jeanette Munro late on the following Wednesday afternoon. She began by telling me how much she had enjoyed visiting my home and meeting the rest of my family. She said she felt that Gina was fortunate in being able to live in such a pleasant neighbourhood, close to school, shops etc. She felt that Gina was pretty much herself; in other words, behaving naturally and not trying to create a particular impression. And as far as she could tell, Gina had settled down well at school, had made friends, and felt that she was a part of the community. Overall, Gina was happy with her day-to-day life; however, she did have some concerns and she was hoping that by meeting with me, she could resolve them.

Of course, I was pleased with what Mrs Munro had to say, and I told her so. As to her concerns, "What, exactly, would you like me to help you clarify?" I asked.

"Well, as I mentioned, for the most part, Gina was pretty relaxed and open with me. However, when it came to discussing her relationship with her mother and her siblings, she seemed to withdraw and I couldn't get her to say much. In fact, she barely said anything. I know there was a lot of trauma at the time Gina came to live with her grandparents, so I didn't push it with her. But we are talking about removing custody from her mother, so I do have to get a better idea of what happened and about her past relationship with her mother. I'm sure you understand…"

"Of course, Mrs Munro," I said, "but I'm just wondering about what Gina told you about her time in Winnipeg and the circumstances leading up to her coming to British Columbia, as well as the circumstances during the time she lived in Winnipeg --- her schooling problems etc. There are also all the circumstances following her arrival in British Columbia, the time when we had to return her to her mother ….when she was abandoned again, and so on. Did you discuss all of this with Gina?"

"Winnipeg! There is very little mention of Winnipeg in my file," Mrs Munro exclaimed, "and nothing about after her return to her grandparents. I do have particulars of when you went to her grandparents and told them you did foster and wanted to know if Gina was available to be a foster child."

I was shocked at her words "*you went to her grandparents and told them you did foster…..*"If that is what the file showed, then the information in the file was incorrect and should be amended.

I turned to Mrs Munro. "If you don't have any information about Winnipeg, then I can certainly understand why you have concerns. That, and also the circumstances under which Gina came to live with us which are not at all as recorded in your file."

"Do I take it that you can help me with all of this?" Mrs Munro responded.

"Yes, I can, I most certainly can, but of course you would have to be satisfied that I was telling the truth because it appears to me that some of the information in your file is quite the opposite of the facts."

"I will bear that in mind, of course," she said "but can you please begin setting the record straight. Oh and by the way, I want to have my secretary type out a record of what you say, so I'm assuming it is okay if I record it?"

"Yes, that's fine," I agreed. Then I took a big breath, and I began recounting the entire story, from the day this lovely little girl showed up in my garden until the court finally placed her in the care of Social Services, who allowed her to remain with our family. The sad little story of what had happened in Winnipeg, the 'on approval' visits to her family members; and on and on, including my current concerns about Gina's visits with her mother, the intervention of Ron and Dave and my concerns in that regard.

I also took the time to explain to Mrs Munro that Gina had a happy relationship with her father in Vancouver and enjoyed her visits with him. I also pointed out that we would soon be leaving for our usual summer at Sandy Bay and I hoped that when we returned in September, the visits with her mother would be less troublesome. An even better situation would be if a hearing date would be set because I was concerned that Gina is settled in the knowledge of where she was going to be living over the next few years. I felt it was very important for her to know that she need no longer worry about yet again having to move back and forth to live with her mother, especially when she was now beginning high school and needed to be able to study without upheaval at home.

Mrs Munro assured me that she would keep in touch over the summer. She would also need to meet again with Gina when we returned in September, and she asked me to say "hi" to Gina and tell her everything was going well.

While Gina was visiting with her dad and Laura on Sunday, Dorrie came over for supper with us. It was a warm June day, ideal for eating outdoors. Steve set up the barbecue and organized the chicken, Dorrie made one of her great salads, I got the potatoes ready for baking. The timing was perfect when Amy and Ben arrived back from the park, and we all sat around chatting and laughing and enjoying our first supper of the year in the great outdoors. It was dark when Gina arrived back. Max accompanied her to the door. He had some questions for me about the custody hearing and I took the opportunity to tell him about my meetings with Mrs Munro. Like me, he was concerned about the things Julia had been saying to Gina, as well as the appearance on the scene of Dave. He told me that the sudden appearance of a boyfriend was a familiar pattern with Julia, something that I was also beginning to realize. He also felt quite strongly that it would be best if Gina's visits to Julia could be cut back, or supervised, or better still stopped until after the hearing. I told him that Mrs Mercer was in favour of stopping visits until the matter of Dave and Ron had been sorted out with Julia's social worker, but I didn't think it was likely that visits could be stopped completely.

Before heading back down to his car, Max commented that Gina's visit had gone well Then came his surprise announcement …Max and Laura were expecting! The baby was due during the Christmas Season, and Gina was very excited about it. I congratulated Max. From our previous conversations, I knew it had taken him some time to rebuild his life after the divorce from Julia. Starting a family together meant a great deal to both Max and Laura. I was pleased for them and I was glad to hear that Gina was happy about it also.

Gina and I talked about the 'new baby' at bedtime that night. We agreed it was a big surprise.

"But I gather from your dad that you liked their surprise?" I queried.

"Oh yes, of course, I do," Gina agreed. "Laura and I get along very well. You know, I have talked with her quite a bit about the time in Winnipeg when I looked after Scott and Lucy, and she said a few times that she loves little kids and would like to be a mom someday, so I just know that she must be really happy about the baby, and I can see that my dad is really happy, too".

"So you don't feel that maybe this new baby may kind of horn in on your dad and you?" I ventured.

"Are you kidding!?" Gina gave me one of her 'knowing' looks, "my dad is the best in the world to me and I know it was very hard for him in the beginning because my mom was so nasty to him. I used to feel afraid because I thought if she kept on being nasty to him, my dad would just give up and not want to see me or have me visit him anymore, but he never gave up."

"I'm sorry, Gina, I didn't know that," I apologized.

"That's okay, mum, you haven't known me right from the very beginning, but my dad tells me that he loves me all the time, and I know he means it. He says the new baby will be my half brother or sister and because I am older and know how to take care of little kids, he and Laura are hoping that I will be able to help them with the baby and sometimes even be a babysitter for them." Her face beamed with happiness.

"That's great, Gina," I smiled right back. "I'm so glad that you will have a chance to be part of another happy family and I know that you'll do a great job of helping with the new baby."

She hopped into bed. I leaned over and gave her a big hug. Then she turned off her night light.

"Sleep well," I said softly as I exited her room. I had no doubt that she would.

Chapter Twenty-Five

We were in June, with the end of year tests looming for all three children. They were all pretty good about getting on with studying. Gina was doing well. At first, she had quite a lot of catching up to do. Fortunately, she had understanding teachers. I was able to meet with them and we were able to put together a plan that had worked well. She wasn't 'top' of her grade, but she was getting a lot of C's and even some B pluses. She had made friends and had by now adapted to most of the 'rules' that had given her trouble in the beginning. When the tests were over, we would do the usual tidying and packing up, get the car serviced and head off for another summer at Sandy Bay. We were all looking forward to that!

In the middle of the first week of June, the phone rang. Julia wanted Gina to come for a sleepover on the coming weekend. I told her this would be difficult as time was limited because Gina was busy studying for her year-end tests. When it was clear that Julia wasn't going to be deterred, I told her I would have to speak to Mrs Mercer and get back to her. Because of the current situation at Julia's place, Mrs Mercer wasn't at all happy about a visit. In turn, she said she would speak to Miss Parks and call me back.

The result of all these communications was an agreement that Gina could visit Julia on the coming Saturday, for the afternoon only – from 2 to 6 p.m., and Julia had agreed that the visit would include herself, Scott and Lucy only. In other words, neither Dave nor Ron would be present. With any luck, that would be the last visit Gina would be making before we left for Sandy Bay.

After her previous visit, Gina wasn't enthusiastic at all about visiting Julia, even for just a few hours. I pointed out that this was the last chance for Scott and Lucy to see her before we left Vancouver for the summer, and it was a reasonable request by her mother. Gina agreed, but she still wasn't happy. On Saturday morning, she dawdled when it was time to get ready. On the trip over to the city, we chatted and she brightened up a lot.

When we drove up to Julia's place on Garden Street, I was relieved to see that there was no sign of Dave's car, nor was there any sign of Dave or Ron themselves. Instead, Julia and the children were waiting for Gina at the top of the steps. I walked Gina to the house and said "hi" to Julia. After that, I said, "Bye, Gina, I'll be back to pick you up at 6 o'clock."

As I drove away, I could see all four of them going into the house. I felt relieved. So far, everything had gone well.

When I arrived back home, Steve, Amy and I went to Ben's soccer game. He was an enthusiastic player and his team won, so the four of us went to the Dairy Queen for celebratory ice cream.

Back at Garden Street around 6 p.m., there didn't appear to be anyone in sight, but after I had parked the car and started up the front path, the front door opened, and Ron walked out onto the porch.

"Hi, there," he said.

"Hi," I responded. "I'm here to pick up Gina."

"Oh yeah, I know why you're here," he said in a loud tone. "They're out, you see. Gina's going to be sleeping over at Julia's tonight."

"Well, Ron," I said, as politely as I could, "that's not the arrangement. Gina is to come home with me at 6 o'clock. That's why I'm here."

"Well," said Ron in the same loud tone, "you are just going to have to change your damn arrangement because Gina's mother has decided she is staying over and, by the way, THIS is Gina's home!"

Just then, there was the sound of a vehicle and I turned to see Dave's car coming down the street. Not wishing to involve me in any further conversation with Ron, I walked down the path and stopped on the sidewalk beside my car. Dave's car pulled up behind it. Julia, Gina and the two little ones were inside.

Dave and Julia got out first.

"Hi, Julia," I said, "I'm here to pick up Gina."

Before Julia could say anything, Dave intervened, "Gina's staying for a sleepover tonight, so you can go back home."

I decided to ignore Dave. Turning towards Julia, I said, "we arranged that I would pick up Gina at 6 o'clock. If you'd like Gina for a sleepover, Julia, then you need to make arrangements with Miss Parks........."

Just then, the back door of Dave's car opened and Gina, Scott and Lucy tumbled out.

"Gina is Julia's daughter. Julia can do anything she damn likes.....", Dave's tone was anything but polite.

It was clear that an argument was brewing. Julia wasn't likely to be of any help, and I certainly wasn't in a mood to be bullied. So I took the 'bull by the horns' and in what I hoped was a very bossy voice, said, "Gina, get in the car NOW!". Fortunately, Gina reacted quickly. She ran around, opened the door and jumped in. As she did so, I jumped in behind the wheel, shut my door, and pressed the master lock. Dave came striding towards me. He didn't look friendly.

"I'm sorry about this, Julia," I said as I shut my window, "but it's up to you to keep to the arrangements you make about visits." With that, I started the engine and drove away as quickly as possible. I didn't look back.

After a few deep breaths, I looked at Gina. She was crying.

"I'm really sorry, Gina," I apologized, "I didn't want to upset you."

"Oh, I'm NOT upset with you, mum," she said weepily, "I'm just so upset about my mum and everything. The whole visit was really bad."

"Bad?"

"Yes, bad! My mom didn't keep her word at all about Dave and Ron. When we went up to her apartment, they were both there! And they all had a big laugh because they had fooled you and the social workers. Ron picked me up and put me on his knee and told me we were all going to have a fantastic day, and I was even going to stay overnight, and we would have a party. When I told him I didn't like parties, he said that it was going to be a special party after Scott and

Lucy went to bed --- just Ron and Dave and my mom and me. And I could even have wine to drink."

"So what did you do all afternoon?" I was almost afraid to ask.

"Well, I said that it would be nice to take Lucy and Scott to the park and maybe they could play on the swings and at the other play area. My mom agreed about that, so we all went there. I was hoping we could walk over there but Dave insisted that we go in the car. I knew he was mad at me. It was awful."

She began sobbing. And I began to realize that I was a bit "shook up" myself.

I turned down a tree-lined residential street and pulled over beside an empty bus stop bench. We both got out of the car and sat there quietly with our arms around each other for a while. Gina was the first one to speak.

"Know something, mum?

"Know. What?" I said.

"I think we are both going to be all right!" She gave me a damp little smile.

"I think you could be right", I made a face back.

Then we both had a good laugh. It was a real laugh!

After that, we got back into the car and sang songs together all the way home.

Chapter Twenty-Six

The first thing I did on Monday morning was to call Mrs Mercer. After we had returned home and were in a calmer mood, Gina confided to me that her mother had told her that at the end of July, she and the children would be moving to a house that Dave and Ron were renting. Julia also told Gina that her lawyer would be 'getting the court to return Gina to her' when we returned from Sandy Bay at the end of August. Naturally, Gina was stressed at this prospect and wanted to know if her mother could do that.

I did my best to give a fair account of what had happened during Gina's afternoon visit. As I expected, Mrs Mercer was upset. She would be in touch with Miss Parks and get back to me after that. In the meantime, she told me to prevent any further communication between Julia and Gina for the time being and to let her know if Julia attempted to reach Gina before we left for Sandy Bay.

After contacting Mrs Mercer, I called Jeanette Munro who asked me to write a detailed report about the matter. I agreed to drop it off at her office before leaving for Vancouver Island. I also gave her our address and telephone number so that she could contact me when more details about the hearing were available.

The rest of June was busy. The three children were doing end of year tests, getting all their chores done, and deciding what 'stuff' they would take along to Sandy Bay. After a family discussion, Steve and I had agreed that each of them could invite a friend over to visit for a week. If the friends came by ferry, we would meet them on arrival and take them to Sandy Bay, and return them by ferry at the end of their visit. Gina decided that she would like to see Kelsey again, so she called her, and Val said that Kelsey could visit us at the beginning of August. It was going to be a busy time and, I hoped, a happy family time far away from complications, such as the events of the past week.

Saturday, June 29th – pack-up and leave day --- arrived! Excitement ran high. Everyone was in a good mood. The final report cards had been received and all three children had done very well, especially Gina who had managed a B plus in English, mainly due to having improved greatly in reading.

Packing to leave was always challenging and would have been impossible without the capacity of two cars. There was all the kids' 'stuff', Steve and my 'stuff', as well as sundry useful items that I didn't have at the cottage and would need. After that, there was our beloved dog, Tessa – who always rode with Steve - our beloved tabby cat, Rascal, who always travelled in my car, and our reasonably beloved guineapigs, Snowy and Spot, complete in their cage. They always occupied Steve's car so as not to distract Rascal who, we thought, had always believed they were some kind of mutated mice! There was a lot more undetermined stuff, such as golf clubs etc. Whatever it was, by the time we had packed and Steve had pronounced us ready to go, there was barely enough room left for me, Amy and Gina in my car, and Ben had trouble squeezing himself into Steve's car along with his dad and the animals!

After a relaxing ride on the ferry, the short drive to Sandy Bay took no time at all. As usual, the business of unpacking was disorganized. For a start, the children always took off down to the beach. Steve went off to get some basic groceries while I went into the cottage and opened the windows etc. to 'air it out'. By the time Steve returned, the children had reappeared and had taken care of setting up the "run" outside Snowy and Spot's cage.

Although we had eaten on the ferry, we were all starting to feel hungry. Steve and Ben rolled out the barbecue and got some burger patties going, while the girls and I made a 'quickie' salad and, as a time-saver, substituted potato chips. We were busy eating in no time and, as we usually did, all of us agreed that there was nothing quite like our first outdoor meal at Sandy Bay!

Our time at Sandy Bay that year was idyllic. From start to finish, the weather was beautiful. Oh, it might have rained a bit on one or two occasions, but otherwise, it was warm, in the 25-degree Celsius range, and dry. Sometimes we spent entire days at the beach when I would hike back up the hill to the beach and drive down with 'supper'. The kids had great fun with the echo which was always great at the top of the hill in the early morning. We visited the falls at Cedar Creek and the Saturday outdoor market at Felton. Then, in our large garden, there was the horseshoe pitch, the volleyball net, the ping pong table and towards the end of that summer and once we had mowed all the grass, we added croquet! I was busy in the kitchen all the time, but it was wonderful to have a break from the tensions of dealing with office life as well as Gina's situation. Steve came over on weekends as well as taking two weeks at the end of August, giving us both time to relax and enjoy uninterrupted time together and with the children.

In mid-July, Amy's friend, Michelle came for a visit, followed by Ben's friend, Lee, a week later. Gina called in to visit her grandparents a couple of times. The visits had gone well and she told me that they hadn't heard from her mother. I also had a few conversations with Mrs Glen who remarked that Gina was a lot better behaved and it was a 'good thing' that she was living with us.

Kelsey came down from Seal Bay at the beginning of August. Gina was delighted to see her and the two girls enjoyed their time together. When she brought Kelsey down, Val stayed for a few days with her in-laws. I invited her over and she spent a day at the beach with all of us.

Towards the end of August, the kids and I had just returned to Sandy Bay from our usual trip to Victoria to get back-to-school needs, when Jeanette Munro called. The hearing into the Ministry's application for permanent custody of Gina had been set for Wednesday, December 14th. She would want to meet with both Gina and me as soon as possible upon our return.

December 14th seemed quite far off at that point, but the hearing was going to happen more or less in the middle of the Christmas season, and before that, we would be dealing with return to school, Thanksgiving, etc. I wondered if Julia had moved into a house with the children and Dave at the end of July. During the summer, I had heard nothing from Mrs Mercer and I hadn't made any effort to contact her. I just wanted to have our family time this summer free of having to deal with Julia and social workers. I felt Gina needed a break from all of that. In fact. all of us needed a break.

As we began our packing up routine, all three children were in great spirits, eagerly anticipating seeing their friends again and wondering who their teachers for the coming year would be. I couldn't bring myself to talk to Gina about it just then. I decided to tell her about the hearing after we had returned home.

Chapter Twenty-Seven

Dorrie came over for dinner on Labour Day and the two of us took the children to the pitch and putt. Steve went golfing, as usual. After that, it was 'back to the old routine'. Gina and Ben went off to high school, Amy began her last year at primary school, and I returned to my job at Lister & Company.

Over the Labour Day weekend, I had a chat with Gina about the hearing. She was feeling a bit apprehensive and we both wondered if her mother had moved in with Dave and what the social workers had done about it. We discussed whether I should call Mrs Mercer or whether Gina should try to call her mother. In the end, we decided to wait and see. It was a busy time of year and Gina wanted to get well organized and make a good start in Grade 10. Gina also began piano lessons. I saw that she was musical and spent quite a bit of time watching and listening to Amy (who was now in her third year) practising. I enrolled her with Amy's teacher at the North Shore School of Music. Gina loved it! She was very serious about practising and it was good to see her developing new talent.

Mrs Mercer called me in the third week of September. She asked how Gina was doing and was pleased to learn how well our summer had gone. Because of the forthcoming hearing date, she wanted to see Gina alone after school the following Wednesday. When I asked if Julia had moved over the summer and what had happened regarding Dave, Ron, etc., all she could tell me was that Julia was still living at the same address and that she hadn't spoken with Miss Parks for over a month. Well, that was something, but it still wasn't clear if Dave and Ron were still in the picture. I reminded her how upsetting the last visit had been for Gina and asked her if she could please ask Miss Parks about the current status so that we would know what was going on when Julia called to arrange a visit. Now that Gina was back, Mrs Mercer said she would contact Miss Parks and let me know the situation as soon as she could. I wasn't too happy being left 'in limbo' but there wasn't much I could do about it. As it turned out, I was soon to learn what was going on with Julia from an entirely new source.

The following Tuesday, when I picked Gina up after music, she jumped into the car, fastened her seatbelt, and announced, "Do I ever have news for you, mum!".

"News, what news?" She was very animated. I was curious.

"About my mum, of course!" came the reply, "my mom is still at Garden Street, but Dave and Ron are gone!"

"How do you know that?" I asked.

"Well, I just saw Alyssa, and she told me all about it!"

"Alyssa! Who is Alyssa?", I asked.

"Oh, I forgot, you don't know Alyssa."

"Who............," I began again.

"Alyssa was a neighbour of ours a long time ago when my mom and dad were together, and I was really little. We lived in Vancouver. Alyssa has a little girl – Pippa -and I used to play with her. Her husband and my dad both work at the hospital and they're good friends. Anyway, while I was waiting outside the music school for you, Alyssa came along on the sidewalk and she saw me. And she came over and asked me what I was doing there."

"How did she know about your mother?"

"Alyssa moved to Alberta for a few years because her husband got a better job. Anyway, they have moved back here and they were talking to my dad and he told them all about me coming to live with you. When Alyssa asked my dad how to get in touch with my mom, he gave them my grandparents' phone number and your phone number. Alyssa couldn't reach you because we were away, so she called my grandparents and got my mom's number and they talked."

"I see. Did your mom tell Alyssa why she didn't move? What happened?"

"She did. I'm not sure why, but my mom had some kind of big fight with Dave. Well, you know what my mom is like. But anyway, Dave and Ron moved away after that. It was in July."

"So your mom and Scott and Lucy are still at Garden Street, then?"

"Yup. They're still there. But Alyssa says that my mom is expecting another baby, too".

"Another baby!", I was flabbergasted. I wasn't prepared for that!. Could it be true?

"Are you sure?" I still couldn't grasp it.

"Yes, she's pregnant. Alyssa says so." Gina was confident.

By that time we had arrived at the house and it was time to get supper. Gina grabbed her books and went downstairs to the piano while I began my labours in the kitchen, thoughts buzzing around in my head. Pregnant! Well, that might certainly explain why Julia hadn't moved. Perhaps the arrival of an additional child had extinguished Dave's enthusiasm for setting up a house with Julia. Perhaps Dave and Ron had had a visit from Miss Parks? There had definitely been some kind of fight.

Some things were now clear: Dave and Ron had departed leaving Julia with Scott and Lucy and another baby on the way! Could Julia convince the Ministry that she was the best person to have custody of Gina? As my old granny would have said, "Everything has gone from bad to worse!". I wondered if Mrs Mercer was aware of the pregnancy. I wondered when the baby was due. In the middle of the hearing, perhaps? For that matter, would the hearing now be cancelled or postponed?

The next day, Wednesday, was Gina's scheduled appointment with Mrs Mercer. I managed to reach her on the phone during my lunch hour. I wanted to find out what Mrs Mercer knew about Julia's pregnancy and what she planned to discuss with Gina. Mrs Mercer had contacted Miss Parks and had learned of the pregnancy for the first time. Before that, she had been planning on talking to Gina about how she was getting along at school. Also, how did she feel about visiting with her mother before the hearing? Was she still happy about the Superintendent having custody of her? Did she understand that the Superintendent felt that it would be much better and less difficult for her mother if she just had to look after Scott and Lucy and the Superintendent would make sure that Gina would have a happy home until she was 18 and even afterwards?

Mrs Mercer wanted to be sure that Gina had a good understanding of what was going to happen and did not have any feelings of guilt about not being with her mother.

I told her about Alyssa and how Gina had learned about Julia's pregnancy. It appeared that I was right. Dave wasn't interested in taking on a pregnant girlfriend, with a baby due in late February or March. In fact, Dave had already disputed his paternity of the baby. A nasty row had taken place in June, resulting in the police being called and a restraining order against Dave. Shortly afterwards, Dave and Ron moved away. A young couple was now living in the downstairs apartment.

Both Mrs Mercer and I agreed, these latest events were a continuation of Julia's ongoing pattern of relationships with men that usually came to sudden, unhappy and damaging endings for her and her children. I was really glad that Mrs Mercer and I were finally on the same 'page' in this regard.

As for Julia, she had gone into one of her frequent depressions but was now starting to function normally. Miss Parks had had several discussions with Julia on the topic of custody, but she still insisted that Gina was her daughter, that she was totally able to look after her, and that Gina should never have been moved away to another home where she would be exposed to 'wrong' influences. As a consequence, the hearing would proceed as scheduled. Because of Julia's hostile attitude, Mrs Mercer felt it would be best if Gina's visits with her mother were suspended until after the hearing, and she also intended to talk to Gina about that.

I called Alyssa on the weekend. We had quite a long chat. She was now living in North Vancouver and I arranged to meet her for coffee the following Friday. Alyssa had gone over to Garden Street and met with Julia. They hadn't seen each other for about five years and Alyssa was dismayed to see how Julia had deteriorated since then. When they became friends back then, both Alyssa and Julia were young mothers, full of fun and happy with their first babies. Julia had been very pretty and full of life. Alyssa said she was still good looking but she wasn't in good shape mentally. Most of the time, Scott and Lucy were left to amuse themselves. Scott – now six - actually got snacks and made sandwiches for himself and Lucy and even Julia! I asked about Dave and the paternity of the baby. All Alyssa could tell me was that when she asked Julia about it, Julia said was that she "wasn't sure" and it might have been someone she "met at a bus stop". Julia was on quite a bit of medication, and Alyssa didn't know what to believe.

From what Gina had told me, it was clear that she had very happy memories and liked Alyssa and Pippa a lot, so I asked Alyssa to come for lunch the next weekend and bring Pippa I wanted Gina to keep the connection to all the good things in her past, and I was pleased when Alyssa agreed to come.

"I don't see why they need you as a witness." Steve was expressing his feelings about my role in the coming hearing. It was November 20th, our twelfth wedding anniversary and we were sitting at a table in a quiet nook in Hy's steakhouse. Hy's was one of our favourite restaurants, and we were both glad of a chance to talk about things that we never seemed to be able to discuss properly at home without constant interruptions of one kind or another.

During that week, Jeanette Munro sent me a bundle of materials outlining the kind of questions she would be asking. I poured over them in the evenings after the kids were all in bed. I even discussed some of the questions with Steve. He felt that, when it came to the hearing, too much of a load was being placed on me. As he put it "all my meetings with Mrs Mercer and Mrs Munro, then taking Gina to meetings with both of them, talking to Max, inviting Alyssa and Pippa over, going over everything with Gina, etc. etc. Steve felt that Julia's history and behaviour towards everyone --- her own family, the social workers, ourselves and her own children over many years, not to mention now being pregnant with another "fatherless" child, should be enough proof that Gina would be much better off in the custody of the Ministry.

Over dinner, I finally convinced Steve that Mrs Munro knew what she was doing and, in any event,, short of flatly refusing to testify, there was nothing I could do to avoid being involved in the hearing. He finally accepted the situation and then, over dessert, he made a perfectly brilliant suggestion: "Well, if you are determined to be well grilled just before Christmas, I think the only fair thing for all of your 'supporters', and definitely the best thing for you, as the Greatest Martyr of all Time, is for all of us to clear off to Hawaii right after the hearing and have a holly, jolly Christmas in Maui. Just like last time, no decorations to be done at home --- well maybe I'll put up the outside lights --- just organize with your mother to look after Tessa, pack our swimsuits and flip-flops, and head for the airport. And as for everything else, we'll all just take a break from the entire "circus" and let the chips fall where they may! Come on Maura, let's have a smile. Don't you go for the idea?"

Well of course I "went for the idea". A break after the end of the hearing was exactly 'what the doctor ordered'. We clinked glasses and then I got up, walked around the table, and gave him a long, intense kiss. It must have appeared impressive because everyone in Hy's applauded!

We were all very excited at the prospect of another Christmas in Hawaii, especially Gina who had missed the trip two years before. Our flight to Honolulu left at 5 p.m. on December 20th, three days after the hearing! In the meantime, we heard nothing from Julia, which was a great relief to all of us. Gina was fine. She had spent a Saturday with Max and Laura. They gave her some spending money for Hawaii and told her they would be in touch in early January when we returned home. All the children had good report cards, including Gina who had not been too badly affected by all the activities and meetings related to the hearing.

On December 8th, I had a final meeting with Jeanette Munro. We discussed the list of possible questions that I might be asked, either by her or the judge, or Bill Fox, the lawyer who would be representing the Ministry, and she updated me on what had been happening during the summer. She met with Mr Fox to discuss her impressions after meeting with Gina and how well she had been getting along since coming to live with us. Mr Fox told her that Julia Niemann would be representing herself, but it was also likely that she would be accompanied by a "support person" which is provided for in family law matters. Neither Mr Fox nor Mrs Munro had been given any information about the support person but they might not know until shortly before the hearing, or even on the day of the hearing – which often happened in this kind of case. Mrs Munro also confirmed that Gina would not have to attend the Court hearing but that she would most likely be interviewed by the judge after the hearing concluded.

PART IX

The Hearing

Chapter Twenty-Eight

It was misty and drizzling as I set off along the highway early in the morning of December 15th, on my way to the East Vancouver Family Court. I had arranged to take the day off work and the kids had been assigned various chores to keep them busy until either Steve or I arrived home. I asked Gina if she would start getting supper ready and, to my surprise, she was enthusiastic at my suggestion.

Jeanette Munro was waiting for me in the entrance lobby of the Court House and she quickly described to me how things would evolve in the court room. Mr Fox, and any assistant he might have from his office, would be seated at the table at front left, facing the judge and Mrs Niemann and her support person would be seated at the table at front right, facing the judge. Mrs Munro and I would be sitting in the front row, behind Mr Fox. Mrs Mercer would also be attending as a witness for the Ministry. Any witnesses who might be appearing for Mrs Niemann would be sitting in one of the rows behind her. Mrs Munro told me that Her Honour Judge Patricia Ferris would be presiding at the hearing. She had a high opinion of Judge Ferris and was pleased about this.

We had scarcely sat down in the court room when the Clerk and Judge Ferris entered and we all stood as the Clerk called the hearing to order. The judge acknowledged the various parties and the hearing began. I noticed that an older, grey-haired woman wearing brown slacks and a beige fleece jacket was sitting with Julia Niemann. I had no idea who she was. Mrs Mercer and Miss Parks had come in and were sitting behind me. Doris Parks, Julia's social worker took a seat across the aisle behind Julia.

Judge Ferris began, "Very well, Mr Fox, please proceed with your opening remarks,"

William Fox stood and addressed the court:

"Regina Niemann – she is generally known as "Gina" – who is the child in this matter, is now fifteen years of age and needs stability in her home life. Her mother, Julia Niemann, who is present here before us, has a long history of instability which, unfortunately, has been the case during most of Gina's life. Gina has been apprehended on several occasions and while it is noted that Mrs Niemann has made efforts to deal with her health and other issues, the evidence strongly suggests that, at this time, it would be in Gina's best interests to place her under the guardianship of the Ministry until she reaches the age of majority." Putting his notes to one side, Mr Fox continued, "Your Honour, I am aware that the matter of removing guardianship of a child from his or her natural mother is a serious matter, not undertaken lightly, but in this case, the Minister is convinced it is the best action to take."

Judge Ferris: "I assume, Mr Fox, that you are prepared to support your application with sufficient evidence to persuade the Court of the wisdom of such action."

Mr Fox: "Yes, your Honour, I am".

Judge Ferris: Mrs Niemann, I understand that you are representing yourself and that the lady seated beside you is a support person?"

Julia stood up, "Yes. Yes….. your honour. I will be speaking for myself. Mrs Lois Ritchie, here, is a friend of mine and she knows about a lot of the things that I have had to deal with, and she has been helping me to get ready for this hearing."

Judge Ferris: "Good, Mrs Niemann, that's good. Now can you proceed.."

Julia: "Okay. Well, okay -Your Honour, I don't agree with the Ministry. I am Gina's mother and I love her. We have always had a loving relationship and she loves her little brother and sister and misses them, and we all miss having her at home with us. She only left us because I was sick. Then her grandparents --- that's my mother and father --- allowed her to visit the Kerrys so that she would have the company of other children. It was always agreed that Gina would come back home to me when I got better.

144

Well, I'm better now and I just want you to give Gina back to me like it was already agreed." As she sat down, it was obvious that Julia was pregnant.

Judge Ferris: "Thank you, Mrs Niemann. Then if everyone is prepared, I will begin to hear the evidence. Mr Fox, you may proceed."

Mr Fox called Mrs Mercer to the stand and she was sworn in.

Mr Fox: "Mrs Mercer, please tell us when you were assigned as Gina's social worker."

Mrs Mercer: "In September of 1974, I was contacted by Social Services at Sandy Bay, and asked to get in touch with the Kerry family. Social Services told me that Gina had been placed with the Kerrys and that it would be necessary to go through the process of having them approved as a foster home for Gina."

Mr Fox: "And did you approve the Kerrys as a foster family for Gina?"

Mrs Mercer: "Yes, we did. I visited the Kerrys home where I met with Mrs Kerry and, of course, I also met with Gina and got to know her."

Mr Fox: "Then I assume that you were satisfied with the arrangements in the Kerry home as well as the way the family functioned."

Mrs Mercer: "Yes, the Kerrys have a lovely home. Gina had her own room, and she was delighted with that. She also got along well with the Kerry children, Ben and Amy."

Mr Fox: "So you were satisfied that Gina was happy there and that her home life was harmonious and stable."

Mrs Mercer: "Very much so."

Mr Fox: "And what about school. Did Gina start a new school? How did that go?"

Mrs Mercer: "Well, Gina had a bit of a struggle at school in the beginning, but she was able to get extra help at school and also the Kerrys gave her a lot of support and encouragement."

Mr Fox: "So Gina adjusted well?"

Mrs Mercer: "Oh yes, very well."

Mr Fox: "Maybe you can clarify something for me, Mrs Mercer. You have said that you first contacted the Kerrys about Gina in September of 1974, but my file shows that Gina returned to Sandy Bay for a short time in December of 1974. Were you aware of that? If so, what was it all about?"

Mrs Mercer: "Oh, yes, Mr Fox. As I recall, in September Gina returned to West Vancouver to live with the Kerrys --- and I met with them and with Gina. Then, at the beginning of December, I think it was, Mrs Kerry received a call from Mrs Niemann. As it turned out, Mrs Niemann had returned to Sandy Bay from Winnipeg, along with her two other little children, and she called Mrs Kerry and told her that she wanted Gina to come home and live with her at Sandy Bay."

Mr Fox: "So, what happened?

Mrs Mercer: "Gina went back to Sandy Bay to live with her mother. Mrs Niemann still had guardianship of Gina, so Mrs Kerry had Gina pack up her things and she brought her to us. We returned her to the social worker at Sandy Bay and after that, she began living with her mother and siblings."

Mr Fox: "But she didn't stay there for long?"

Mrs Mercer: "No. Well of course I wasn't there, but apparently, when Gina came home from school one day in January, her mother and little brother and sister had left the motel and Gina's clothes were left there in a box."

Mr Fox: "Do you know what happened?"

Mrs Mercer: "Well, yes, I know what Gina told me. She said that she had walked along to her grandparents' home. She told them what had happened and she asked them to call Mrs Kerry and ask if she could go back to live with the Kerrys in West Vancouver...."

Mr Fox:"…..and….."

Mrs Mercer: "Gina's grandmother --- a Mrs Spencer, I think, called Mrs Kerry. And then Mrs Kerry came over to Sandy Bay with her children and picked Gina up. I remember it took a while because there was a lot of snow and they had to wait for a few days at a motel for the court hearing……."

Mr Fox: "Court hearing?"

Mrs Mercer: "Yes. Nobody knew where Mrs Niemann had gone. She wasn't to be found! You must understand, it was quite a shock to the Kerrys when Mrs Niemann reappeared so suddenly. They had no idea that this was a possibility and it was very disruptive --- especially returning Gina just before Christmas. Mrs Kerry was okay with Gina returning to live with the Kerrys, but she asked that something is done to prevent this kind of thing from happening again."

Mr Fox: "And where was Mrs Niemann?

Mrs Mercer: "At that point, nobody knew. As I said, Mrs Kerry went over to Sandy Bay. It's a circuit court over there and she waited with the children at a motel for two days until the court made an order that Gina was to be placed with the Kerrys until a full hearing could be scheduled.

Mr Fox: "Thank you, Mrs Mercer, you have been very helpful. So are we to understand that a further hearing didn't take place until May?"

Mrs Mercer: "Yes. Mrs Niemann eventually returned to Sandy Bay and wanted to have Gina returned to her. I believe the Kerrys brought Gina over to Sandy Bay and attended that hearing"

Mr Fox: "Thank you, again, Mrs Mercer, Mrs Kerry will be testifying shortly and I'm sure she will be able to clarify what occurred. But before I finish, I would like you to tell me why you support placing permanent guardianship with the Ministry rather than leaving open the possibility of Gina being returned to her mother."

Mrs Mercer: "Well, Mr Fox, Gina has now been in a happy, stable environment for over two years. But as you can see during the time that I have been involved with her placement, there has been a considerable amount of difficulty in dealing with Mrs Niemann. This has given me great cause for concern. In just 3 years, Gina will be 18 years old, and I'm afraid that if she's returned to her mother, there's a considerable risk that this stability will be lost and that, among a lot of things, she may not be able to complete her education."

Mr Fox: "So you believe that Gina's overall well-being and stability will be lost if she returns to live with her mother.

Mrs Mercer: "Yes, I do."

Mr Fox: "Thank you, Mrs Mercer, that's all." Then, turning to Julia, "Mrs Niemann, can question Mrs Mercer now."

Julia (remains sitting at her table): "Hi, Mrs Mercer, how long have you known Gina?

Mrs Mercer: "I've known her since she came to the mainland in September of 1974 – that's about two years."

Julia: "And do you think that if you only know someone for two years, you can know what's best for them?

Mrs Mercer: "Well, Mrs Niemann, it's true that I've only known Gina for two years or so, but we have good talks. Gina tells me how she feels about things, and from what she's said to me, I believe she would be happier if she stays where she is."

Julia: "Well, Mrs Mercer, I'm her mother and I know where she is happiest. I don't need to talk to her about that. I just know. She's only happy where she is because she has her own room and material things like that. And that's all wrong. She needs to come home and get her head straightened out."

Mrs Mercer: "Well, Mrs Niemann, that's why we are all here. We all want the best for Gina.

Julia: "You don't know anything. You don't love her."

Judge Ferris: "Mrs Mercer, I think you can step down for now." Then, to Julia: "Mrs Niemann, you can call your witnesses now."

Julia leaned in towards her support person, Mrs Ritchie, who nodded. Then she spoke to Judge Ferris." Your Honour, I would like to ask my social worker, Doris Parks, to come forward to be a witness."

"Will Doris Parks please come forward," the Court Clerk called Miss Parks who was sworn.

Julia began. "Doris, you've been my social worker since I moved to Vancouver with Scott and Lucy in 1975, right?"

Doris Parks: "Yes"

Julia: "And haven't I always taken good care of my kids?"

Doris Parks: "Yes"

Julia: "And when Gina has come to visit, has she ever told you that she didn't want to come to see us?"

Doris Parks: "No".

Julia: "Is Gina happy when she comes to see us?"

Doris Parks: "Yes"

Julia: "And she plays with Scott and Lucy and we all have a happy time together?"

Doris Parks: "Yes".

Julia: "Do you think I'm a good mother?"

Doris Parks: "I think that you always do your best to take care of your children"

Julia: "But am I a good mother?"

Doris Parks: "Yes, you are good to your children, but there are other things ---" Julie interrupted.

Julia: "What 'things'?"

Doris Parks: "Well, things like making sure they eat a good diet, correcting them when their behaviour isn't good, helping them to dress appropriately....things like that".

Julia: "You don't think I am doing that?

Doris Parks: "Yes, you are doing that but I'm there to help you manage these things."

Julia: "So you don't think I'm a good mother?

Doris Parks: "No. I'm not saying that."

Julia, in a somewhat impatient tone. "Well, what are you saying then?"

Doris Parks: "I'm saying that you have had a lot of problems managing. You're doing very well but you are a single mother with two small children to raise, and you need help."

Julia frowned and looked towards Mrs Ritchie. Then, turning towards Judge Ferris, she said, "You see, I am a good mother. Gina should be back home with me."

Judge Ferris: "Do you have any more questions for Miss Parks?"

Julia, in a rather perfunctory tone. "No, she can go now."

Judge Ferris: "Mr Fox, do you have any questions for Miss Parks?"

Mr Fox: "Yes, Your Honour." Then, turning to Doris Parks, "Miss Parks, you have testified that you were assigned as Mrs Niemann's social worker in 1975 when she moved to Vancouver from Vancouver Island. Can you tell me how that came about?"

Doris Parks: Well, she was referred to me by Social Services in Tofino. Apparently Mrs Niemann had been in a relationship with a man who lived in Tofino but the relationship had broken up and Mrs Niemann had left Tofino. After that, I believe she went to Social Services because she wanted to move to Vancouver and had no available funds or place to live when she arrived there."

Mr Fox: "The file shows that Mrs Niemann's parents live at Sandy Bay. Didn't she want to return to Sandy Bay?"

Doris Parks: "Apparently not."

Mr Fox: "So Mrs Niemann and her children simply travelled over to Vancouver where you were assigned to assist her?"

Doris Parks: "Yes, Mrs Niemann had been with Social Services in the past and they knew her file."

Mr Fox: "Can you please describe the type of assistance you have given Mrs Niemann since her arrival."

Doris Parks: "Well, the first thing I did was to find her a temporary place until we were able to find her an apartment."

Mr Fox: "And do I take it that Mrs Niemann is expecting another child at this point?"

Doris Parks: "Yes. In late January."

Mr Fox: "I understand that Mrs Niemann has been divorced for some time. Is she receiving child support for the children?"

Doris Parks: "Mrs Niemann's ex-husband, Max Niemann, has paid child support from time to time. Gina has told me that she visits often with her dad and he is helping. I think Gina's foster mother, Mrs Kerry, can tell you more about that. The remaining children are from different relationships."

Mr Fox: "What about child support for them?"

Doris Parks: "Social Services had made some efforts to trace Scott's father but they've been unsuccessful so far. I understand that Lucy's father has left the country."

Mr Fox: "So Mrs Niemann is entirely dependent upon Social Assistance?"

Doris Parks: "She is."

Mr Fox: "Raising two little children on social assistance can't be easy. How is she doing?"

Doris Parks: "She has great difficulty in managing. Just recently, we arranged for a financial worker to assist her."

Mr Fox: "It seems to me that the addition of a new baby, as well as Gina, would create more problems than it solved."

Doris Parks: "Yes, it would create a difficult situation for everyone, and a lot of additional stress for Mrs Niemann."

At that juncture, Julia Niemann suddenly jumped to her feet and shouted: "Your Honour, that's not true! That's not fair at all! Everything will be totally happier and easier when Gina comes back."

Judge Ferris frowned. "Please don't shout, Mrs Niemann. Mr Fox is conducting his examination."

At that comment, Bill Fox turned towards Julia and asked: "Perhaps you can clarify for me, Mrs Niemann, how the addition of two more children could make things easier?"

Julia retorted quickly: "How? Because Gina would be able to help. She's so good with Scott and Lucy --- she used to look after your parents all the time when we lived in Winnipeg. They love being looked after by Gina. So everything would be much easier."

Mr Fox: So you mean it would be easier for you?"

Julia: "Of course, and Gina would be back with her family."

Judge Ferris: "Do you have any further questions for Miss Parks, Mr Fox."

Mr Fox: "No, Your Honour, that's all."

Judge Ferris: "Time has flown! I see by my watch that it's almost
noon. I'm adjourning until 1 p.m."

With that, she banged her gavel.
This meant I would be on the witness stand next.

Jeanette Munro caught up with me out in the hall. She led the
way to the Court House self-serve cafeteria where we found a table
and sat down to enjoy the soup and sandwich special.

"Well, Maura," she asked, "how do you think it's going?"

"You mean, so far?" I asked.

"Yes, is this what you expected. What do you think of what Julia
has said, her behaviour, her argument?"

I tried to collect my thoughts. "I guess I'm not surprised. She's
acting in just the same way as I have experienced over the time I've
been involved with Gina. Also, I think Bill Fox is doing a great job
of drawing out the background details of Julia's life so that we have a
clear picture of the kind of life she and the children have been living."

"And are still living," Jeanette Munro continued, "That's what
I'm intending to show this afternoon when you are on the witness
stand. I think your evidence will be extremely important in confirm-
ing Julia's pattern of constant upheaval."

All I could say to her in response was, "Well, I hope you're right.
I'm feeling pretty nervous and I don't mind telling you, I'll be glad
when it's over."

She smiled at me. "I know. Hearings are no picnic. But I'm
sure you will do a good job. In the meantime, if you'll excuse me I'm
going to go out in the hall to find Bill Fox. We need to discuss how
we are going to approach this afternoon's proceedings. See you back
in court."

With that remark, she disappeared out into the hall, leaving me to sip my coffee while I tried unsuccessfully to distract myself by gazing at the dripping wet shrubs outside the cafeteria window.

Judge Ferris entered the court room promptly at 1 p.m. and the hearing reconvened.

Judge: "Are we ready to proceed with hearing the remaining witnesses? Mr Fox, I believe we have heard from all of your witnesses. Bill Fox nodded

Judge Ferris: "Then, Mrs Niemann, the court is ready to hear from your witnesses."

Julia stood up slowly: "Your Honour, I intend to appear as my own witness."

Judge Ferris: "That's fine, Mrs Niemann. Then, to the Court Clerk, "Will you please swear Mrs Niemann in."

Julia was sworn in and entered the witness stand.

Looking towards Judge Ferris, Julia began. "Your Honour, I am a good mother and I don't understand why the Ministry wants to take Gina away from me. It's true that Gina hasn't been living with me for some time, but that's because I was ill and couldn't look after the children. That happened when I was in Winnipeg. Lucy's father left us and I was trying to work part-time. You see, we didn't have very much money, so everything was very stressful and hard. Gina really tried to help me a lot but I had a nervous breakdown and was in the hospital. So my father and mother agreed to help and my father came from Sandy Bay to Winnipeg and he took Gina back to live with them--- but that was just until I was better. Gina was 11 years old. That was the first time she ever went to live away from home --- and she went to live with her family. It took me a while to recover and I kept in touch with Gina all that time and I knew she was all right and happy. But when I was better and returned to Sandy Bay late in 1974, I was shocked to find that Gina wasn't living with my mother and father any longer. They told me that after she came to live with them in the summer of 1973, Gina became friends with a family – the Kerrys --- whose house was very close to their house. Gina was with these Kerrys all the time. They didn't know the Kerrys or anything about them --- they lived in West Vancouver but came to the house in Sandy Bay every summer. Gina was happily playing there, nearby, so they didn't worry about it. Gina started school in Sandy Bay and things were going along well until, suddenly, near the end of the summer in 1974, Mrs Kerry came to see my mother and told her that they – the Kerry's – wanted to have Gina as a foster child. My parents were a bit shocked but they went to Kerry's house and talked with them. They said the Kerrys were very keen about having Gina come back to Vancouver and live with them --- and in the end, my parents decided to let Gina go for a while, at least until I was better. There was never any plan to have Gina stay with the Kerrys because my parents knew that I would soon be better and return with the little ones. Anyway, when I did return and I found out where Gina was, I called Mrs Kerry and thanked her for looking after Gina in the meantime, and I asked her to send Gina back to me. So Gina returned and we found a lovely little cottage to live in at Sandy Bay and Gina went back to school. Everything was going well until January when Mrs Kerry called my mother and said she wanted to come over to visit Gina. I agreed, and Mrs Kerry came over and I allowed Gina to go out with her for the afternoon. That was a big mistake because Gina was never happy after that. She went out for walks all the time, or just wanted to read her schoolbooks and she didn't play with Scott or Lucy like before.

We weren't happy and then I decided we would be happier if we returned to Winnipeg, so I got a bus ticket but the day we were to leave, Gina must have gone off somewhere after school and she didn't turn up in time, so we had to get the bus without her. But I was going to phone and tell her to catch another bus and we would meet her in Winnipeg. Well, anyway, on the bus I met a friend who lived in Calgary and we got off there and visited him for a week. After that my money ran out. The Women's Shelter in Calgary arranged for me to return to Sandy Bay --- but by that time, Mrs Kerry had come over and gone to the court and Gina went back to live with them. That's not what should have happened and ever since then I've been trying to get Gina to come back to us but Social Services just don't seem to want to help me. I even moved back to Vancouver to be near Gina --- you can ask Miss Parks, my social worker. It was always the plan that Gina would return to live with me and I don't understand why the Minister doesn't want to help us."

With that, Julia leaned over, put her head in her hands, and began sobbing.

Judge Ferris: "Mrs Niemann --- do you feel you can continue. Mr Fox, here, would like to ask you some questions."

"That's okay. He can ask." Julia mopped her eyes and sat up straight.

Mr Fox: "Mrs Niemann, how long is it since your divorce from Mr Niemann?"

Julia: Oh --- about 15 years."

Mr Fox: "And how old would Gina have been at the time of your divorce?"

Julia: "About six"

Mr Fox: "I see. And I see from your file that you lived in Vancouver during your marriage. Can you tell me what year you moved to Winnipeg?"

Julia: "I think it was about 1969."

Mr Fox: "So Gina was about 7."

Julia: "Yes, I guess so."

Mr Fox: "Why did you move to Winnipeg. It's a long way from Vancouver."

Julia: "Oh, I had met Scott's father and he was from Winnipeg, so we moved there to be with him."

Mr Fox: "So Scott is your son and what age is he?"

Julia: "Well, he's six. He was born in 1969"

Mr Fox: "And you also had a daughter?"

Julia: "Lucy. Lucy was born in 1971. She's three now. But that was after I split with Pete."

Mr Fox: "Pete?"

Julia: "Yes, Pete was Scott's dad. Lucy's dad was after that --- Norm."

Mr Fox: "And I seem to recall from earlier evidence that neither of these men has been providing child support. Is that right?"

Julia: "Yes."

Mr Fox after pausing to review his notes: "Mrs Niemann, you mentioned that when you were hospitalized in Winnipeg, arrangements were made for Gina to live with your parents. Can you clarify for me who took care of the little ones, Scott and Lucy?"

Julia: "Social Services put them into foster care in Winnipeg."

Mr Fox: "Let me see, Scott would have been 4 years old, and Lucy 1 ½. Is that about right?"

Julia: "yes"

Mr Fox: "So, Mrs Niemann, would it be correct to say that since you recovered and left the hospital in Winnipeg, you have been in the care of Social Services?

Julia: "yes"

Mr Fox: "One last thing. Mrs Niemann, I gather from your testimony that you are unhappy about Gina living with the Kerry family. Can you explain why?"

Julia: "Okay --- I think the Kerrys just wanted Gina so they can receive payment for foster care. That's why they're always so nice to everyone. It's really all about the money."

Mr Fox: "But, Mrs Niemann, you just testified that when you left the hospital and returned to Sandy Bay you called Mrs Kerry and asked her to return Gina to you, did you not?"

Julie: "Yes."

Mr Fox: "And did Mrs Kerry argue with you? As I recall, she returned Gina to you right away, didn't she?"

Julia: "Well, yes…."

Mr Fox: "Thank you, Mrs Niemann, that's all."

Judge Ferris: "Mrs Niemann, do you have any other witnesses?"

Julia: "Yes, Your Honour, I would like to call my Social Worker, Miss Doris Parks, back to the stand."

Miss Parks is sworn in by the Court Clerk and takes the witness stand.

Julia: "Miss Parks, how long have you been my social worker?"
Miss Parks: "Since late 1975 when you came to Vancouver..... I guess that's nearly a year and a half."
Julia: "Have I always taken good care of my children."
Miss Parks: "yes"
Julia: "When you've seen Gina with us, hasn't Gina always been happy"
Miss Parks: "I believe so."
Julia: "Miss Parks, don't you think that Gina will be much happier when she comes back to live with us."
Miss Parks: "Well, it's always difficult to tell how a child will behave when a big change is made......."
Julia, interrupting: "but don't you think that Gina will be happy to be back with Scott and Lucy?"
Miss Parks: "Of course, Gina likes to be with Scott and Lucy ... but....."
Julia: "So there is no reason why Gina can't come home to live with us?"
Miss Parks: "Well, there are some things that would need attention so that we would be sure the transition would go well..."
Julia: "But we can easily look after that because you and I get along well, don't we?"
Miss Parks: "Yes, we get along ....."
Julia, in a triumphant tone: "That's all. Thanks, Doris."
Judge Ferris: "Any questions Mr Fox?"
Bill Fox: "Yes, your Honour, I have just a few questions."

Mr Fox, turning to Miss Parks: "Miss Parks, what kind of assistance are you providing for Mrs Niemann."

Miss Parks: "When she first arrived, I assisted Mrs Niemann to find accommodation for herself and the children. Since then I generally meet with her or call to see her and the children once or twice a month, to see how they are getting along."

Mr Fox: "And is that all the assistance she has needed?"

Miss Parks: "We give Mrs Niemann assistance with her finances. In addition to myself, we have a financial worker who helps Mrs Niemann with budgeting. We also help with the children if Mrs Niemann has to go to an appointment --- such as the doctor --- that kind of thing."

Mr Fox: "And I take it you work with Mrs Mercer and Mrs Kerry to make arrangements when Gina comes to visit?"

Miss Parks: "Yes, we have been coordinating that."

Mr Fox: "And how has that been going? Have the visits been going well?"

Miss Parks: "Fairly well. Gina always seems to enjoy her visits."

Mr Fox: "So there have been no problems or difficulties when it comes to Gina's visits."

Miss Parks: "Well, earlier this year there were some problems."

Mr Fox: "What kind of problems?"

Miss Parks: "We had problems with two men who were renting the downstairs apartment where Mrs Niemann lives."

Mr Fox: "Can you be more detailed?"

Miss Parks: "Apparently one of the men, Ron, took Gina for a ride on his motorcycle without asking Mrs Niemann's permission."

Mr Fox: "And did it get resolved."

Miss Parks: "Mrs Mercer called me about it. Gina told Mrs Kerry that she felt uncomfortable about the way this man, Ron, spoke to her."

Mr Fox: "Did you or Mrs Niemann speak to this man, Ron?"

Miss Parks: "Yes, I spoke to him and also to his roommate, Dave."

Mr Fox: "And what happened?"

Miss Parks: "They weren't very cooperative."

Mr Fox: "So the problem continued?"

Miss Parks: "Actually, no. Both Ron and Dave moved out of the apartment in August."

Mr Fox: "Thank you, Miss Parks. That is all."

Judge Ferris: "Have you any other witnesses, Mrs Niemann?"

Julia: "Yes, Your Honour, I would like to have my support person here, Lois Ritchie, testify for me."

Lois Ritchie was sworn in and took the witness stand.

Julia: "Mrs Ritchie, how long have you known me?"

Mrs Ritchie: "About a year"

Mr Fox to the Judge: "Your Honour, it would be helpful if we knew how and where Mrs Ritchie came to know Mrs Niemann."

Julia: "Sorry about that. Mrs. Ritchie was my neighbour for over a year at Hobbit Court, the motel at Sandy Bay where I was living with my children when I came back from Winnipeg."

Judge Ferris: "Fine, Mrs Niemann, please go on….."

Julia: "So you know me and my children very well?"

Mrs Ritchie: "Yes, we were neighbours. Our kids played together."

Julia: "And you were my neighbour when Gina was living with me?"

Mrs Ritchie: "Yes, I saw Gina all the time."

Julia: "And Gina was walking to school with your kids. And she was happy?"

Mrs Ritchie: "Yes."

Julia: "And when you chatted with Gina, did she ever say she wasn't happy?"

Mrs Ritchie: "No. She loved being back at home with you and Scott and Lucy."

Julia: "And was there ever a time when she wasn't happy?"

Mrs Ritchie: "Well, the only time I can think of when Gina wasn't happy was the time when Mrs Kerry came over and took her away with her for a day."

Julia: "How do you know Gina wasn't happy."

Mrs Ritchie: "Well, she was sad … not her usual happy self, and she told me that she wished she had gone back to Vancouver with Mrs Kerry when she had the chance."

Julia: "So Mrs Kerry wanted to take Gina back to Vancouver with her?"

Mrs Ritchie: "Yes, that's what happened, but Gina told her she wanted to stay home with you."

Julia: "Do you think Gina would be happy if she was able to come home to live with me and Scott and Lucy."

Mrs Ritchie: "Oh, yes, I'm sure she would."

Julia: "Thank Mrs Ritchie, that's all."

Judge Ferris: "Mr Fox, do you have any questions?"

Mr Fox: "Yes. Just a couple." Then to Mrs Ritchie: "Mrs Ritchie, you mentioned that Gina walked to school with your children every day."

Mrs Ritchie: "Most days."

Mr Fox: "So were there some days when Gina didn't walk to school with them."

Mrs Ritchie: "Yes. Some days."

Mr Fox: "Would that be a lot of days or just a few days?"

Mrs Ritchie: "Well, I can't remember. I mean, I wasn't counting. Sometimes a few"

Mr Fox: "Maybe you can remember one or two occasions.................."

Mrs Ritchie: "Well, of course, sometimes Julia wasn't too well and Gina would stay home to help?"

Mr Fox: "Help?"

Mrs Ritchie: "Yes. Gina is so good at looking after the little ones. And then Julia could rest."

Mr Fox: "And how about Gina. Was she well? Did she get sick and have to stay home?"

Mrs Ritchie: "I guess a few times. She seemed to get a lot of colds and when she came into my place, she didn't have much appetite."

Mr Fox: "Thanks, Mrs Ritchie. That's all."

Judge Ferris, looking towards Jeanette Munro. "I see that our next witness will be Mrs Kerry who will first be examined by Mrs Munro who is acting on behalf of Gina. But before we begin, I'm going to hold a brief half-hour recess to give us all a chance to stretch our legs etc." She looked at her watch: "I suggest we reconvene at 3 p.m."

It seemed to me that, everyone in the court room welcomed the recess. For those unaccustomed to the goings-on during the hearing of witnesses in a court room, the day had, so far, been heavy going. I wondered if we would be able to finish the hearing by 4:30 p.m., the customary end of the court's day. After a trip to the washroom, I found my way back to the cafeteria and sat down with a coffee. I was relieved to find that Jeanette Munro was nowhere in sight. I felt I needed to sit quietly, but struggled to keep the day's evidence from running around in my mind. On the one hand, it seemed to me that the Ministry's case was definitely going well. On the other hand, and somewhat to my surprise, I felt sad about it. I thought "wasn't it sad that every time she was questioned, Julia Niemann just seemed to dig herself into a deeper hole in her effort to keep her daughter". I was beginning to realize that, way back in the beginning when I went to the Spencer's home and spoke to them about having Gina come to us, I had no idea what a Pandora's Box I was opening. No idea at all! Compared to what I had heard today, the events of my own childhood and life to date seemed extraordinarily humdrum! Whatever had happened, I asked myself, to transform Julia Niemann, from Miss Sandy Bay of 1960 into this mixed-up, messed-up, sad woman. I had no doubt Julia loved all her children but something had caused her to lose her way a long time ago, to a point where she didn't seem capable of understanding how unprepared she was to care for them.

"Time to go back in..." Jeanette Munro tapped me on the shoulder, and we hurried back down the hall to court the court room.

As we returned to our seats, I noticed that Julia and Mrs Ritchie were missing. However, they hurried into the room as Judge Ferris took her seat. Julia looked tired. Not surprising, I thought, remembering how tired I had been in the afternoons when I was near the end of my pregnancies.

Judge Ferris addressed the court: "Mrs Munro, as the Ministry's appointee to represent the interests of Regina --- that is "Gina" Niemann, the Court is now ready to hear from you."

Mrs Munro: "Thank you, Your Honour. I would like to advise the court that I have met with Gina on several occasions and I believe I have established a good relationship with her. I first met with Gina at her foster home where I felt she would be most comfortable in talking with me. She has also come to my office. I would say that our relationship is a very friendly one and I believe Gina has been open and honest in expressing her feelings to me. I have also met on several occasions with Maura Kerry, Gina's foster mother. Mrs Kerry has been most cooperative with me and I believe that she has Gina's best interests at heart."

Judge Ferris: "Have you met personally with Mrs Niemann?

Mrs Munro: "No, I have not. However, over these past few months, since I was appointed to represent Gina, I have met with both Mrs Mercer and Miss Parks on several occasions."

Judge Ferris: "Do you feel that this is sufficient for you to make recommendations in this matter?"

Mrs Munro: "Yes, I do, your Honour."

Judge Ferris: "I understand that you wish to call Mrs Kerry as a witness."

Mrs Munro: "Yes. Gina has now been living with the Kerry family for over two years. When the Kerrys first met Gina, she was 12 years old. Very soon, this coming January, she will have her 15th birthday. Growing children change. Gina is now a teenager. Mrs Kerry is the person best qualified to attest to Gina's development over the past few years."

Judge Ferris: "Yes. Will Mrs Kerry please come forward."

Chapter Twenty-Nine

Once I was sworn in and sitting on the witness stand, it didn't seem all that formidable. Somewhat of a relief, in fact.

Mrs Munro: "Mrs Kerry, thank you for attending today on Gina's behalf. Would you briefly describe to the court how you came to know Gina?"

Me: "Yes. We have a summer cottage at Sandy Beach on the Island where I spend every summer with our children. My husband comes over on weekends and takes holiday time there. And Gina's grandparents live a few houses away down a lane."

Mrs Munro: "Can you tell us about your family."

Me: "Yes. My husband, Steve, is an accountant – a tax consultant --- he has his own business. We have two children. Ben (he is 12 years old now) and Amy (she's just had her 9th birthday). That's it – except we have a dog, Tessa, and a cat, Rascal!"

Judge Ferris smiled.

Mrs Munro: "And what about you?"

Me: "I have a part-time job. Otherwise, I am a homemaker."

Mrs Munro: "What kind of part-time job?"

Me: "I'm a paralegal and the firm where I worked before my marriage now employs me part-time. I leave early so that I am at home when the children get home from school. And I have the summer months off."

Judge Ferris: "They must like you!"

Me: "I think I'm good at my work and it makes a change from the house."

Mrs Munro: "So, can you tell us why you wanted to be a foster parent?"

Me: "I never thought of being a foster parent at all. In fact, at that time I hadn't much of an idea of what is involved in being a foster parent."

Mrs Munro: "Then why did you go to the Spencer's --- the grandparents – and offer to be a foster parent to Gina?"

Me: "Well, it didn't actually happen like that. You see, we first met Gina in the summer of 1973. We had just arrived at the cottage for the summer and Gina turned up in the garden one day and was playing with Ben and Amy. The children had a great time together and Gina began coming over just about every day. She came with us to the beach and on picnics and she usually went home when Ben and Amy went to bed."

Mrs Munro: "And didn't you think that was a bit strange?"

Me: "Yes. I asked Gina if her grandparents wouldn't worry if she wasn't home for meals but she told me that they were okay with her coming over to our house and they always left food in their fridge if she needed it. Her grandmother worked at the drugstore up in the village. Anyway, Gina told me that it was okay for her to be with us and I guess I didn't think any more about it. The children were always with me and Gina behaved well."

Mrs Munro: "Did Gina say anything about her mother?"

Me: "She said her mother was sick and she was in Winnipeg and she had a baby sister and a little brother – and her grandpa had brought her from Winnipeg to stay with them at Sandy Bay until her mom was better."

Mrs Munro: "So you didn't talk to her grandparents?"

Me: "No. After all, I just thought that her grandparents were taking care of her --- they would be older and probably glad Gina had found some friends. During the summer, it's very relaxed at Sandy Bay. Anyhow, when we said goodbye to Gina and went back to the mainland at the end of August, I expected that her mother and siblings would be back before long and that would be that."

Mrs Munro: "When was the next time you saw Gina?"

Me: "I guess it was almost a year later, in May of 1974. My mother was visiting from Ontario and we took her over to the cottage for a few days. Gina turned up when she saw our car outside. I seem to remember we all went to her school concert."

Mrs Munro: "And had her mother returned."

Me: "I don't believe so. We saw Gina very briefly. We were only there for a couple of days."

Mrs Munro: "But you saw Gina that summer, didn't you?"

Me: "Actually, no. We were really surprised because we expected her to turn up as soon as she saw our car and Ben and Amy in the garden. But there was no sign of her all summer."

Mrs Munro: "Didn't you wonder where she was?"

Me. "Yes, we did. Around the middle of August when I was in the drugstore I mentioned to her grandmother that we missed seeing Gina. Mrs Spencer said that Gina was over on the mainland with her father. When I asked her if we would see Gina before left at the end of August, Mrs Spencer remarked that they didn't have room for Gina anymore and they were hoping that Gina's father would keep her with him."

Mrs Munro: "Is that why you went to Mrs Spencer?"

Me: "Well, of course, we didn't know anything about Gina's family – just that the Spencers were her grandparents; but when Mrs Spencer told me they didn't have room for Gina anymore, I was upset. Maybe it wasn't any of my business, but Gina had spent so much time with us and we were so fond of her that I just couldn't bear the thought of her not being wanted anywhere? I think I stewed over it for a couple of days and then I spoke to my husband about the idea of going to the Spencers and offering to have Gina, and he was okay with it."

Mrs Munro:" So that's what motivated you to go to the Spencers?"

Me: "Yes. It looked like Gina's mom still wasn't well enough to come back home. We didn't know anything about her father and we just wanted Gina to have a happy place to live."

Mrs Munro: "So you weren't interested in being a foster parent."

Me: "I just didn't think of it like that. I mean – we didn't know about her mother or anything."

Mrs Munro: "So when did Gina actually come to live with your family?"

Me: "Well, after I went and spoke to Mr and Mrs Spencer, they called me a couple of days later and told me that Gina's father said he couldn't keep her with him --- so they came over to my house to discuss having Gina live with us."

Mrs Munro: "And you agreed that she would come"

Me: "The Spencers told me all about Julia being hospitalized in Winnipeg and about her other children, Scott and Lucy, and of course how Mr Spencer had flown to Winnipeg and had brought Gina to live with them."

Mrs Munro: "And so you agreed that Gina would come to live with you if she wanted."

Me: "Oh, the Spencers had already called Gina before they came over to see me, and they said she was just thrilled at the idea of coming to live with us."

Mrs Munro: "And when did Gina come to live with you."

Me: "She came back on the ferry two days later, packed her things and moved over to our cottage and back to the mainland with us."

Mrs Munro: "What happened after that?"

Me: "Well, the children began school – all of them went to Pine Park Elementary."

Mrs Munro: "Did Gina settle in well."

Me: "Fairly well. It took her a little time to get used to our family rules, etc. That's normal. There were no major difficulties. She did have quite a bit of catching up to do, though."

Mrs Munro: "Why was there a problem with catching up?"

Me: "After she started Pine Park, Gina and I had a few chats about it. She told me that she hadn't started school until she was almost eight and she had also missed a lot of school when she was in Winnipeg – so she had to work hard to catch up and her reading was still slow."

Mrs Munro: "Do you know why she was so late in starting school. And the cause of missing school. Was she sick?"

Me: "I'm not clear on all of it, but I gather that after Mrs Niemann's divorce they moved around a lot and that resulted in Gina not starting school. As far as missing a lot of school in Winnipeg, when I asked her, Gina said that she often had to stay home to help with Scott and Lucy because of her mother's work shifts."

Mrs Munro: "Surely there was a babysitter?"

Me: "Apparently not. Gina took care of them. .In fact, it was very touching to me to see how motherly she was towards them both. But she told me that she was always getting into trouble at school because they thought she was playing hooky."

Mrs Munro: "Didn't Mrs Niemann send a note."

Me: " I don't think so."

Mrs Munro: "And were your children okay with Gina? After all, she is older than they are."

Me: "I know that can be a problem but I guess I was lucky --- and my children were just great. Things went well."

Mrs Munro: "Mrs Kerry, my file shows that Mrs Niemann returned to Sandy Bay in November of 1974 and she called you in early December and asked you to return Gina to her."

Me: "Yes, that's correct."

Mrs Munro: "How did you feel about that?"

Me: "Well, it was a bit of a surprise. Of course, we expected that Mrs Niemann would eventually recover but when the Spencers discussed Gina coming to live with us, they never said that they expected Mrs Niemann to return to Sandy Bay any time soon. Otherwise, quite frankly, if we had thought she would be returning in a few weeks, there would have been no reason for us to offer to have Gina."

Mrs Munro: "So when Mrs Niemann called you, what happened?"

Me: "We were all going to Hawaii that Christmas --- so I called Mrs Mercer and arrangements were made to return Gina right away after school closed."

Mrs Munro: "How did Gina feel about that?"

Me: "Gina was totally thrilled that her mother had returned and wanted her to come home."

Mrs Munro: "She wasn't upset to miss going to Hawaii or to be leaving your home?"

Me: "No. Not at all. I could see that Gina loves her mother very much, and still does, and she also loves Scott and Lucy. And

Julia still had custody of Gina – so it was quite right that Gina should return home."

Mrs Munro: "So there were no hurt feelings?"

Me: "No. Except I have to say, I wished this had all happened sooner. Adding another child to a family causes something of an upheaval at any time."

Mrs Munro: "So Gina returned to Sandy Bay and the Kerry family went to Hawaii for Christmas."

Me: "Yes."

Mrs Munro: "When was the next time you heard from Gina?"

Me: "I guess it was about a week or ten days after we returned at the beginning of January. I got a letter from Gina."

Mrs Munro: "Can you give us some idea of what Gina said in that letter?"

Me: "Well, she said she hoped we had a good time in Hawaii. Also, she said that she was back at school in Sandy Bay and she was glad to be with Scott and Amy."

Mrs Munro: "Anything else?"

Me: "Yes. Gina said she wasn't happy. She was having difficulty getting along with her mother. She told me she would like to come back to live with us and she asked me to come over and get her."

Mrs Munro: "What did you do?"

Me: "I wrote a short letter back to Gina telling her that the best place for her to be was with her mother and brother and sister. I told her to be helpful to her mother and to do her best to get along. I also said that I would see if I could come over to see her and maybe we could spend a day together. After that, I believe I called Mrs Mercer to ask her advice about going over to see Gina."

Mrs Munro: "And did you go?"

Me: "Yes. Mrs Mercer thought it would be all right. I didn't have a phone number for Julia so I called Gina's grandmother and asked her if she would ask Julia if it would be all right with her if I came over and took Gina out for a day. I didn't want to take Gina out unless it was okay with Julia."

Mrs Munro: "And did you get approval?"

Me: "Yes. Julia agreed that I could come over and take Gina out for an afternoon on a Saturday. And that's what I did."

Mrs Munro: "And how did the visit go?"

Me: "Well, I took the ferry over and picked Gina up at Hobbit Court in the late morning."

Mrs Munro: "And did you see Julia."

Me: "No, Gina was waiting on the steps when I arrived. There was no sign of Julia."

Mrs Munro: "Please continue…."

Me: "We drove down to Nanaimo and had a meal. Gina is very partial to steak --- so we went to a steakhouse. She was her usual talkative self, but she looked very pale and she had lost weight. She also complained of feeling a bit dizzy. Anyway, she said that she missed eating meat. I understand Julia doesn't believe in eating meat, so they ate mostly vegetables and pasta. When I asked her what they would eat for supper, Gina said that sometimes her mother would ask Scott what they should have, and if Scott said "bananas", then they would have bananas."

Mrs Munro: "And how was school going?"

Me: "Gina said that she was staying at home quite a bit to help with the children."

Mrs Munro: "Anything else?"

Me: "Yes, when we finished eating Gina asked me not to take her back to Sandy Bay. She wanted me to take her back with me on the ferry, to live with us."

Mrs Munro: How did you deal with that?

Me: "I just told her that she and Scott and Lucy and her mother were her family and she must learn to make the best of things and to understand that things were difficult for her mother. I said that I would speak to Mrs Mercer and see if she could talk to the social workers over at Sandy Bay about possibly giving the family more assistance."

Mrs Munro: "And did Gina accept that?"

Me: "Yes, she did. She told me that she really loved her mum but that she just didn't want to live with her anymore. And I told her that I couldn't interfere, but I would speak to the social workers."

Mrs Munro: "So you returned to the mainland; and did you speak to Mrs Mercer."

Me: "Yes, I did. I was concerned about Gina. I was concerned about her missing school. I could see that she was really unhappy and I wanted to see if something could be done to make her situation better."

Mrs Munro: "Did you hear anything back from Mrs Mercer."

Me: "No. I don't suppose there was enough time -- because a couple of weeks after my visit, I got a call from Gina's grandmother asking me if Gina could come back to live with us. She said that when Gina had arrived home from school the previous day, she found her clothes in a box in the middle of the kitchen floor and her mother and the little ones had gone!"

Mrs. Munro: "Gone?"

Me: "Yes. No one had seen them. They were nowhere to be found!"

Mrs Munro: "They left Gina behind?!"

Me: "Yes."

Mrs Munro: "Did Mrs Spencer know why that was?"

Me: "No. She just said that Julia had gone."

Mrs Munro: "Have you any idea why Mrs. Niemann would do such a thing. When you took Gina out, did she say anything to you about her mother leaving Sandy Bay? And have you any idea why Gina was left behind?"

Me: "No. Gina didn't say anything. But I think I may understand why?"

Mrs Munro: "Please tell us what you think?"

Me: "Well, when Gina was living with us, as time went by she began to tell me about a lot of the things that had happened before she came to live with us. And from what she told me, I started to realize that Gina believed that she was responsible for all kinds of trouble – that she had caused a lot of trouble for her mother and little brother and sister. She still feels guilty about it and she believes that her mother blames her for it. So I think that when she came home and discovered that her mother had left Sandy

Bay without taking her along, she felt that she had been left behind as a punishment."

"That's a lie, that's a lie!" Julia Niemann stood up and shouted across the court room.

Judge Ferris: "Mrs Niemann, please sit down and please do not interrupt Mrs Kerry's testimony. You will have an opportunity to cross-examine and ask your own questions when Mrs Munro finishes."

Julia sat down and began whispering angrily to Mrs Ritchie.

Judge Ferris: "Please continue Mrs Munro."
Mrs Munro to me: "Mrs Kerry, perhaps you can explain to the court what Mrs Niemann is blaming Gina for."
Me: "All I can do is tell the court what Gina told me."
Mrs Munro: "All right. Please continue."
Me: "Gina told me that when they were living in Winnipeg, they had a one-bedroom basement apartment. She said that her mother and the little ones slept in the bedroom and she slept in a big box in the kitchen. Anyway, one night she was wakened up because her mother was yelling and screaming loudly in the bedroom, so she got up and ran into the bedroom to see what was wrong. Her mother was very angry and yelled at her "get out, get out!" but Gina said she didn't want to go because the little ones were wakened up and started crying. She felt scared because her mother yelled and yelled, so in the end she ran outside and went down the street. She told me that she often played with a girl who lived three houses down and she went there and found the basement door open. It was very late and it was so quiet that she decided everyone in the house was asleep. Finally, she fell asleep on a couch in their rec room. The next morning when she woke up it was very early and she decided she needed to hurry home because her mother would be leaving for work and she would have to feed Scott and Lucy. Anyway,

as she was walking back to her house, a police car came along and stopped her and the police asked her what she was doing. She said they put her in their car and drove her home, and then when they spoke to her mother, her mother began yelling again, so they took all of them to the hospital. After that, her mother was put in a bed and then a lady came and took Scott and Lucy away. Another lady came and took Gina to her office where they phoned her grandfather. Gina said she spent a night at a lady's house and then her grandfather came and took her back on the plane to Sandy Bay. That's when she met us."

Mrs Munro: "So, how does that lead you to believe that Gina believes her mum is punishing her?"

Me: "Well, when she told me about it, I asked Gina why the police had picked her up in their cruiser and taken her back home. After all, she was just walking along on the sidewalk? And Gina said that when the police stopped her, she was still in her nighty and bare feet, and it was twenty below zero. Then I understood why they would have stopped. But the reason I believe Gina thinks her mother is angry with her because, when she finished telling me all about it, Gina said "And my mother got into all this trouble --- and IT WAS ALL MY FAULT!"

Mrs. Munro: "So Gina believes that what happened was her fault?"

Me: "Yes. She feels if she hadn't been out on the sidewalk and the police hadn't stopped her, none of it would have happened. She has a great sense of guilt about it......."

Mrs Munro: "But surely Mrs Niemann would have explained to Gina that this isn't so."

Me: "I don't know if she did. All I know is that Gina always worries that she might do something that would cause more trouble. Ever since she told me about it, I have on many occasions tried to reassure her that it wasn't her fault, but I know it's still there in her head."

"That's a bunch of lies. It's all lies!" Julia Niemann jumped up again, waving her arms at the Judge.

"Mrs Niemann," Judge Ferris's tone was firm, "I have explained to you that you will have an opportunity to cross-examine Mrs

Kerry when Mrs Munro finishes this examination. So I am asking you once more to be patient and wait until it is your turn."

Julia sat down again, but not before glowering in my direction.

Mrs Munro: "I understand that Gina then returned to live with your
    family?"

Me: "Yes. Ben and Amy and I made a trip over to Sandy Bay and
    Mrs Spencer brought Gina to us. We had to wait for three days
    until the circuit court sat so that the social workers could appear
    before a judge. At that point, Gina was considered abandoned,
    and they needed to get a temporary order before she could be
    placed with us."

Mrs Munro: "Why was that?"

Me: "Well, as I mentioned, we were happy to have Gina return to live
    with us, but I was concerned about what would happen if Mrs
    Niemann turned up again, as she did just a couple of months
    before, and we would have to return Gina once more. I didn't
    want any more disruption from the point of view of our house-
    hold, and I didn't want any more disruption from the point of
    view of Gina. I don't think it's good for anyone to be shuffled
    back and forth. In Gina's case, it doesn't help with schooling."

Mrs Munro: "So Gina returned and settled in again."

Me: "Yes, but when the court at Sandy Bay made the interim order,
    the judge set a date for a proper hearing in May. So, we all trav-
    elled over there in May for that hearing."

Mrs Munro: "And did that all go smoothly?"

Me: "Unfortunately, no! Mrs Niemann returned to Sandy Bay in
    April, I think it was, and she wanted Gina to be returned to
    her."

Mrs Munro: "And did Mrs Niemann give a reason for leaving Sandy
    Bay and abandoning Gina?"

Me: "As I remember it, Mrs Niemann told the judge that she hadn't
    abandoned Gina. She said that she had just left town without
    telling Gina where she was going."

Mrs Munro: "And did she say where she had gone?"

Me: "I believe she said she had decided to return to Winnipeg. However, she didn't go there in the end because she got off the bus in Calgary. I believe there will be a court transcript of the evidence."

Mrs Munro: "Yes, I have the transcript of that hearing….. which I would like to enter into evidence as Exhibit "A", your Honour."

Judge Ferris to the Court Clerk: "Please enter the transcript of the May hearing as Exhibit "A"."

Mrs Munro: "The transcript of that hearing shows that His Honour Judge Sperling, made an order for temporary custody."

Mrs Munro: "So after the hearing in May of 1975, Gina returned to live with your family in West Vancouver and has been living with you for about three years in total?"

Me: "Yes."

Mrs Munro: "How often has she seen her mother during that time?"

Me: "Since Mrs Niemann moved over to Vancouver --- I believe that was in late 19756 --- Gina visited her about once a month."

Mrs Munro: "And I understand that Gina visits her father?"

Me: "Yes. Max came over to introduce himself to us just after Gina came to us in the fall of 1974. He helps out occasionally with things she needs. And Gina visits her dad at least once a month. She usually stays with him and Laura, her stepmother, overnight. She enjoys her visits and gets along very well with both of them."

Mrs Munro: "You say he helps out?"

Me: "Yes, if there's something she needs that is a costly item --- he helps. For instance, he got her a bike for Christmas 1975 so that she could ride with Ben and Amy. Things like that."

Mrs Munro: "And how have Gina's visits with her mother been going?"

Me: "Fairly well until just recently."

Mrs Munro: "Can you describe the problem?"

Me: "There were two male tenants on the ground floor of the house where Mrs Niemann lives. I gather they were friends of her mother and one of them began acting in a way that embarrassed Gina."

Mrs Munro: "What kind of way?"

Me: "Mrs Munro, Gina is now a teenager and like a lot of young girls she is quite sensitive and self-conscious about the way her body is changing. I gather that one of the guys made remarks that made her not want to be in the room if he was there."

Mrs Munro: "What was done about it."

Me: "Gina and I talked it over and then we spoke to Mrs Mercer. I gather that Mrs Mercer talked to Miss Parks who I assume spoke to the guys in question. I really don't know because we went over to Sandy Bay for the summer, as usual, and since we returned, I understand the two of them have moved out of the apartment."

Mrs Munro: "So they are no longer a problem."

Me: "No."

Judge Ferris: "Mrs Munro, I'm looking at my watch and I see that it's just about 4:30 – so I think this might be a good time to adjourn for the day. How much of Mrs Kerry's testimony remains?"

Mrs Munro: "Not a lot, your Honour. Perhaps 15 minutes or so."

Judge Ferris: "I see Mrs Niemann looking in my direction and I want to assure her that she will be given ample time to cross-examine. But I think that we have done enough for today. It would have been nice to conclude this hearing today but that just isn't possible. I'll give instructions to the Clerk to reschedule the hearing on the first available date in the new year that's convenient to all parties. Until then, this hearing is adjourned."

With a quick 'bang' of the gavel, Judge Ferris departed from the Court Room. It was clear from Julia Niemann's reaction that she wasn't at all happy with the adjournment. Considering that her baby was due in January, that was understandable. In fact, from my point of view, it was also a great disappointment. This meant that I would have to wait in suspense for God knows how many weeks before I was cross-examined. Remembering Julia Niemann's hostility, I wasn't overjoyed with that prospect. And of course, the delay would also mean a delay in knowing the outcome of the Ministry's application.

When she caught up with me in the car park, all Jeanette Munro had to say was "I'll give you a call tomorrow". Then, as I drove home through the torrential rain, I remembered that we were leaving for sunny Hawaii in three days and I thought "Thank God for Steve and his brilliant idea!"

PART X

Respite

Chapter Thirty

Just three days later, viewed from my comfortable Boeing 747 window seat at an altitude of 20,000 feet, the scenic metropolis of Vancouver with its surrounding snowcapped mountains became a distant, miniature world. As our plane veered out over the blue Pacific Ocean, all the tensions of the court hearing, attending to last-minute details at work, and getting three excited children to put their schoolbooks away, tidy up their rooms, and pack a bare minimum of clothes (bearing in mind that we all expected to spend most of the holiday in t-shirts, shorts and flipflops) began to ebb and float away like the wispy white clouds outside the window.

I heaved a sigh of relief. Free at last, I thought. Well, not exactly, the hearing wasn't over, but for the next ten days, we could all enjoy fun in the sun. Seated beside me, Steve had already begun to unwind and was reading the newspaper, one of his favourite 'escapes'! The children were across the aisle from us, in the centre row which had a good view of the movie screen --- a definite must.

When I arrived home after the hearing, I told them it had all gone well. They were satisfied with that. I didn't mention that the hearing hadn't finished and would continue in the new year because I didn't want any of them, particularly Gina, to be worrying about events on our return. I had, of course, told Steve who wasn't very happy about it, even when I explained that Jeanette Munro had called me to say that she was very pleased with the way it had gone to date and she didn't anticipate any real difficulties when Julia Niemann cross-examined me. However, I just couldn't hide the fact that I was quite apprehensive about being cross-examined, considering Julia Niemann's hostility, the fact that she had called me a liar, and her insinuations that I was somehow trying to 'steal' Gina from her.

Steve was both annoyed and concerned, mainly on my account. Although he never said so to me, I knew he felt that having Gina living with us was proving to be altogether too much trouble and perhaps it would make more sense to return her to her mother and let the social workers figure it all out, rather than leave it all to us, which most of the time was 'me'! When I tried to see it from Steve's point of view, I could understand his feelings but I just couldn't resign myself to the idea of Gina returning to live with Julia. In the beginning, what I wanted to do was provide a loving home for a little girl whose mother was sick. But what I knew at the beginning was just the tip of the iceberg and the more I learned, particularly since listening to the testimony at the hearing, the more convinced I was that Gina shouldn't be returned to Julia. In a way, I felt I was becoming quite hard-hearted. After all, I had children of my own and I knew how I would feel at the thought of anyone taking them away. But when the focus is on the well-being of a child, everything changes.

I sat there thinking. I thought about Judge Ferris, that white-haired, quiet woman with the kind blue eyes sitting up there on the Bench, faced with making such an important decision, a decision which would so greatly affect the life of a mother or father or child. I asked myself a lot of questions. What is a good mother or a good father? How do you define it? Don't we all generally expect our mother to do whatever is necessary to meet our needs? We even expect her to know all our needs and then be able to fill them! Ditto for our father. But can every mother or father do that? If circumstances arise which prevent a mother from fulfilling the needs of her child, then isn't it only reasonable that the child's needs can be met by another 'mother" on a temporary basis? That would be me!? Again, what is a mother?

I dozed off before I could reach a conclusion! Mercifully, maybe? About an hour before we landed in Honolulu, Steve woke me up and handed me a snack. He had booked the trip, which began with three days and nights at the Outrigger on Waikiki Beach. It was around 6 p.m. Hawaiian time when we finally cleared U.S. Customs and Immigration. We managed to squeeze all our bags into one taxi and reached the hotel at around 8 p.m. We had two lovely airy rooms on the third floor overlooking the beach and pool. The kids loved it. After a light supper at a restaurant, we decided to call it a day. All of us were very tired. We had three whole days to enjoy while we showed Gina around Honolulu.

And the Kerry family really did make the most of Honolulu: the beach, a day trip to the Hawaiian Cultural Centre, an afternoon at the AlaMoana Shopping Centre, etc. etc. Gina just lapped it up. One evening we hired two bicycle rickshaws and raced --- Gina and Ben in one rickshaw and Amy and me in the other. The guys operating the rickshaws thought we were mad! I suppose we were quite a sight as we raced along, hooting and hollering. I can't remember who won! Anyway, that didn't matter. Steve opted out of the escapade. He hid out in a coffee shop as far away from his crazy family as possible. Of course, we didn't think we were crazy. We considered ourselves "cool"!

Three days later, we boarded an afternoon Hawaiian Airlines flight and landed in Maui in the middle of the afternoon. Steve had booked a condo at the Kona Kai, just north of Kihei and right on the beach. Every condo came along with a car for the duration of the stay, which was ideal for us. The kids were beginning to appreciate the wisdom of travelling light. It only took a half-hour taxi ride from the airport and twenty minutes or so to check into the Kona Kai, and we were on the beach about 90 minutes later.

The Kona Kai was a rectangular, seven-storey concrete building, set at an angle of approximately 45 degrees to the beach, with its lobby facing the beach and a car park on the other side. We were all delighted because our condo was on the very top floor --- a penthouse! It was furnished Japanese style with a large ensuite master bedroom near the entrance, living, dining and kitchen areas opposite, and a second bedroom on the other side, also ensuite. The girls agreed to share the bedroom and Ben was happy with the convertible bed in the large living area. But, hey, who worried about that when you could look out over the ocean and the beach way down below?

The Kerry family was more than ready for a holiday and we enjoyed it to the full. Although this was their second trip, Ben and Amy enjoyed it all over again as they shared it with Gina. As for Gina, she was one happy almost fifteen-year-old girl. We had a family conference and decided that for Christmas we would just give each other small 'fun' gifts. I received plastic pineapple earrings, Steve received a small 'hip flask' which someone?! had filled with pineapple juice, and Gina received a glow in the dark grass skirt and matching wig, to name but a few of the more exotic treasures. On Christmas Day, we had dinner at the 'posh' restaurant at the Napili Golf and Country Club. For that occasion, we all donned our finest garb. Gina and Amy wore the puff-sleeved dresses I had made for them, puff sleeves being "in" at the time. Gina's dress was a lovely shade of mauve with white trim, and Amy's dress was white, with mauve trim. I thought they both looked beautiful. So did they. Dinner was enjoyed all, especially Gina because there was steak on the menu!

On Boxing Day, we drove along the windward side of the island to Hana. The children decided to count the bridges as we went, to verify that there actually were 201 of them as stated in the tourist literature in the hotel lobby! Gina brought along a notebook to keep tally. The girls and I made sandwiches etc. and we found a lovely spot down by the beach where we enjoyed a picnic. There was a mini crisis when we decided it was time to return because the car wouldn't start. Our car – a Mustang - was okay but, shall we say, the cars at the Kona Kai had 'seen a lot of action'. Fortunately, Steve who was never cut out to be a mechanic managed to fiddle around with the wires and get the car going, a real stroke of luck since there are no gas stations or similar at Hana. The children, of course, thought all of this was hilarious.

For most of the time, we enjoyed the beach. The children got along so well that Steve and I felt comfortable leaving them at the Kona Kai on two occasions while we took ourselves out to dinner. All of us drove up to Kaanapali where we spent the day on the beach and exploring in Lahaina. Steve did a bit of golfing. When he was golfing near Kahului, the kids and I found some interesting shops including a quaint little shop specializing in all kinds of things made out of shells where they bought gifts for friends and family at home.

Finally, all our days used up, we found ourselves, suntanned and laid back, boarding a Boeing jet for Canada. Were we really going back --- back to damp, cold days, back to school, back to work and back to a hearing? Right now, we were about to go up in the air, but at the other end we would come back down to earth and with a bump.

Chapter Thirty-One

Why is it that, even after a wonderful, happy holiday, about two days after arriving home, it feels like you have never been away at all? Surely this is one of the great injustices of our time! The Kerry family scarcely had time to unpack their bags and throw their sandy t-shirts in the wash before the telephone began to ring. First, it was Mrs Mercer who wanted to arrange to meet with Gina. After the conclusion of the hearing, Gina would be interviewed by Judge Ferris and Mrs Mercer wanted to be able to prepare Gina so that she would understand what would happen if the Ministry became her guardians until she was eighteen years of age. Gina would go after school on Tuesday.

Mrs Mercer had heard from Doris Parks and it looked like Julia's baby would be arriving sometime around mid-January, which meant that the hearing wasn't likely to resume until the end of January or early February.

Next came a call from Max Niemann, again wishing us a Happy New Year. With the baby due in three weeks, he and Laura invited Gina for a sleepover on the coming weekend so that they could hear all about her trip. John would pick Gina up on Saturday morning at 10 o'clock!

After that, I had a call from Alyssa who had visited with Julia during our absence. She confirmed my belief that Julia felt that I was trying to usurp her place as Gina's mother, and she was impossible to reason with. Alyssa said she would pop in to see Gina after music.

Next, Jeanette Munro called me to set up an appointment at her office so that we could discuss possible questions during my cross-examination. This was something I didn't relish thinking about but knew it must be dealt with. We would meet on Friday! She would let me know when she had a Court date. It would likely be only half a day but there would still be the matter of Judge Ferris's interview. I told her about Gina's appointment with Mrs Mercer.

And last but not least, Dorrie called to report that Tessa had been a 'good dog' and when could she bring her back home to us. So Dorrie was bringing Tessa home and staying for supper on Sunday!

Those first three days at home were such a zoo that I think Steve was glad to escape back to his office. I was even glad to return to my orderly work files and court schedules!

After their trip, the kids returned to school full of energy and high spirits. Gina carefully wrapped the little shell gifts she had bought in Kahului for Max and Laura and wore her TIKI necklace when Max picked her up on Saturday morning. And Steve took Ben and Amy off in the car to a 'mysterious' destination. I wasn't allowed to ask where.

With the house all to myself, I did a quick tidy-up and then had a chat on the phone with Bette Vogt who was glad to hear how well the holiday had gone for all of us.

When Dorrie came to supper on Sunday, she was pleased that all the children had brought back a little gift for her, including Gina, even though Dorrie wasn't her 'real' grandmother. For me, it was an indicator that Gina felt 'included' and part of our family to the extent that my mother was her grandmother too. It was a small thing but it meant a lot to me. Over supper, Gina shared with all of us how she and Laura had put up the shell mobile gift and how good it looked in the nursery.

Gina walked over to Mrs Mercer's office after school on Wednesday. I picked her up there at around 5 o'clock. "How did it go?" was my first question. After my comments at the hearing about Gina's sense of guilt and of being punished, I knew that Mrs Mercer was anxious that Gina understand what a transfer of guardianship to the Ministry would mean. Both Mrs Mercer and I felt it was important for Gina's ongoing happiness and progress in her development as an adult, that Gina learn to deal with her relationship with her mother in a more reasoned and less emotional way. Although I was anxious, I now understood better that as Gina's social worker and the person responsible for Gina's overall well-being, this was Mrs Mercer's role. As a foster mother, my role was to be 'back-up' for Mrs Mercer.

Afterwards, I asked Gina how their meeting went.

"Okay," Gina replied. Then, after a short pause, "Actually, I think it helped a lot."

I wanted to know more. "How? What did she say?"

'Mmmmmmmm She's not as easy to talk to as you, mum, you know". Another pause, "She explained what it would be like if the Ministry is given guardianship of me. Like, things won't change all that much ---- from the way they are now, I mean. I can still live with you and go to the same school, and visit with my dad, and take music lessons ..... all that stuff. And oh yes, I can still visit my mom. It's just that I won't ever have to go back to live with my mom unless I want to go. I can still see Scott and Lucy and the new baby – whoever that will be – and I can even stay longer like in the summer, but Mrs Mercer will be the person who helps me work things out."

"That's good," I said, "it sounds like you understand it well.

"Oh, and I forgot," she interrupted, "it will go on until I'm 18 and after that, I'm the boss of me! It will all work out much better, especially for me because my mom will just have three kids to look after, and that's enough!?"

"I guess so," I smiled.

"BUT", as she spoke, Gina screwed up her face into one of her 'ugh, I hate this medicine' faces, as she added "will my mother see it this way? You know what she's like. She makes up her mind one minute and then changes it the next minute."

"I think this is one of those times when we will just have to hope for the best" I advised.

"Anyway," Gina added, "I will have a chance to talk to the Judge before she decides."

"How do you feel about that?" I asked.

"Judges are supposed to know everything. So I suppose she will know what's best," Gina spoke in a quiet tone. "You saw her already, mum, what do you think?"

"Yes, I saw her, Gina. She has a very kind face I think people with kind faces are usually very good people. I think you will like her and I think she will make the best decision for you. But you must be sure to tell her how you really, really feel right deep down in your heart. You shouldn't be afraid of Judge Ferris. I believe you can trust her to do the right thing for you and your mum."

"Well, anyway, Mrs Mercer thinks it's best I don't see my mom until after the hearing is over and her baby is born."

"I think that makes good sense" I replied.

At that we pulled into our driveway, Gina grabbed her books. It was supper time.

Chapter Thirty-Two

Alyssa picked Gina up after music the next day and the two of them turned up at the house around 4:30 p.m. After a snack, Gina went downstairs to practice, leaving Alyssa and myself drinking coffee in the kitchen. Over Christmas, while we were away, Alyssa had gone over to visit Julia and the children. She said that Julia seemed to be very listless and lacking in energy. Of course, she was in her third trimester and rather big, with two small children at home most of the time. Scott, at the age of six, was a great little helper, but Lucy was very demanding and prone to tantrums which Julia was quite unable to control. From what she had been able to find out, Alyssa said that Doris Parks was very seldom on the scene. There were a lot of people like Julia living in that area and the word was that she had a caseload that was much too high for one social worker to manage properly.

Alyssa did as much tidying up and cleaning of Julia's apartment as she could but the problem was that Julia seemed incapable of doing anything in an orderly fashion. The place was a shambles. In addition, Julia slept a lot and only prepared meals sporadically, which doesn't work with two small children who get hungry frequently. And when Julia was awake, for most of the time she was ranting on and on about how I had stolen her daughter. According to Alyssa, Julia regarded me as some kind of "Evil Witch" determined to steal her child and corrupt her with bad habits! And Julia says all of this in front of Scott and Lucy and anyone else who will listen.

I asked Alyssa what kind of help the Financial Worker was giving. Again, Alyssa said that the financial worker came once a month when she sat down with Julia to prepare a budget for the month, based on Julia's income. However, since Julia's style was to buy one or two items at a time from the corner store, the monthly budget just didn't work. Alyssa felt Julia was quite incapable of dealing with money at all. Alyssa's overall feeling was that the addition of one more child was simply going to add to an already impossible situation.

In the end, we both agreed that Julia's setup was unworkable Neither of us wanted to use the word "hopeless", but both of us were thinking it. Perhaps it would be a great blessing for all concerned if the Ministry's application for guardianship of Gina was successful.

After coffee, Alyssa went downstairs for a chat with Gina. I told her I would let her know when the hearing was over.

And then it was Friday and I was sitting in the reception area of Harris & Harris waiting to see Jeanette Munro. "Aloha, Maura! How's Hawaii these days?" Jeanette Munro was standing in front of me smiling and holding out her hand.

"Very sunny, mahalo" I replied as we entered her office and I settled into a chair in front of her desk.

"It sounds like you made the most of your holiday. One thing for sure, you were all ready for it?"

"Yes. It was great. We needed a break and it did us all a lot of good."

"Yes, as I recall, Hawaii is a great stress reliever". She leaned forward and opened her, by this time rather voluminous, file. "So now we get ready for the 'home stretch'?"

"I have to admit, I'm dreading it quite a bit," I said.

"Be careful you don't beat yourself up, over this, Maura. Yes, you are being cross-examined, but bear in mind that you are being cross-examined by Julia Niemann. I doubt that she will request any assistance, professional or otherwise with it. I've read over the transcript to date and in my view, there isn't anything there for her to latch onto that will in any way persuade the court that she should continue to have custody and guardianship of Gina. Surely you must see that?"

"Okay, what you say makes sense. But at the hearing, Julia seemed to be intent on proving that I somehow decided to get Gina to come and live with my family for the money. I know we pretty well refuted that, but I still think she's going to come back at me on this point" I said.

"Okay then, Maura," Mrs Munro continued, "but you know that there's no truth at all to that and if she continues with it, it will most likely work against her with the court. Judge Ferris has dealt with a lot of similar applications. She will know immediately what is going on. And in any event, it isn't you but the Ministry that will have custody and guardianship. I let out a sigh. "I suppose it's just nerves. One always tends to focus on what could go wrong rather than what is going right, And I had a visit on Wednesday from Alyssa Brooks. You remember, she's an old friend of Julia's. While we were away, she visited Julia twice and what she had to say was quite disturbing."

"Just exactly what did she say?" Mrs Munro asked, and I found myself recounting to her almost all of the conversation.

"Thanks for letting me know," she said, "When you have a minute, would you type up a summary of it and fax it to me?"

"Of course," I replied

As we walked to her door, she said, "Don't forget, I represent Gina and I'm totally on her side in all of this. I'll let you know just as soon as I have the date."

In the meantime, our busy life continued. Gina's fifteenth birthday was on the coming Saturday and after we discussed it, the plan was that Gina would invite her two best friends over for dinner and a movie or two? (we would have to get those from the video store) and a sleepover. I was in charge of catering, except that Gina was going to bake a bunch of brownies. We were organized or at least I thought so. But there is always the unexpected, isn't there? Max called on Saturday morning and asked for Gina. I put the extension down on the hall table, called "Gina, it's your dad," and returned to party preparations in the kitchen. I heard Gina clattering down the stairs and then an almighty squeal, "Mom, mom, the baby has arrived! Laura went into Children's Hospital last night and he arrived at 7 a.m. this morning! Isn't that the most exciting thing? He's born on MY birthday. Can you talk to my dad.........."?

I hurried down the hall. "Hi, Max, Congratulations," I said, "do I understand it's a boy?"

"Yes, a 6 lb. 10 oz. healthy boy!"

"That's wonderful, Max. And Laura's okay?" I asked.

"Yes, she's very okay and glad to be a lot slimmer!". He laughed.

"Well, your daughter is jumping around beside me like a jack-in-the-box," I said. "You realize it's HER birthday too?"

"Oh my God, so it is," he exclaimed, "I'm afraid I've been so caught up in the action around here I forgot".

"I'm sure she'll forgive you," I said. As I spoke, Gina put her arms around my waist, stood on tiptoe and whispered in my ear, "When can I see the baby?"

"I don't know if you heard that, Max," I said, "Gina is asking when she can see the baby.'

"I'm going to go home now for a shower and shave," Max continued, "but how about I pick Gina up after lunch and take her to the hospital?"

"I've got a better idea," I said, "It sounds like you could use a rest, so why don't I drive over to Children's. We can meet outside the door, and I can take Gina home afterwards for her birthday party and give you a break."

"That would be great if you don't mind" Max sounded relieved.

"No trouble at all," I said, "After all, it isn't every day that you become the father of a baby boy!"

We arranged to meet at Children's Hospital, Vancouver, at 3 o'clock, giving us time to have lunch before leaving for the hospital. When I told Gina, she did what any fifteen-year-old girl would do --- she ran downstairs to her room to decide what to wear!

This was certainly a day for the unexpected because when told Steve what had happened, he insisted that he would drive us all over, including Ben and Amy. Gina's friends weren't getting dropped off at our place until 5:30, so we would be back in time. I couldn't see the sense in all of it, but Steve was determined, so I gave up arguing and got lunch ready.

As arranged, Max was waiting at the hospital door when we arrived. Gina was worried in case they wouldn't let her in but Max assured her that she would be allowed in because she was "family". I don't have words to describe the expression on Gina's face when she heard this. Until that moment, I hadn't realized what a magic word "family" can be to a child who has never really had a chance to realize the relationship between "family" and "belonging".

While Gina was visiting her new little brother, Steve, Ben, Amy and myself went to a coffee shop. And that is where Steve explained why he had insisted on coming along with us. The mysterious trip he had taken with Ben and Amy just after our return from Hawaii was to arrange a surprise birthday party for Gina, who had told Ben and Amy that she had never had one. The plan was for all of us to go to The Firebrick Steakhouse at Ambleside Beach, near our place. And not to worry, Steve had already called Gina's friends' parents and arranged for them to be dropped off there. I had an amazing husband! We decided that we would ask Max to come along too. That would probably be the best 'icing' on Gina's cake.

When Max and Gina came out of the hospital, Steve took Max to one side and explained the secret plan. Of course, Max was delighted to drive over to the Firebrick and join the party.

As we drove home from the hospital, Steve's master plan went into action. He pretended to suddenly remember that he had to stop by the Firebrick to pick up a file that a client had left there for him. Gina was very disturbed by this development and said she was "sure" her friends would arrive for the party and find our house empty. As soon as we had parked the car at the Firebrick, both Ben and Amy 'faked' needing to use the washroom. At that, Steve leaned over towards me and whispered, "give us 10 minutes and then bring Gina in". As we sat waiting, Gina was bouncing up and down like a fly on a hot griddle. Finally, I said, "All right, Gina, let's go and get those guys to stop clowning around and take all of us home NOW.

Gina was at least ten feet ahead of me as we walked into the restaurant. Fortunately, a young waiter stepped in front of her. "Would you be Miss Gina Niemann?" he asked. Startled, Gina stopped and blurted out: "Yes". Please come this way." Leading Gina, with myself in tow, we rounded the corner into the private dining area, to be greeted by an enormous roar of "Surprise" and "Happy

Birthday Gina" from all the family including Max, and Gina's friends Jenny and Madison.

Over dinner, I talked with Max about the hearing. He said he appreciated everything we were doing for Gina and he had never seen her happier. When I told Max him how much Gina loved him and how she thought he was the best dad in the world, his eyes glistened with tears, reminding me that life is a two-way street and that dads need to know that they are loved by their children in return.

As for Gina, she had a great fifteenth birthday. She would have been happy with just the steak! But in addition to that, she was among family and friends, and she had fun reading all the cards and opening all the gifts. Her short, but heartfelt speech was: "Thanks, everyone. This is my best birthday ever. Love you all."

As for me, I began to realize that although he wasn't one for saying a lot, Steve saw and understood much more than I had imagined.

Three days after Gina's birthday dinner, the phone rang. It was Julia's social worker, Miss Parks. Julia had given birth to a little girl at Children's Hospital "yesterday" -the day following Gina's birthday. Both of them were doing well and, of course, Julia was anxious for Gina to meet her new little sister. Miss Parks had been in touch with Mrs Mercer who suggested that perhaps the best way to deal with it was for Miss Parks to take Gina over to Children's to see the baby the next day after school.

The visit to Children's went well and Gina arrived home in an excited mood. "What a week!", she exclaimed, "First I have a new brother. By the way, did I tell you they are calling him Theodore and some other name, but I've decided to call him Teddy --- he is just as cute and cuddly as a real teddy! Then I have a fantastic surprise birthday party, and now I have a new little sister. My mom is going to call her Rosalie --- she is very sweet!" I think I may have to crack open my piggy bank to get them each a gift." Then, to me, "Mom, I'm gonna be poor! Do you think you could find some extra chores so that I can get a bit more allowance?"

"Well," and I smiled "I'm sure there is some kind of miserable, messy chore that needs to be done. Leave it with me.............." She disappeared downstairs before I finished the sentence!

On Friday of that week, Jeanette Munro called me at the office to tell me that the hearing had been set to resume on the morning of Tuesday, February 10th. Now that Julia's baby had been born, it made sense that the court would set a date. I told her about Gina's visit to Children's. Mrs. Mercer agreed with her that Gina would not visit again with Julia until after the hearing had adjourned and Gina had been interviewed by Judge Ferris.

In the meantime, I should 'relax' and she would check with me again a day or so before the resumption of the hearing. It sounded like a good idea but I didn't know about relaxing. I decided I would keep busy. I was much better at that than I was at relaxing!

Chapter Thirty-Three

"Guess what?" Gina chirped on Sunday as we sat sharing what we had been doing during the week ."We've got a new girl in our class.. Her name is Isabella DeSantos.."

"So?..............." said Ben, in his usual 'why bother us with something so mundane' way.

"So, she's from Mexico!", retorted Gina.

"Mexico?", always the curious one, Amy was interested. "why did they come here? Are they immigrants?"

"I'm not sure," Gina replied, "but I think her father works for the Mexican government. Um – I think she said he is the Mexican Ambassador or something."

By this time, Steve had pricked up his ears. "The Mexican Ambassador would be in Ottawa, I think. But he just might be the new Mexican Consul. It was in the paper last week."

"What's a Consul" Even Ben was curious now.

"A Consul is Mexico's representative outside of Mexico. There is usually a consulate building. Consuls look after Mexican citizens in other countries, they issue visas to people wanting to visit Mexico, if they need a visa, they promote trade between the countries…." I offered. My job involved dealing with immigration law and similar matters so I knew quite a bit about it.

"Oh ….Then I guess Isabella's dad is the "big boss" of the Mexican Consulate?" Gina exclaimed.

"Does she speak good English?", Ben wanted to know.

"Of course,' said Gina, "but she has a kind of foreign accent. She's really nice. She has a brother – his name is Marco – and he's going to UBC. Mom, could I invite her back here after school one day, and she could maybe stay for dinner and you could drive her home after that? She doesn't know many people and I know what that's like."

"Sure, Gina, do that," I said, "I hope she'll be okay with just joining in with whatever we have for dinner."

"I'm sure that'll be okay, mom, thanks."

Gina brought Isabella DeSantos home after school the following week. She was a petite girl with a long dark hair and possibly the most enormous black eyes I have ever seen. She was also quite shy. After all, she was in a strange house in a different culture. But she was a smart visitor --- she complimented me on my meatloaf!

After dinner, I left Gina to do some kitchen chores while I drove Isabella home. Their house was further up the hill from us, in an area where the houses were larger and more expensive. Before leaving our house, Isabella called to make sure the gates at the end of their drive were open for us. The drive was very long and ended at a circular parking area to the right of the house. As she got out of the car, Isabella said "Please, Mrs Kerry, you must come in and meet my mama."

We climbed a fan-shaped flight of steps onto a wide terrace overlooking the city. The front door was opened by a gentleman who I judged to be the Mexican equivalent of a butler. He led us into a large room overlooking the terrace where we were immediately approached by Elena DeSantos, a tall, willowy woman who walked like a fashion model. She greeted me warmly, "Meeses Kerry, I am so pleased to meet you. Eet is so kind of you to invite Eesabel;a to your home."

"How do you do, Mrs De Santos," I said, "Gina's told us quite a lot about you. When I was much younger, my family moved around a lot, and I know how difficult it is when you begin a new school where you don't know anyone. I think Isabella enjoyed her visit."

"Yes, eet is very much appreciated. Also, may I say, if our girls are going to be friends, I hope that my hawsband and I may have the opportunity to meet the rest of your family," she said.

"Yes, that would be nice...." I began, but she continued,

"Do you go often to the Country Club? Eet is so close to these house. We might meet there....."

"I'm afraid we aren't members," I began,

"Then the golf club?" she suggested again, "Isabella says that your husband plays golf."

"Yes," I replied, "when he has time. He belongs to the University Golf Club in Vancouver."

"Well, it looks as eef we wives must make some arrangements once we are settled." She made a circle in the air with her arms, "these house ees beeg and I still have to find more maids to help me put theens the right way." Then she waved at me, "But when eet is complete, we will have a reception. You must come."

"Thanks," I said, "that's very kind, Mrs DeSantos."

"Please call me Elena," she continued as we walked to the door, "I hope that we can meet again soon."

Clearly the Kerrys were not on the same economic level as the DeSantos family, but the two girls got along well, and that was my main concern.

PART XI

Back to Court

Chapter Thirty-Four

It was raining hard on February 10th as I drove once again through the busy morning traffic to the Family Court, but a few rays of sunshine finally emerged from behind the clouds as I walked into the Court House. Jeanette Munro met me in the lobby and we went straight to the courtroom. Julia and her friend were already there.

Judge Ferris took her seat promptly at 10 o'clock. After stating a summary about the purpose of the hearing, she asked me to take the witness stand once again, reminding me that I was still under oath. She directed Julia to continue.

Julia got up and walked towards me. She looked much better than she had in December – just a bit tired, which didn't surprise me considering she now had a newborn baby at home.

Julia: "Maura" – then turning toward the judge, "I hope it's okay if I call Mrs Kerry Maura. It just isn't comfortable for me to call her Mrs Kerry."

Judge Ferris: "That's fine, Mrs Niemann, just say Maura. I'm sure Mrs Kerry won't mind."

Me: 'That's fine."

Julia: "Mrs Kerry, did you know Gina before you went to spend the summer at Sandy Bay?"

Me: "No."

Julia: "So you had never met my daughter until you saw her on the road outside your house at Sandy Bay and asked her to come in to play with your children?"

Me: "The first time I saw Gina, she was already in my garden, playing with my children."

Julia: "Yes, as I said, you asked her to come in to play."

Me: "No. I didn't ask her to come in. I was busy in my house and when I went out to see what my children were doing, Gina was there, playing with them."

Julia: "So you kept Gina with you and your children all that day."

Me: "When lunchtime arrived, I asked Gina if she would like to stay for lunch and she said she would. I asked her if she needed to call home and she said she was staying with her grandparents and they allowed her to stay out for lunch.

Julia: "And you didn't call them to ask if Gina could stay."

Me: "Gina told me they lived just across the road and frankly, the lunch was ready and it was all very casual. As you know, your parents' house is close to ours – only about two blocks away at most."

Julia: "Well, anyway, you kept Gina with you almost every day and took her out on picnics and away from Sandy Bay and you never once asked permission to do that?"

Me: "No, I guess I didn't. When we went to picnic spots in other places, Gina just came along. I mean, as I testified before, Gina told me that you were in Winnipeg and she was staying with her grandparents. She said they put food in the fridge for her to eat when she wanted something. I never actually invited Gina to come along. She always just turned up every morning and she went back home every evening. I suppose I expected that her grandparents would get in touch with me if they were concerned about her --- but they didn't, although she told me they knew where she was. I felt that it was okay to include Gina in our outings."

Julia: "But you just took Gina along and never got permission……"

Judge Ferris interrupted. "Mrs Niemann, Mrs Kerry has already testified about what happened when she met Gina. I suggest that you move on with your examination."

Julia: "Why did you go to my mother and ask her to give Gina to you and your family?"

Me: "I've already testified about this, Mrs Niemann. Your mother told me that they wouldn't have room for Gina in the fall, and Gina's father couldn't give her a home. Having spent a lot of time with Gina, I cared about her--- all of us in my family care about Gina, so I decided to offer to have Gina come to live with us. I just wanted her to be happy."

Julia: "But you knew you would get a lot of money for giving Gina a home......."

Me: "No. I didn't. I never really thought about getting money. All I wanted was to provide a happy place for Gina to live."

Julia: "But you are a foster parent and you get money for her, don't you?"

Me: "At that time, I didn't know the first thing about foster parents. I think mainly because I had never thought of another child coming to live with us. But when it was decided that Gina would come to us, your mother told me she would have the social workers contact me to get me approved. Apparently, your own parents were approved as foster parents for Gina when she came from Winnipeg. I didn't think of being a foster parent until they mentioned it."

Julia: "But you like having the money?"

Judge Ferris interrupted again: "Mrs Niemann, I must again remind you that Mrs Kerry has already testified about these matters. Please move on."

Julia, frowning: "Why did you come to visit Gina after you returned from Hawaii last January?"

Me: "Just after we returned, I received a letter from Gina. She wasn't feeling happy. While she was glad to be back with Scott and Lucy, she said that she would like to return to live with us. I didn't know what to do but I felt I should do something to encourage Gina to settle down back at Sandy Bay with you. So I had the idea of going over for a little visit with her and talking to her. Then I called your mother and she said she would talk to you and Gina about a visit...."

Julia – her tone was angry: "Well, that's a load of nonsense about Gina being unhappy. For a start, my daughter would never write such a letter. She would talk to me. That's what she would do."

Me: "Are you saying that I am lying to you about it?" I was annoyed.

Mrs Munro interrupted, speaking to Judge Ferris: "Your Honour, I have here Gina's letter to Mrs Kerry. I would like to enter it as Exhibit "B" to this hearing."

Judge Ferris: "May I see it, please."

The Court Clerk handed the letter to Judge Ferris who read it:

Judge Ferris: "Please note this letter is to be entered as Exhibit "B". Then please give it to Mrs Niemann to read."

After reading the letter, Julia Niemann threw it furiously on her desk ."My daughter never wrote such a letter...."

Mrs Munro: "May it please the court, I have discussed the contents of this letter with Gina and she told me that she wrote it."

Judge Ferris: "Mrs Niemann, I would like to remind you again that the purpose of this hearing is to determine whether it is in the best interests of your daughter to remain with you as her guardian or to transfer guardianship to the Minister. Mrs Kerry has been approved as a foster parent for Gina. She is NOT Gina's guardian. So what I need you to tell me is why it would be better for you to remain as Gina's guardian, instead of the Minister."

Julia sat down and brushed a strand of hair away from her eyes. She leaned over to her friend, Mrs Ritchie, and they whispered for a brief minute. Judge Ferris looked annoyed but she waited patiently. Julia stood up and spoke:

Julia: "I am the best person to be Gina's guardian because I am her mother and I love her, and she should be with her brother Scott and her sister Lucy, and her new little sister, Rosalie. Nobody can love Gina as much as me and the kids!"

Judge Ferris: "So you have no further questions for Mrs Kerry?"

Julia to me: "You already said that Gina was thrilled when I came back from Winnipeg and asked for her to be sent home to me. She loves me, right?"

Me: "Yes."

Julia: "Then you should just get out of her life and she should come home to me. That's it."

Judge Ferris to me: " Thank you, Mrs Kerry, you can step down now."

Mrs Munro to Judge Ferris: "Your Honour, I have a few more questions that I would like to put to Mrs Niemann, if I may."

Judge Ferris: "Very well, Mrs Munro, but I don't want to take up more time than necessary.

Mrs Niemann, would you be kind enough to go to the witness stand, and I remind you that you are still under oath."

Julia went to the witness stand.

Mrs Munro: "Mrs Niemann, I understand that congratulations are in order. I am told that you had a lovely little girl about three weeks ago."

Julia: "Yes, thanks. Her name is Rosalie."

Mrs Munro: "So how are things going. You must be busy with three children to look after?"

Julia: "It's going okay. Miss Parks has arranged for some extra help. Scott is in Grade One now, so I just have Lucy and the baby at home."

Mrs Munro: "And Lucy is?....."

Julia: "Lucy is four."

Mrs Munro: "So how do you see things going if Gina comes home?"

Julia: "Oh, it will be great. Gina is just wonderful with the little ones. She helped so much when Scott and Lucy were babies in Winnipeg."

Mrs Munro: "But of course, Gina will be going to school every day?"

Julia: "Oh yeah, but she can help after school and on weekends."

Mrs Munro: "How long has it been since Gina was last living at home – on a continuous basis, I mean."

Julia: "Oh .... Let's see.......I guess she was 11 when she came back with dad to Sandy Bay."

Mrs Munro: "And now she has just turned fifteen. That's quite a long time. She is growing up."

Julia: "Oh, yes. I notice that."

Mrs Munro: "I think there's quite a difference between being 11 and being 15. Have you thought about the time Gina needs to study for school and hanging out with friends?"

Julia : "I suppose so. But she will soon be 18 and won't have to go to school."

Mrs Munro: "What do you think Gina should do when she finishes school."

Julia: "Well, she could get a job, maybe even buy a used car so that we could all go places together. I hardly ever get out much now, you know. Gina will make a big difference to us."

Mrs Munro: "Do you know how Gina is doing at school. Has she any ideas about what career she might pursue?"

Julia: "We don't talk about that stuff --- we're always too busy with the little ones. But Gina loves us. She will get a job. Maybe she might go to night school or something like that."

Mrs Munro: "So there is no clear plan?"

Julia: "No."

Mrs Munro: "And what about her father. I understand from Mrs Kerry that he has been helpful."

Julia: "Nothing! We don't need that bum in our lives. There will be no more visits with him after she comes home to me."

Mrs Munro: "You don't want her to see her father?"

Julia: "No."

Mrs Munro: "But what if Gina wants to continue her visits."

Julia: "If I'm her guardian and I say 'no', Gina will do as I tell her."

Mrs Munro: "That's all, Mrs Niemann. Thank you."

Judge Ferris: "In the absence of anything further, this hearing is adjourned. Mrs Munro, I will contact you shortly to set up an appointment for me to meet with Gina before I make my ruling."

Judge Ferris banged her gavel, and we all left the courtroom. Julia and her friend exited first, followed by me and Jeanette Munro. Turning to me, she said, "Maura, I'm really pleased with the way things went today. All the testimony clearly shows how unprepared Julia Niemann is for the challenges of parenthood --- any kind of parenthood. It's sad but it's a fact. I see a lot of this kind of thing in my practice."

"I'm just glad it's all over --- at least my part as a witness is over. I feel bad that we had to enter Gina's sad little letter as evidence that Julia had to read. I know how I would feel if I had to read a letter like that, written by one of my own children."

"Sometimes we are left with little choice in these matters," Mrs Munro said consolingly. "You did what was right. Just go home now and get back to the everyday stuff! I expect I'll be hearing from the Court soon with an interview date for Gina." With that, she was off down the hall.

I took my time going home, stopping at Starbucks to enjoy a coffee and to appreciate that the weather had cleared up entirely and a wintery sun was shining. Gina would soon meet with Judge Ferris, and after that, we would have a decision. In the beginning, I found it easy to believe that Gina would be infinitely better off living with us, away from her emotionally ill mother; but after having seen Julia's situation laid bare in a courtroom, while I still had the same opinion, now it was tempered by a kind of sadness for the plight of any woman facing the loss of her child, for whatever reason. And I felt immensely relieved that such a potentially life-changing decision would be made by a judge.

Chapter Thirty-Five

With the weight of testifying at the hearing now removed from my shoulders, the rest of the week rolled by easily as we all pursued our individual routines. On Thursday, I agreed that it was okay if Isabella DeSantos came to dinner. She was dropped off at our house in the late afternoon and seemed to generally enjoy herself. At our house, dinner time was when we all shared what we had been doing during the day or the week. We argued and laughed and quite often Steve had to remind us that we were supposed to be a civilized family – which usually made us argue and laugh even more. While Isabella participated, she was still a bit shy of our lively banter, but by the end of the meal, she was making comments and laughing as loudly as all of us. My general impression, however, was that mealtimes at the Mexican Embassy were considerably more formal. Gina came along later when I drove Isabella home and there was a lot of whispering and giggling on the way there. I was pleased to see Gina cultivating a friendship by herself.

Jeanette Munro called my office on Monday to tell me that Judge Ferris wanted to interview Gina on February 24th, just a week away. Mrs Munro decided that she wouldn't meet again with Gina before then because she didn't want to make a 'big deal' out of it and possibly create more stress for Gina. Both of us knew that Gina would have to deal with feelings of guilt when it came to saying that she didn't want to live with her mother again. We agreed the whole thing would be kept 'low key. I would drive Gina over to the Family Court that morning and bring her home afterwards. Since Gina would be missing a day of school, I decided I would take her out to lunch. Mrs Munro would arrange to come by the house to speak to Gina a few days after the interview. We were happy with our plan of action!

When I went to our mailbox on February 18th, among other mail I found an envelope addressed to Gina. It was from 10 Garden Street. I was sure it was from Julia. With the interview date with Judge Ferris just six days away, it made sense that Julia would write to Gina. It also made sense to guess that Julia would be putting pressure on Gina to tell Judge Ferris that she wanted to return 'home'. I had already told Gina about the appointment with Judge Ferris and she had listened calmly but when I looked at the envelope in my hands, I was really dismayed. I didn't want to give the envelope to Gina at all. Should I hold onto it? I wanted to tear it up and throw it in the garbage. Temptation!!! I agonized about it all afternoon and the next morning, I called Mrs Mercer. After all, she was Gina's social worker and it was her 'call'. As it transpired, Mrs Mercer had already spoken to Mrs Munro about the last day of the hearing and she also felt that it would be best not to give the letter to Gina until after the interview with Judge Ferris. I was to bring the letter to Mrs Mercer and she would assume total responsibility. What a relief!

On Thursday Gina arrived home from school all flushed and excited. Isabella had invited her to join their family on a ski trip to Whistler on the weekend after the interview. Some friends had a ski cabin there with lots of room for guests.

"Oh, mum, please say I can go. Isabel's parents and her brother Marco will be there too. They will be skiing with us and keeping an eye on us. It's gonna be great…. Can I go, can I?" I agreed. After all, I had already met Elena DeSantos and it was clear they were a nice family if living life at a more highly elevated level than the Kerrys. Also, it would be good for Gina to experience life at a different economic level and to become aware of different cultures. Gina was ecstatic!

But before life on the slopes, came the interview with Judge Ferris.

Chapter Thirty-Six

On the early morning of February 24th, as I got ready to take Gina to her interview at the Family Court, I had a lot on my mind. Maybe too much. I should have been busy tidying the kitchen and checking that the kids' school lunches were ready in the fridge. Instead, I lingered at the table trying to decide what I should or shouldn't say to Gina during the forty-minute drive to the courthouse. On the one hand, I wanted to ask her how she was feeling about discussing her mother and little brother and sisters with the judge; and on the other hand, I felt that I didn't want to say anything judgmental. Of course, there were a lot of things I could say but my 'inner voice' kept telling me that I should do my very best to remain neutral and allow Gina to decide for herself without too much pressure. It was going to be hard to remain neutral. I consoled myself with the knowledge that Mrs Mercer had asked me to bring Gina to her office on our way home after the interview. Naturally, Mrs Mercer wanted to find out firsthand how it went and I knew that she was going to give Julia's letter to Gina.

It was very quiet in the car. For once, Gina and I were mute. It was a sunny morning and the traffic was less congested than usual. As I pulled into the courthouse parking lot, I ventured, "Are you okay, Gina?".

"Do you mean am I nervous?" she asked.

"Well – yes --- I know this is a bit difficult for you…." I replied.

"I'll be okay," she reassured me, "don't worry, mum."

It was a short walk to the main door of the courthouse. Inside was the familiar hall with its waiting area and two corridors --- the one on the left leading to the courtrooms, and the one straight ahead leading to the judges' chambers.

As soon as we made our way through the heavy doors into the hall, my heart sank. Right there in front of us, seated beside the corner of the corridor leading to the judges' chambers were Julia Niemann and all three children. Scott and Lucy were crammed onto another chair while Julia clutched the baby, Rosalie in her arms.

I hadn't expected this. But it made sense. Julia would have been advised of the interview date and it was just like her to attend. She had perched herself and the children right at the corner of the corridor so that Gina couldn't possibly go down it without squeezing past them. I was annoyed. It was so unfair to Gina.

But I had forgotten that Gina knew her mother much, much better than I, and Gina handled the situation very well indeed. She walked directly over to Julia, said "Hi Mom", gave Scott and Lucy great big hugs, and tickled Rosalie under the chin. Julia said, "Hi, Gina, we're so happy to see you. We're looking forward to having you come home at last. And Scott and Lucy have been making you some late birthday presents. It will be so great when we are all together again…….."

Gina took a little step back and smiled. She said, "Bye, mom, I have to go see the judge now," and with that, she reached back, took my hand, and we continued down the corridor. I knocked on the door of Judge Ferris's chambers and Gina gave me a little wink as she walked in. After that, **(deletion)** I returned past Julia and the children, out to the car and down the street for a quick coffee while I waited. When I returned about half an hour later, there was no sign of Julia and Judge Ferris's clerk brought Gina back to me soon after that. The interview had taken just over an hour.

In the car, I gave Gina a searching look. She seemed quite composed. Did I imagine it or did she have a happy look. "Why don't we go to the White Spot for lunch before we see Mrs Mercer?" I suggested.

"Great idea, mum. I'm really starved!", came the reply.

As we sat munching our burgers, I ventured a few more questions. "How did it go?"

"Oh, it was pretty much what I expected," she replied. "You were right, mum, Judge Ferris is nice. She has a kind face. I liked her a lot."

"So were you able to tell her how you feel?" I needed to know.

"Yes, mum, I did."

"Good, Gina, good," was all I could manage to say.

When we arrived at Mrs Mercer's office, I sat in the waiting room. After about half an hour, they both came out. As the three of us stood together in the hallway, Mrs Mercer raised the matter of Julia's letter.

"Mrs Kerry," she began, "Gina tells me that her mother and the children were present at the family court when she arrived to see Judge Ferris?"

"Yes," I said, "it was a bit of a surprise but Gina did stop and say 'hi' to them on her way to the judge's chambers."

"Yes," Mrs Mercer continued, "Judge Ferris's clerk called and told me about it. It isn't what is supposed to happen but it did happen and the interview went ahead."

"Yes"

"Gina and I have had a good chat about it and she tells me that she liked talking to Judge Ferris. I've also spoken with Judge Ferris and she is happy with the way it went, too."

"Well, I think both Gina and I are glad it's over….." I began.

"Oh, and Mrs Kerry, I explained to Gina about the letter from her mother and I've given it to her to read" she added.

"That's good," I agreed.

"Well, Gina, as you know, we must all wait now for Judge Ferris to decide what's best for you". Mrs Mercer smiled and gave Gina's shoulder a squeeze.

"Yup," Gina smiled back.

When we arrived back at the house, Gina disappeared to her room – most likely to read Julia's letter, I surmised. I hoped it wouldn't inflict a sense of guilt. Whatever it said, it was up to Gina whether or not to share its contents with me.

Chapter Thirty-Seven

The Kerry family led a busy life, so it wasn't surprising that Spring Break and Easter seemed to come upon us with record speed. Since the end of the hearing, we had managed to lead a relatively uneventful family life for almost four weeks! After Gina's visit following the Judge's interview, Mrs Mercer called to tell me that Julia's letter to Gina simply said that they were looking forward to Gina returning home etc. Mrs Mercer felt that unless Julia called or requested a visit, we should make no effort to contact her. The feedback from Miss Parks was that Julia was struggling to cope with the new baby and it wasn't likely that she would want to see Gina for a while. After all the court attendances and upheaval over the past three months, I welcomed any opportunity for 'normalcy' for all of us.

Gina was in a state of high excitement about her ski trip to Whistler with the DeSantos family. We had great debates about what to pack, what would she wear, what did you wear if you went out après ski and how much spending money would she need .... After numerous telephone 'consultations' with Isabella, and a trip to the bank to take some money out of her savings account, the packing was finally done and Marco, the DeSantos' dark-haired, rather good-looking son came in his sports car to pick Gina up. I must say we were all very impressed, especially Gina!

As for the Kerrys, we enjoyed Spring Break immensely, even if we didn't go to Whistler.

Steve arranged for Ben and Amy to go skiing on Grouse Mountain over the weekend, and we all went out to the Firebrick after skiing on the Saturday for a fabulous dinner. And I had lunch with Bette Vogt and updated her on the hearing etc.

Elena DeSantos called me on the following Thursday evening and insisted that I come up to the house for a drink before I brought Gina home. This time, she answered the door in person.

"Meeses Kerry, how very nice to see you again. Please do come een….". I followed her down the hall into the living room which had a wonderful view over the harbour, the Lion's Gate Bridge and all the way out to UBC. At the far end of the room, a log fire was blazing in a huge fireplace and Marco was standing in a corner beside a cocktail cabinet.

"Meeses Kerry, these ees my son, Marco," Elena began, "I theenk you met him when he picked up Gina?"

"Yes," I said, "Hello again, Marco."

Elena and I sat down by the fire while Marco did a great job of getting drinks for the two of us.

"The girls will be down soon," Elena continued, "they are up in Isabella's room, trying on clothes!!!" She laughed. "You must know what yong girls are like. Isabella will soon be attending a special reception at the Consulate an she has to decide about a new dress to wear ---- so I theenk Gina is being her – how do you say eet - advisor?"

I laughed too. "Well, if Gina is being her advisor, the two of them may be busy up there for the rest of this week ---- at the least!!!"

Elena smiled."Your Gina, she ees a very energetic girl and a good skier. Of course, she ees learning, but she has done very well. My husband and Marco spent much time weeth her."

"That's great", I said, "she was so excited about going. It was very good of you to invite her. I do hope she was tidy and helpful in the kitchen."

"Oh, there was no problem," Elena replied, "you see, here we have a cook and a housemaid. We breeng them along so that we can all enjoy the skiing and we don't have to do the housework! It's a good idea … no?"

"It's a great idea!" I replied.

Just then, amid a flurry of giggles and laughs, Gina and Isabella danced in from the hall.

"Well, mom, what do you think". Gina was standing in front of me, twirling around. When she stopped twirling, I couldn't quite believe what I saw. Was it Gina, or wasn't it Gina? Whatever it was, it definitely wasn't the Gina I knew!

In front of me stood a young woman with a fantastic figure, wearing a square-necked sheath dress in the most incredible shade of violet. Incredible, because it matched her eyes. Her fair hair with its blonde highlights was swept up into a curled braid and secured on the top of her head by a purple velvet bow. Her eyebrows had been darkened just a little bit, her cheeks were flushed (that was natural), her lips were just a little bit pink, she wore small glinting stud earrings, and on her feet were high heeled silver pumps. She was absolutely stunning! And as I looked around the room, it was clear to me from the expression on Elena DeSantos face and especially from the way Marco was looking at her, that I wasn't the only one in the room who was spellbound.

Isabella was there too, looking just lovely in a soft pink dress with a pleated skirt that flattered her beautiful eyes and classic dark hair.

But there was no question that Gina had taken the room by storm.

"Gosh, Gina," I finally managed to blurt out, "I hardly know you. You both look so grown up."

"I think Gina should be a model," Isabella stated firmly.

Before I could say anything else, Elena spoke, "You both are looking very beautiful. But eeit's time for Gina to go home. So, my yong ladies, please go upstairs and change and then Gina should come down and Marco will take your bags to the car."

While we waited for the girls to get changed, I chatted with Marco about his studies. He was in second-year medicine at the University of British Columbia where he was enjoying his courses and had already made some friends. He impressed me as quite self-assured but as we talked, I realized that because of moving to different locations and countries with his family, he would naturally become more sophisticated than many young men his age.

I was pleased when Gina made a point of thanking Mrs DeSantos quite eloquently for inviting her along and for such a wonderful trip.

Gina was a non-stop chatterbox on the drive home.

"Mom, you won't believe how great it was," she began. "I think the DeSantos' are really rich. We didn't even have to make our beds or cook or tidy up …. THE WHOLE TIME! They have a cook and a maid and they came along and did all that kind of work. So all that we had to do was just get up and get dressed and go skiing! Can you believe that? It was fabulous!. And Marco and Mr DeSantos spent a lot of time with me helping me to improve my technique. And we went out to a different restaurant for dinner every evening. And we could order anything we wanted!"

I couldn't help smiling. "So did you eat a lot of rare steaks?" I ventured.

"Well, I certainly did!" came the retort. "But they got me to try Posoli - that's a big deal in Mexico, and it was great. I think I would like it in Mexico. They have warm weather almost all the time. Of course, I knew that from Socials. But they have two villas. In the summer they go to their mountain villa where it's cooler and they have a swimming pool there. Oh My God, mum, what a life!!!! They might even invite me to visit there." She stopped to catch her breath.

"Well, Gina, I guess this would be the first time you have learned what it is like to have a lot of money."

"Mom, I had no idea, did I? Do you know, when I mentioned to Mrs DeSantos how lucky I thought they were, she told me that it isn't hard to have that kind of life."

"Really?" I commented, "did she tell you how to do it?"

"Well," Gina continued, "she said that for me it would be easy to have that life. She said that for a girl who is clever and good look-ing like me, it is always possible to find a rich husband and then everything is possible."

"Do you think that finding a rich husband is a good idea?" I asked.

"Well, I'm not too sure, mum. I mean Mrs DeSantos is good looking and Isabella told me that her mother didn't come from a rich family but she was a very important model and her father fell in love with her, and he has a lot of money. So I suppose it could happen that you fall in love with a rich man but, I mean, you might fall in love with someone who isn't rich. Right?"

'Well, Gina, what I know is that life isn't always like a fairy story or a romance novel. And there are more middling rich people and poor people than there are rich people. At least that's what I have discovered in my life."

"But that's another thing that Mrs DeSantos said, mom. She said that sometimes people could be rich but they miss out because they don't do the right things."

"Oh? Like what?" I asked.

"Well, take you and dad, for instance. I know you have a good job, but maybe you could get an even better job. Get to know more important lawyers or their wives and get them interested in giving you a job."

"Uh, huh"

"And Dad. Like, dad has his own consulting firm and that's great. But maybe he could get a job with a very big company and make a lot more money. And if he joined the expensive clubs he would meet more important people and get them as clients."

"Did Mrs DeSantos suggest something like that?" I asked.

"Well, kinda….I think she was just trying to be helpful because she knows you work and that we don't have a lot of money like them."

"Well, Gina, Mrs DeSantos is a rich person who has been rich for a long time and she likes being rich. That's just great. But I've learned that many people don't want to be that kind of rich. A lot of people just want to make enough money so that they can pay their bills and have holidays and have a nice little house --- or maybe like us--- be able to have a little house at Sandy Bay. You must realize that Mr DeSantos has an important government job and he is paid a lot of money. Because of having to move a lot, his life is not usual --- even for people in Mexico."

"I never thought about it like that," Gina commented. "But you know my mum never has any money and when you are like that, you never really have much fun or even much food. Living with you has been way, way better … but I never imagined that people could live like Isabella's family --- except in storybooks."

"Well, Gina, now you know and now you have something to think about…." I pulled up in the carport and the two of us began unloading her 'stuff'.

The weeks between Easter and the beginning of May sped by in a flash for the Kerry family. We rooted for Ben's team at his soccer games, we attended a piano recital at Gina's music school and were amazed at her progress and how well she could now play, we were amazed by Amy's art project, a series of sketches of horses – her favourite subject; and we were thrilled when Steve hit a hole in one towards the end of April. On that particular Saturday, he had accidentally put on mismatched socks --- a black sock on his left foot and a white sock on his right foot, which we all agreed had been the key to his luck! And as for me, work was going well and it felt good to see my little family in such happy spirits.

During April, Gina spent a weekend with Max and Laura and Teddy. She adored Teddy and her role in taking care of him. These visits meant a lot to her.

With the arrival of warmer spring weather, Alyssa and Pippa picked Gina up and they spent a couple of afternoons at the park. Gina's friendship with Isabella continued to blossom and she visited at the DeSantos house after school at least two days a week. While I was glad to see Gina making new friends, I was at times concerned that she was spending too much time with Isabella. It was plain to see that Gina was very impressed by the DeSantos family – by their wealth and lifestyle. Because of her past background, this kind of lifestyle was completely new to Gina and I began to notice it was exerting a powerful influence. I would have felt better if Gina had wanted to spend more time with her friends who were closer to our social level, but for the moment I couldn't see a way to change the situation. Anyway, June was fast approaching. We would be leaving for another summer at Sandy Bay, and it would most likely sort itself out by September – or so I reasoned.

Chapter Thirty-Eight

The phone on my desk rang at the end of my workday on Friday, May 2nd. It was Jeanette Munro.

"Hello, Maura," she began, "how are things?"

'Just great," I said.

"Good, good," she continued, "Maura, I have more good news. We have a decision!"

"You mean Judge Ferris has decided?" I gasped.

"Yes, and it's in our favour. Guardianship has been granted to the Minister".

"It has?" Somehow, after all this time, it was hard for me to get my head around it.

"Yes, with effect from May 1st --- that's yesterday! And by the way, Mrs Mercer has been advised."

"So what now?" I asked.

"Well, Maura, first of all, Gina must be told."

"Of course," I agreed.

"Maura, it's important that she be told in a 'good way. I know how close you two are, but I would appreciate it if I could come over to your home and tell Gina about it there. I know it's a big "ask" but I'm asking you not to tell her --- I'm asking you to let me come over and deliver the news and also explain to her what it means and what her future life will be."

"Yes," I said, "yes, I understand what you're saying. This is a big thing for Gina. She should be clear about what it means for her future. And I guess she may have questions ---. Yes, I can see how it would be best for you to tell her. And anyway, you're her lawyer who 'went to bat' for her."

"I'm so glad you agree. Is there any possibility I could come to your house maybe after lunch tomorrow? Would that work for you?" she asked.

"I think after lunch will be fine," I said, "about 2 o'clock?"

"Okay. Two o'clock it is. And thanks a lot, Maura."

"Well, I think I'm the one who should be thanking you," I said, "but to be honest, I'm still trying to get my head around it."

"I think it's a really good decision; the best for all concerned." Her tone was reassuring.

"I think so. I certainly hope so," was all I could manage.

"Well, then, I'll see you and Gina tomorrow at two. Goodbye" and she hung up.

My brain was buzzing all the way home in the car! True, it was only six months since the hearing had begun, but it seemed like a lifetime had been lived or a mountain had been climbed. It had certainly been an emotional rollercoaster for everyone. And now it was over. At least the 'hard part' was over. After all, Gina was a young adolescent girl with a lot more to learn and a lot more of life to experience. But maybe now it would all be much easier for her. At least that was my great hope for her.

That night I tapped on Gina's door at bedtime.

"Can I come in?" I asked.

"Sure, mom," She was sitting on the end of her bed brushing her hair.

"Gina, I had a call from Mrs Munro today, just as I was leaving for home." I began.

"Oh?"

"She asked me if she could come to see you here at home tomorrow."

"Why, mom, what's up?" Gina frowned.

"Well, there's something she wants to discuss with you," I said.

"I hope it's not something about my mom. Like I hope she hasn't been creating some kind of fuss about me..."

"No, Gina, it's not about your mom" I hadn't realized Gina was worried about this kind of thing.

"But if she didn't say what it's about, you know I haven't spoken to my mom since I saw the judge. And after I got her letter, I just didn't want to talk to her because she makes me feel bad that I don't want to go back to live with her. You know, she's my mom and I love her but I just can't go back there….."

"Gina, Mrs Munro would have told me if she they had heard from your mum. You know Mrs Munro is your lawyer and she's your good friend --- so let's just wait and talk to her tomorrow. Okay?"

"Okay mom, I guess you're right."

I gave her a hug. "Good night, Gina. Tomorrow's going to be great, I just know it".

I slipped out of the room and shut the door quietly behind me.

Saturday was a sunny day. Ben and Steve left for Ben's soccer game. Amy went to her friend Mimi's house to work on a school project, and Gina went down to the family room after breakfast to do her piano practice.

Jeanette Munro drove up promptly at 2 o'clock. I made an excuse about feeding the cat and left the two of them together in the living room. It wasn't long before Gina came bouncing into the laundry room, grabbed me by the hand and hauled me into the living room. "Mom, Mrs Munro says I don't have to go back to living with my mom again! Judge Ferris decided it would be better for me to be looked after by the Ministry and I can just go on living here. Isn't that awesome!" she squeaked.

Gina looked quite radiant. I felt like crying for joy. Instead, I smiled and said, "I don't know about awesome – but I think it's good news for everyone."

"Yup, mom. No more court hearings for you. No more worrying for you or me! Isn't this the best news ever?" She did a little jig around the room.

"Well, I hope you thanked Mrs Munro, Gina. No more worrying for her either?".

"Gosh, yes," Gina explained. "Thank you so, so much Mrs Munro……" and she bounced over to Mrs Munro and gave her a hug.

"Gina and I are going to keep in touch. And of course, I've explained to Gina that Mrs Mercer will continue to be in touch with you about how things are going for Gina. That part won't change until Gina is 18. And I've explained to Gina that in future, decisions about where she is to live, her schooling etc. will be made by Mrs Mercer on behalf of the Ministry. And Gina can continue to visit her mom --- but she doesn't have to visit her mom unless she wants to do that…"

"Yes, I get it, I get it!" Gina nodded her head at us both.

"Well, in that case, I'd better be going," Mrs Munro stood up and moved towards the doorway. "Gina, you've got my card if you ever need to talk." And to me, "Maura, I wish you all the best. It's been a real pleasure working with you. Your help made my work a lot easier. Take care of each other. Goodbye, Gina, be happy."

Gina and I waved goodbye.

After she had gone, Gina turned to me, "Mom --- you're a sneak. You knew all along why Mrs. Munro was coming, didn't you?"

"Yes, I did," I smiled sheepishly.

"But you didn't tell me!"

"Mrs Munro wanted to be the one to tell you, Gina. She asked me not to tell you. After all, she was the one who did all the hard work in court for you. So I agreed to let her tell you. I think it was the right thing to do, don't you?"

"I guess so," Gina frowned, "but if it had been me, I wouldn't have been able to keep the secret. I bet I would have blurted it out".

I laughed. "That's what we call giving in to temptation. You will probably find that kind of thing happens a lot to you as you go through life. And sometimes it's more important to be fair than to do what you would like to do."

"I think you are better at that kind of thing than me," she rolled her eyes and waved her arms in the air.

"Not all the time," I admitted, "but I am older than you, so I've had more practice at it. Now, why don't the two of us sit down and have a cup of tea or something to celebrate?"

"Great idea," Gina grabbed my hand, and we went into the kitchen to forage together.

Chapter Thirty-Nine

Early the next week, Mrs Mercer called and we had a good talk. She was genuinely pleased with the outcome of the hearing and we arranged for her to see Gina at her office after school on the coming Thursday. During our conversation, Mrs Mercer pointed out that at this point Gina was officially a temporary foster placement with our family. However, because of the Judge's decision, the possibility now existed of changing Gina's status to that of a "permanent foster placement" with us until she reached the age of 18, in just three years. I hadn't realized this. Mrs Mercer asked me if we would consider having Gina on a permanent basis. If so, there would be the usual paperwork which would, of course, involve consulting with Gina to determine if she wanted to be placed permanently. Since this would mean talking the entire matter over with Steve and Ben and Amy, we agreed that the matter wouldn't be discussed with Gina until I had spoken with Steve about it.

We were all very busy the following week. It was Mother's Day on the coming Saturday and I decided to take Dorrie out to lunch. If everything went as usual, I would order in for the kids and Steve would take me out to dinner. If I was really lucky, he would bring home a bunch of roses for me that same evening. If I had any concerns about how the change in her status might affect Gina, I need not have worried. She remained her usual self. I reminded myself that children tend to be more flexible than adults when it comes to adjusting to changes in life circumstances, and in her short fifteen years, Gina had certainly had lots of practice in adjusting to change. However, we did have a rather unexpected discussion on Thursday evening.

I was in the living room, scanning through Steve's newspaper when Gina walked in and sat down in the chair opposite to mine.

"Mom, can I talk to you for a minute," she began.

"Sure," I said somewhat vaguely as I continued with the newspaper.

"It's about Mother's Day," she continued.

"Okay," I said, "what about it?"

"Well, mom, it's just that I don't know what to do about it".

I pricked up my ears. She sounded worried. I paid attention.

"Well, what do you mean, Gina?" Mother's Day had always seemed straightforward to me. I was puzzled.

Gina continued, "Well it's just that I know on Mother's Day, kids are supposed to send a card or a gift to their mother. But it's just that – like, I don't live with my mom. Of course, I could send her a card. But I live with you in our family here now --- so in a way, you're my mom; and then I got to thinking that I lived for quite a while with my grandma at Sandy Bay and she's like a mom, and when I visit my dad and Laura, Laura always lets me call her mom. So if I send a card to my real mom, it won't be fair to you and my grandma and Laura. I don't want to ...not be fair. I mean, who is my mother? So what should I do?"

I realized with a shock that I hadn't thought about what Mother's Day would mean for a child in Gina's circumstances. I realized, too, that there must be many children like Gina. What should she do? What could I say to her? What should I say to her? She was there, sitting opposite me, looking so worried, asking for my advice. I struggled to find an answer. Finally, I said: "You know, Gina, I hadn't realized that Mother's Day is a bit different for you, isn't it? Honestly, if I was you, I think I would feel the same. All I know is that sometimes when you find yourself not knowing the right answer about something, or not knowing the right thing to do, the best thing is not to do anything. If your mom calls you, then just say "Happy Mother's Day" and if it comes up, say the same thing to your grandma and Laura. I think eventually you will be able to decide about this. Sometimes, we have to wait and see, and that's okay."

"So it's okay to wait and see," she asked.

"Yes, I believe it's okay. Better to do nothing than to do something you feel isn't fair."

Gina perked up visibly, "Pheeeew…. What a relief! Thanks, mom." And with that, she got up and disappeared downstairs.

I smiled. From Gina's point of view, the problem had been solved, at least for the immediate future, but in my mind, the questions she had raised remained to a large extent unanswered. For the rest of the day, I wrestled with them those questions. Mother's Day! That's the day we all think of remembering our mother --- our birth mother. Our society attaches great importance to motherhood, to the role of a mother. We honour that role. And Mother's Day is the special day each year when we honour the mother's of our nation. But we are all aware that many women aren't actual birth mothers, yet who fill the role of 'mother' to untold numbers of children. What about the 'step-mothers' and, yes, 'foster mothers' as I had now become. And the women who step in and raise children without the benefit of being acknowledged or asked. Are such women any less 'real' than a birth mother? It seemed to me, in my reverie, that to the children in their care, all such mothers are equally real. In Gina's case, the other option would be to send a card to all of her 'mothers' but that didn't seem like a good solution or answer her question.

What is a mother? If asked to write a 'job description', I know it would go on for many pages. And when it came to Gina's question, "Who is my mother?", I found myself reasoning that while Julia is truly Gina's birth mother, it seems to me that in the course of a lifetime, many of us come in contact with other older or even younger women who for periods of time, fulfil the role of 'mother' to us. At least that's what I discovered when I searched for an answer to, "Who is my mother?". In the end, I believe that if each of us asks ourselves that same question, we may be surprised to learn that we have had other 'mothers' in our life experience. My hope for Gina was that as she matured, she would be able to find her own answer.

Dorrie and I always enjoyed our 'traditional' Mother's Day lunch. My mother was a frequent visitor for Sunday dinner at home, and she usually came over to Sandy Bay for a week each year, but apart from that and conversations on the phone, we didn't see a lot of each other. She was an independent person, still very active and busy with her own friends and interests, and I was busy with work and home and the children's activities. All of which made our annual Mother's Day lunch more precious.

I had been giving a lot of thought to what Jeanette Munro and Mrs Mercer had said about the possibility of applying to have Gina placed with us permanently and I decided to ask Dorrie what she thought about the idea. She listened to what I had to say --- how I felt it was important that Gina know that she had a family to be with until she was eighteen. I wanted her to feel safe and secure so that she could finish school well. Dorrie gave me her full attention. Then she said: "Maura, I think you've done enough. Don't you think that after everything that you've all been through, you've really done enough for Gina?"

I was disappointed by her reply. "But if Gina knows she has a permanent home for the next three years.........".

"I don't think that's going to mean as much to Gina as you think," Dorrie interrupted. "You and Steve have done more for Gina than anyone else in her life to date," Dorrie continued, "and that includes Gina's own family, for God's sake! See Gina through to 18 if you want, but don't go putting yourself on record as permanent."

"But....", I began again.

"Maura, sometimes you can be so pigheaded," Dorrie sounded exasperated, "you know how I feel about all of this, I've said it from the beginning. Kids don't take things as seriously as you think, especially not kids like Gina who have been bounced around. Oh, I believe she likes you and she's really happy she can now stay with you instead of with her 'loser' mother, but don't read into it more than is there. She is 15 now and God knows what will happen between now and 18 --- you know how teenagers are. And you have Ben and Amy to consider. Take my advice, dear, and just leave things as they are."

The waiter appeared just then with dessert, and I let the conversation drop. There wasn't any point in continuing. Dorrie's opinion was clear. Our attention turned to other things.

After my discussion with Dorrie, I was very hesitant about raising the subject with Steve, but I knew it needed to be confronted sooner rather than later. So I brought it up during our Mother's Day dinner. Probably not the best time, but I just wanted to get it done.

Just as with Dorrie, I outlined my view that if we went ahead and applied to have Gina with us on a 'permanent' basis until she was 18, it would be reassuring to her, etc. etc.

When I had finished my little speech, Steve finished his steak, put down his knife and fork, leaned back in his chair and smiled at me. Then he said, "Maura, you are a wonderful wife and a great mother. At times I just don't know how you do it all, but you do. No wonder I love you! But, Maura, here's what I think......I think, I really DO think, that the time has come for all of us to have a rest. By 'rest', I mean a total rest ---- from court hearings, social workers, well-meaning lawyers, upset mothers, judges. The whole lot of them. I don't know about you, but I'm relieved that finally, we all have a chance to just get back to a kind of normal existence. In just a few weeks, we can once again head for Sandy Bay. God, what a thought. The beach, the garden, out in the dinghy, bike riding, picnics. No deadlines. Just days in the sun. Maura, give yourself a break. You've been amazing. But as far as I can tell, Gina is happy with the way things have turned out. Why don't we all just get on with family life now.... see how it goes. Maybe give it more thought in September after the summer. What say you......."

Of course, Steve was right. What he said made a lot of sense. I was ready for a total rest and this year at Sandy Bay was going to be different --- no court dates looming, no tension about Gina's future. I looked at my long-suffering husband, our eyes met, and I said, "Okay. Yes, let's make this the best year yet at Sandy Bay!"

Steve took the wine bottle and divided the wine that remained between our two glasses,

"Okay! Maura says okay!. Here's to okay and a great summer at Sandy Bay", and we clinked and swallowed the last of the Mother's Day wine.

I knew this should have settled the entire matter for me. Somehow it didn't, but I had said "okay", so I would keep my word.

A few weeks later, I had lunch with Bette Vogt. She was delighted to learn the outcome of the hearing. I thanked her again. After all, if she hadn't intervened on my behalf, the hearing might never have happened. I was grateful. Of course, I asked Bette what she thought about the idea of Gina becoming a permanent placement with us. I don't know what I expected, but Bette's reaction was much like Steve's. Among other things, she said, "Maura, you have been so personally involved for so long, that it's easy to lose one's perspective. I think now would be a good time for you to step back and let things settle down. Take time to enjoy your summer with Steve and all the kids at Sandy Bay. You've certainly earned a rest. Time to take care of yourself."

With all these sensible people around me making the same recommendation, what could I do other than heed their advice? Yes, I decided, this year at Sandy Bay would definitely be the best ever.

Chapter Forty

The rest of May was very busy. The kids were studying for tests. Ben had soccer finals. Gina had a piano recital. Amy and Clare were rehearsing their parts for a year-end play at school.

Max and Laura were delighted with Judge Ferris's decision. As Max remarked to me, he was finally free from past tensions with Julia over Gina's visits. Both he and Laura were very happy with the way Gina and Teddy were bonding. Teddy was always very excited when Gina came to visit. It was clear that he adored Gina and Gina felt the same way about Teddy.

Gina's friendship with Isabella continued and the two of them continued to visit back and forth.

Then, around the second week in June, matters took an unexpected turn. After spending the afternoon with Isabella, Gina arrived home in a high state of excitement, "Guess what, mom?" she explained in her typical "Gina' way, "Marco wants me to be his date at a dance at UBC?"

I was surprised. "Marco?" I began.....

"Can I go, mom? It's going to be great. Please – can I go? She was jumping up and down with impatience.

"Well, Gina, when is it? We're going to be leaving for Sandy Bay as soon as school is out. I just don't know…….."

"I'm not sure, but I think it's before we leave. And anyway, I can stay at their house and go with Marco, and then they could put me on the ferry over to you after that….."

But a lot of things were running through my brain. Was this really a good idea? Marco was in second-year university. Gina wasn't quite sixteen and had never been to this kind of dance. I was sure it would be formal. The more I thought about it, the less I liked the idea,

"Gina, this is probably going to be a formal dance. I don't know if it's a good idea for you to go."

"Why not?", she sounded a bit upset.

"Well, because you're only 15 and this is a formal event."

"Oh, mom, I know it's formal. Isabella and I have talked about it and Isabella can easily lend me a dress to wear. And anyway, I don't look like I'm 15 --- Isabella says so and so does Marco."

I still didn't feel happy about it. So I said, "Gina, I need to think about it before we decide. I tell you what, I'll call Mrs DeSantos and talk to her about it, and then we'll decide."

"That's so unfair. You're not being fair!". Gina was upset.

"I'm afraid you are going to have to wait until I've spoken to Mrs DeSantos, Gina," I tried to reason, "then I will decide. You're just going to have to wait."

But I was talking to the air. Gina had already left the kitchen and I could hear her thumping down the steps to her room.

That evening, I called Elena DeSantos. She knew that Marco had asked Gina to be his date. She said that Marco had a crush on Gina and she understood my concern that perhaps Gina was just a bit too young to go. However, she assured me that Marco was sensible and didn't drink a lot of alcohol – in other words, Gina would be in good hands. And of course, it was absolutely fine for Gina to borrow one of Isabella's party dresses. "You know, Meeses Kerry, when Marco saw Gina in the lovely mauve dress a couple of months ago, he was very, how do you say, 'blown away". You must know that Gina ees a very pretty girl."

"I do know, Elena," I said, "perhaps that's why I am reluctant to let her go to dances where there is alcohol and not so much supervision. University is quite different to high school."

"Yes, I totally agree," she replied, "but Marco will take good care of her."

So we gave Gina permission to attend a dance at UBC as Marco DeSantos' date. She would stay overnight at the DeSantos' home and they would put her on the ferry to Sandy Bay the next morning. In addition, we invited Isabella to visit Sandy Bay during the last week in August, and Gina would return with Isabella to spend the last week of the holidays at their home. Both girls were in a state of mad joy over all of this!

PART XII

The Summer From Hell

Chapter Forty-One

Beautiful sunny weather arrived at the beginning of June, putting all of us in a holiday mood. Gina spent a weekend with her dad and Laura and Teddy, Ben invited his friend Lee to visit for a week at Sandy Bay in early August and Amy booked her friend Susie in at the same time. From my point of view, Sandy Bay was going to see a lot of action during August, there would be lots of sand in the bath and enormous quantities of food would be consumed!

At the beginning of June, Kelsey called Gina. Val and Kelsey were driving down from Seal Bay to Sandy Bay to visit the in-laws at the beginning of August, and Gina was invited to go back and stay with them at Seal Bay for a week when they returned home – to which we said "yes".

When Steve realized what a 'zoo' August was going to be, he decided to come over for the last two weeks in July when things were 'quiet'. And Dorrie was coming over at the beginning of August when Gina was at Seal Bay and there was a spare bed!

It was all very chaotic, but on June 25th, a Friday, with the car packed to the brim and the dog and cat forced to ride on various knees, Ben, Amy and I headed off to the ferry terminal. The highway was clogged with holiday traffic, there was a one-hour ferry line-up, and we didn't arrive at Sandy Bay until around 10 p.m. All of us, dog included, were very tired. We unpacked hastily, dumping most of the load in the living room, and collapsed into bed. Plenty of time tomorrow to deal with all of that. Right? The fun had begun.

Our summer at Sandy Bay got off to a great start. Looking back, it's hard to imagine the way it all ended. As arranged, the DeSantos's put Gina on the ferry on the day following the dance at the university. The kids and I drove down to Nanaimo to pick her up. She had a great time describing how much she had enjoyed herself. I thought 'perhaps I shouldn't have been so concerned about letting her go.' But Gina WAS my responsibility in a different way to my own children. Maybe that was why?

July passed quickly. Steve came over for the last two weeks of the month and we all had a wonderful, relaxing time. Lots of barbecues, bike riding, picnics at the beach, trips to Cedar Creek where the water was icy cold off the mountains, shopping trips to the Ferndale Market and the Wooden Shoe junk shop, and quite a few visits to the Dairy Queen on hot evenings. We always had a large jigsaw puzzle in progress on a big sheet of plywood in one corner of the living room (for rainy days?) and out in our large garden we had the well-used ping pong table etc. There wasn't any excuse for complaining that there was 'nothing to do'. And when all else failed, we could turn up the volume on the radio and bask in the sun all day long!

Yes, July was fun!

We were delighted to see Val and Kelsey when they came by at the beginning of August to pick Gina up and take her to Seal Bay. Kelsey had grown about two inches taller and, like Gina, was maturing into a young woman. Her curly locks were shaped into a more organized 'hairdo' now but her nose remained cutely turned up. Val assured me there was no need to go to Seal Bay to pick Gina up as Greg had to drive to Victoria at the end of the week and would drop Gina off with us on his way. After they left, the kids and I drove down to Nanaimo to pick Dorrie up from the ferry. Dorrie loved visits at Sandy Bay because it reminded her so much of the little coastal town in Ireland where she was born. The four of us had a good time. Dorrie enjoyed being with her grandchildren and in the absence of my busy day-to-day city life, the two of us got to spend some quality mother/daughter time together. She was tanned and relaxed when we put her back on the ferry to the mainland. Ben's friend, Lee arrived a day later on the same ferry with Amy's friend, Suzie. All of them enjoyed the beach and fooling around in the dinghy. Finally, Greg dropped Gina back home on his way down to Victoria. Remembering it now, I can see that our wonderful summer began to fall apart after that.

Gina was in high spirits. The big news was that Kelsey, who had just had her sixteenth birthday, had got her Learner's Licence and with Val along in the car, they had been 'practice' driving all-around Seal Bay. Gina told us about this one afternoon when I was driving back home from the village, with Gina sitting in the front passenger 'seat of honour, and the rest of the kids packed in the back along with Tessa. It began when Gina said, "Driving is so fun, mom. When can I get my learners?".

"Not until you're sixteen." I said. The matter of driving and Learner's Licenses hadn't occurred to me until that moment and my initial thought was that we would probably have to discuss it with Mrs Mercer first. We'll probably have to talk to Mrs Mercer about it before you can apply," I continued.

"Wait!!! Talk to Mrs Mercer!," Gina sounded outraged, "She won't understand."

"It's much too soon to talk about that, Gina," I said, "but first you have to realize that driving is a big responsibility........"

"But it's so easy, mom. Kelsey's mom let me have a turn at the wheel." With that Gina suddenly shifted in her seat, leaned across me and grabbed the steering wheel." I was shocked! Fortunately, we were travelling on a side road I wrestled with her to get control of the wheel. "Gina, please don't do that....Please get back in your seat...." I shouted but she kept laughing and just wouldn't let go. Finally, I was able to steer the car over to the side of the road and stop. Gina released her grip and slid back into the passenger seat. I looked quickly into the back of the car. "Everyone back there okay?" I asked. It was very quiet. "We're fine," Ben said. I turned to Gina, "Please don't ever do anything like that again. You could have caused an accident. We might all have been hurt!"

"Well, there wasn't any traffic!", Gina scowled back.

"That's not the point, and you know it," I said firmly. I was in no mood for arguments.

We drove the rest of the way home in silence.

After I calmed myself down, I pretty much dismissed the incident in the car as an isolated one … just 'one of those things". Isabella would be arriving at the end of the week, Gina would settle down.

But Gina didn't settle down and, if anything, things got worse. Two days later when I was reading a book and sunning myself in the garden, Gina came up from the beach and found me ."Mum, we're all going along the beach to visit my friend Jake," she announced.

"Jake?" I said.

"Yes, I know Jake from when I went to school here. He lives in one of those houses out near the point. We can easily walk there."

It was a fair walk to the farthest point on the beach and I was about to go into the house to prepare supper. It was about 4 o'clock, so I asked Gina to make sure they were all back at the house by 6 o'clock for supper. Two hours was a reasonable amount of time to walk there and back and have a visit. She said "Okay" and headed back to the beach..

After I finished my book, I went into the house and got busy preparing supper --- salads, cold meat and the crusty rolls from the village bakery that the kids liked so much. Six o'clock arrived but there was no sign of the kids. Oh well, it was summer, and we were all taking it easy, I thought. By six-thirty, the kids still hadn't arrived. I began to feel uneasy. When the tide came in all the way, it cut off the point so that the only way back to our house was to leave the beach, walk inland up to the highway and follow it back to our turnoff. Gina knew about the tide. She would surely have mentioned to me if it was going to be a problem. All the same, I was worried. When they weren't back at 7 o'clock, I decided to walk down to the beach to check the tide. By this time, twilight was beginning. About halfway to the beach, I met them all ...... walking back up the road to the house!

I was annoyed. "Where have you been!!!?? Don't you realize I've had supper ready since six o'clock?! Hurry up, the lot of you." I marched furiously ahead of them back to the house.

We all sat down at the supper table in stony silence. Gina was the first one to speak, "Honestly, mom, I don't understand why you're so upset, we were just visiting."

"But you knew I was getting supper ready! If you were going to be late, you could at least have phoned. Doesn't Jake have a phone? " I was not to be easily mollified.

"I guess we were just hanging out and didn't keep track of the time" Gina replied.

I turned to Lee and Suzie, "I'm sorry, Lee and Suzie. I'm sorry to be having a row in front of you."

"That's okay, Mrs Kerry," Suzie ventured, "we sometimes have arguments at our house."

"I'm just mad because it's bad manners to be late, especially when someone has gone to some trouble for you," I said, looking straight at Gina, "please remember this in future." I don't know what I was expecting, but Gina just scowled at me.

After supper when I was watering the flower beds, Ben came out to see me. "I'm really sorry about all of this, mum", he apologized, "I guess we didn't realize that we had to be home by 6 o'clock…."

"But I told Gina that supper was going to be ready at 6 o'clock and to be home," I explained.

"Gina never told us that," Ben said, "I guess she must have misunderstood."

I couldn't see how Gina could misunderstand. Was it all intentional? If so, why? But it was clear that she was the cause of the upset. I asked myself, what was going on in that girl's head?

On Saturday morning, I drove to the ferry terminal. Lee and Suzie were going home and being met by their parents at the other end. And the DeSantos's were sending Isabella to us for a week. After the suppertime row, Gina had spent a lot of time alone in her room and had been generally uncommunicative, but I knew that she had been looking forward to Isabella's visit all summer. I hoped that she would settle down now.

Chapter Forty-Two

Isabella was both excited and happy to join us. She admired the lovely countryside and our 'charming little house' as she described it. But after the initial excitement of Isabella's arrival, it was clear that Gina was nowhere near settling down.

Since Isabella had never visited Sandy Bay before, I had planned several outings we could all do together, to acquaint Isabella with our summer lifestyle and the variety of activities we enjoyed. But every time I proposed an outing, Gina proposed something different or didn't want to go at all. When I suggested that Gina might like to take Isabella across the road for a visit with her grandparents, Gina's response was "I don't want to see them at all." The two girls spent most of the time huddled together, chatting and laughing, either in the bedroom or outside. Ben and Amy weren't included. We had our meals together but there was almost no communication between us and any time I started a conversation with Gina, it became somehow uncomfortable. There was a kind of tension that I couldn't explain. As the week progressed, I became more and more perplexed. It seemed like Gina had an entirely different person since returning from her visit with Kelsey. Why? By now I knew it wasn't a figment of my imagination. Had something happened to cause such a change in Gina's attitude? I simply couldn't come up with an explanation and that worried me even more.

One Thursday, I suggested that we should all go to Horne Lake, take the dinghy along, and have a picnic. Horne Lake was a delightful little lake up in the hills, surrounded by Christmas tree farms. It took about 40 minutes by logging road to get there. Usually, we were the only people at the lake which was crystal clear and great for swimming and rowing around in the dinghy. Ben and Amy were enthusiastic, but Gina didn't want to go. "I thought Isabella and I could go out to the Atlees' farm and pick raspberries for supper," she explained. "Why don't you guys go to the lake and meet us back here at supper time? "I wasn't too happy with the idea of leaving the two of them alone back at Sandy Bay, but it was an easy walk to and from the Atlees' farm, so I agreed. We would see them back at the house at around 5:30.

The picnic having already been packed away in the car, Ben, Amy, Tessa and I set off for Horne Lake. As usual, we were the only people there and did our usual stunt of yelling at the top of our lungs like crazy people, for the sheer delight of not being heard by anyone else but ourselves! And with uncanny timing, we rolled up outside the cottage at 5:20 p.m.

The house was quiet. The door was locked. Rascal was stretched out on the mat in the sun. There were no raspberries in the kitchen. There was no sign of Gina and Isabella.

Ben and Amy could see that I was annoyed. Amy unpacked our wet swimsuits and began pinning them outside on the clothesline to dry. Ben unpacked the car and hung the dinghy up at the back of the garage. Still no sign of the girls. We were all really hungry, so at 6:30 I decided to go ahead with supper.

After supper, the three of us began working on the jigsaw puzzle which was still very much in progress, although I confess I kept looking at my watch and mentally trying to decide at what point I should get in the car and drive to the Atlees to investigate. Just before dark, at around 9 o'clock, the sound of giggling floated in through the open kitchen door. Tessa gave a 'woof' and bounded forwards as Gina and Isabella strolled in.

Amy spoke first, "Where did you guys get to? You were supposed to be here at 5:30."

"Yeah," Ben replied. "We waited and waited for you. And where are the raspberries?"

Gina looked unconcerned, "Oh, we never got to the Atlees!" She laughed.

"Where did you go then?" Amy asked.

"Oh, we met my friend Jake on the way into town and we all went to the drive-through and had burgers."

"And are you telling us that took three and a half hours?" My tone was sharp.

"Well, no," Gina replied, "we went over to Jake's place and hung out, listened to some of his music, and then we decided to come home."

"Gina," I exclaimed, "I just don't understand you. We agreed that you were going to the Atlees. You told me you were going to the Atlees. You even agreed to bring raspberries back for supper .... And then you didn't bother to come home or let me know where you were....."

Gina's reply was very matter of fact. "Sorry. We just changed our plan. I didn't think the raspberries were that important."

"It's not that they were important," I continued, "it's just that you didn't think to call and let me know where you were. That's really inconsiderate."

Isabella spoke: "Meeses Kerry, I am so sorry. Gina has been so good to me. We had a very good time. I thought it would be all right to buy the lunch for everyone, to say thank you for everything. Eef we have upset you, I am sorry ---- eet ees my fault."

"No, Isabella, it isn't your fault. And it was very generous of you to take everyone to lunch, but Gina knows she is expected to let me know if she changes a plan or will be late home. I'm sure your mother asks you to do the same thing?"

"Of course," Isabella nodded her head. "I always tell my mamita where I am going to be."

"You see, Gina," I turned in her direction, "I am just asking you to be considerate."

Gina said nothing. She turned and walked out of the room and Isabella followed her. The tension in the room was palpable.

The next day, Friday, was Isabella's last day with us. She would be returning home on Saturday and, as planned, Gina would be going with her to spend the last week of the holidays with the DeSantos family. Now that the children were growing older, I had for the past two years given each of them what I considered to be a fair allowance to purchase their back-to-school needs - - socks, t-shirts, jeans etc. I gave them cash, with the understanding that if they spent a big heap of money on t-shirts and didn't have enough left for socks, then they would just have to live without enough socks until next time. I wanted them to learn how to budget money. So far, the plan had been working quite well. Now I was about to give Gina her back-to-school allowance and send her back with Isabella. The problem was that, after this latest incident, I felt that Gina's behaviour over the past three weeks had been so difficult that she really shouldn't be allowed the 'reward' of spending the last week at the DeSantos' with Isabella. What I **should** do was 'ground' her until her behaviour improved.

While we were all at the beach on Friday afternoon, I sat and agonized over what to do. I was angry, annoyed, perplexed and, yes, hurt by Gina's attitude. Where was the happy little girl I first met? We had always been able to talk to each other. She seemed like a stranger. Had I done something wrong? I didn't think so. What could I do to get things back on a good footing? Yes, the children were becoming teenagers, but that didn't have to mean that we were at war.

I decided to try talking to Gina about it. We would be leaving for the ferry the next morning, so that night at bedtime, I asked Gina to see me in the kitchen – alone. All I could do was talk to her from my heart, "Gina," I began, "after the way you have been behaving since you got back from Seal Bay, quite frankly you don't deserve to go back with Isabella to spend the last week with the DeSantos family --- but at this point, I need a break from these constant disagreements or misunderstandings, or whatever you call them. So I've decided to allow you to go. Maybe after we have a break from each other, the two of us can sit down together when I return home and get our friendship back. I really hope so."

She said, "Okay". Nothing more. Then she turned and went back to her room. I felt empty and sad inside.

Ben, Amy and I had the cottage all to ourselves for the last week of the holidays and we made the most of it. We had a few days of unsettled weather during which we drove down to Victoria and stayed at a motel for a night while the two of them did their back-to-school shopping, I had my hair done and we all went out to dinner at their favourite – "Earl's". There was even time for another picnic at Horne Lake and lazing around in the garden or at the beach. With Gina's departure, all the tension had evaporated. It was a very relaxing week. Gina had not called me since she left, and I decided to let it go. I had confidence that the DeSantos's would call me if there was a problem.

On the Wednesday before Labour Day weekend, the three of us worked all day to tidy the house and load up all our 'gear' so that we could head for the ferry early on Thursday morning and, hopefully, avoid the holiday rush. It was incredibly exhausting. It always was. But on Thursday morning, the key having been turned in the lock, the three of us together with Tessa and Rascal squeezed ourselves into my overloaded hatchback and began the journey back to city life.

Chapter Forty-Three

We arrived home around mid-afternoon, the first order of business being to unload the car and put things away. When I was halfway down the hall to the laundry room, weighed down under a bundle of dirty towels, the phone rang.

Ben hopped into the kitchen and picked it up: "It's for you, mum," he called.

Dumping the clothes beside the washer, I went into the kitchen to answer. "Hi?" I said.

"Hello, Mrs Kerry, I hope this isn't a bad time," It was Mrs Mercer.

"Oh hi, Mrs Mercer, we've just arrived back from Sandy Bay. I'm in the process of unloading the car."

"I'm sorry to interrupt," she continued, "but I need to talk to you."

I was a bit surprised, "What is it?" I asked, "Gina's not here at the moment...."

She interrupted again, "I know, Mrs Kerry. There's been a bit of trouble."

"Trouble?" I exclaimed.

"Yes, Mrs Kerry. I understand that Gina came back about a week ago to visit with her friend Isabella."

"Yes, that's right," I said, "Isabella spent a week with us and Isabella's family invited Gina to spend the last week of the holidays with them. The girls are great friends. They planned to do their back-to-school shopping together."

"I see," said Mrs Mercer, "but I'm afraid that Gina's been in trouble."

"Trouble?" I asked.

"Yes, Mrs Kerry, Gina was arrested for shoplifting at the mall on Tuesday."

I was shocked, "I don't know what to say, Mrs Mercer. It doesn't make any sense. Before Gina left, I gave her her shopping budget money ---- it was over $350.00 in cash! She had plenty of money...."

"Well, of course, I was contacted when it happened," Mrs Mercer continued. "I have spent some time talking to Gina."

"I still don't know what to say" I repeated.

"Mrs Kerry," Mrs Mercer continued "I'm sorry to have to tell you this, but Gina says that she isn't happy living with your family. She feels you are not treating her well. She doesn't want to return......"

A wave of total shock rolled over me. This all seemed unreal. I couldn't get my mind around it, "Wasn't happy?........."

"Mrs Mercer," I said, "I am really sorry to hear this. As you know, from the very beginning all I have ever wanted is for Gina to be happy. Over the summer, she has seemed restless and difficult to get along with. I put it down to fallout from the hearing and dealing with her mother and I told her we would get together and talk about it when we all got back from the cottage. But if the problem is that she truly isn't happy living with us any longer, then we would never insist that she stay." I heard my voice, a long way off, saying the words.

"All right, Mrs Kerry. I think the best thing at this point is to find another placement for Gina. Sometimes these things happen."

"What about her things?" I found myself asking.

Mrs. Mercer continued: "She doesn't seem to want to pick them up. So perhaps I can come up on Tuesday, after the weekend, and get them?"

"That'll be fine. I'll have them ready. About what time?" I replied.

"I'll come on my way home after work," she said, "How about between 5 and 5:30?"

"That's just fine," I said.

"Goodbye". She hung up.

I went into the living room and flopped down on the couch. I felt as if I had fallen from a great height.

Ben looked in and saw me as he walked along the hall. I guess he noticed that I looked a bit stunned because he came in and sat down beside me. "Are you okay, mum?" he asked.

"Gina's gone!" was all I could say.

"Gone? Gone where?" Ben was puzzled.

Then the whole story tumbled out. Amy came into the room when I was halfway through. She sat there and listened, big-eyed. When I finished, Ben, always the level-headed one, said, "Okay, mum, so it's a shock, but it's not our fault. I don't understand what happened, or Gina wanting to leave. I think that's sad for her but not for us. You know, we are still 'us' the Kerry family."

"Ben's right, mum," Amy chimed in, "Gina's crazy. She'll be sorry."

I didn't realize it right at that moment, but I have two of the best kids you could ever imagine.

"Okay," I said, "we'd better get on with unloading and tidy up before dad arrives home from work. What is it they always say, "keeping busy is the solution to many a problem"? So we got back to work!

PART XIII

Living with Loss

Chapter Forty-Four

My memory of the events of the next few weeks is still quite blurred. I don't know how to describe my mental condition.. I was plunged into a state of grief, regret, sadness, disappointment..... all feelings so jumbled together that I didn't know which end was 'up'. The days went by. Steve was told. He was very honest with me about his feelings, "You know, Maura, I have always had doubts that made me hesitant about Gina. I could see how much of yourself you have invested in her. Somehow, I was afraid that you would be disappointed. But I must say I never imagined anything quite as rough as this. I think we have to decide that this is for the best. I don't think anyone could have done more for Gina than you but --- and I know this may sound hard-hearted --- it's time to let go." Dorrie's response was somewhat similar. She didn't say "I told you so" but she didn't encourage me to remain involved. Ben and Amy just continued to be their agreeable selves --- perhaps a bit more helpful than usual – their way of comforting me. The one thing they never said was "We're glad she's gone" --- a testament to their generous nature!

Mrs Mercer arrived after 5 o'clock on Tuesday. We had packed all Gina's clothes and nick-nacks and cleaned up her bike. As I helped load things in her car, Mrs Mercer remarked that they had decided to place Gina in a group home about three miles away, at Glenoak Bay.

"There are several other foster kids at the home," she explained "They all meet every week as a 'council' with the couple who run the home. They set the rules and are expected to keep to them. Gina's 15 now, and I think the experience will be good for her. I'm taking her over there tomorrow."

"Is she still staying with the DeSantos's, then?" I asked.

"Oh, no. After Gina was arrested, I spent quite a bit of time talking to her. It seems that she and Isabella had been planning that Gina would move to live permanently with the DeSantos family. They had it all worked out. I gather Mr DeSantos is the Mexican Consul and they are quite well off money-wise. Isabella was sure that Gina would have her own room and that there would be no problem with money. It was quite a plan they had made."

"I had no idea….." I began.

Mrs Mercer smiled wryly, "Unfortunately, Isabella didn't consult with her family about it until Gina came back from Sandy Bay with Isabaella, and the DeSantos family said absolutely "NO". They told Gina to go back home. Later that day she did the shoplifting."

"Now I'm beginning to understand," I said.

"Yes, the shoplifting was just a cry for help. After I spoke to Gina, we returned the necklace she stole --- it was a piece of cheap costume jewelry --- they aren't going to press charges."

"That's good!" I said.

Mrs Mercer continued, "I think Gina needs to realize that just because she is out from under her mother's custody now, that doesn't mean that she is free to do anything she likes." With that, she put Gina's duffle bag on the back seat, got into her car and said, "Thanks, Mrs Kerry" as she drove away.

Gina was gone! She was no longer part of the Kerry family. She had disappeared just as suddenly as she had appeared on that sunny summer morning four years ago. It took a bit of getting used to. At least, for me it did. How do you express everything you feel when someone you really care about is no longer with you? As the days and weeks passed, I grappled with my inner thoughts and feelings. Of course, the rest of my little family were understanding, but their day-to-day lives continued much as usual. After a while, we were more or less back to the way we had been "before Gina". At least, that was the way it was for them. But not for me. Every day there were little reminders of her. For the first few weeks after she was gone, I kept setting five places at the supper table, then remembering and having to take put the extra setting away. I found myself shopping for too many vegetables or looking for a good buy on steak because that was

Gina's favourite. Things like that. I remember thinking that it's much easier, in a way, when a person dies because they are gone from everyone. But when a person just isn't there, when you know that they are living just a few miles away among other people, it's more like an amputation. You find yourself wondering if they are okay. You wish you could see them if only for a minute, to be sure they are happy. For quite a while, I lived in this inner 'thought world'. I was grieving.

As time passed, I felt better. Dorrie came over on weekends and we went to the pitch and putt. Things were going well at work. The kids were busy at school and Steve and I revived our social life which, I had to admit, had suffered somewhat during the time I was involved with the court hearings. I heard nothing at all about Gina. Although she was still at the same high school as Ben, he never said anything about her. She was in a different grade of course, but I knew they would probably see each other at recess. I suppose I could have asked him about her, but I didn't. I felt I just couldn't bear it, especially if the news wasn't good.

We spent Christmas at home. Dorrie came over and stayed with us from Christmas Eve through to New Year. The two of us created a marvellous Christmas Feast and Dorrie stayed with the kids while Steve and I went over to the Vogts to bring in the new year. Then, during the first week in January, I ran into Alyssa at the supermarket. I hadn't seen her since Gina left us but as soon as we began talking, it was clear that she knew about it. Julia had told her. Alyssa said she went over every so often to see Julia who had been pretty devastated when she lost custody of Gina. Julia's social worker had told the two of them that Gina had moved to another foster home. I asked Alyssa if Gina had visited Julia.

"No! That's just it," Alyssa remarked, "Gina has told the social workers that she doesn't want to see her mother ever again."

"Really?" I was surprised.

"Julia just couldn't understand it. Neither could I, for that matter. I know things have been difficult, but Gina always wanted to see Scott and **Lucy**. Of course, now that we know the entire situation, it's not surprising."

"What? What situation?"

253

"Oh, well ...... you know. You did your best. You were just great to Gina. I think even Julia would agree with me about that. You shouldn't feel bad........"

Just then, the cashier interrupted with, "that's a total of $110.25", and by the time I had fished around in my purse and paid my bill, Alyssa was wheeling her buggy towards the door. I tried to catch up with her. What was she talking about? What had happened to Gina? By the time I reached the door, Alyssa was gone and there was no sign of her in the parking lot.

My mind was whirling for the rest of the day. What had happened? I told myself it was no longer anything to do with me, but it made no difference. I HAD to know. But how? I no longer had Alyssa's number. Should I call Mrs Mercer? No. I would feel stupid doing that.

Then I had a brilliant idea. I could ask Ben. Or Amy. I tackled Ben after supper when he was helping me load the dishwasher.

"Do you see anything of Gina, these days?" I began tenuously.

"Sometimes." He sounded vague.

"It's just that I saw Alyssa at the supermarket today and she happened to mention that --- well that there's a situation with Gina. I just thought that you might have some idea what she meant."

"Uh-huh," Ben sounded reluctant.

"Well, can you tell me about it? If there's something wrong, you would've told me, wouldn't you?"

"Look, mum," he said, "Amy and I just don't want you to be upset anymore."

"It can't be all that bad, can it?" I pleaded.

Ben took a deep breath. "Mum, Gina's pregnant."

"Pregnant?!" I just hadn't been prepared for that.

"I don't know anything else, mum. She's pregnant."

"I see," I said, "I see. Thanks, Ben. Thanks for telling me."

"Amy and I, well, we knew you would be upset. We thought if we didn't say anything, you wouldn't have to know."

I gave him a hug. "That's kind of you. Thanks."

He escaped downstairs to watch television. I tidied up the kitchen with a lot of unanswered questions floating around in my head. I had had my doubts about whether Gina was ready for a Group Home situation. Most of all, I remembered the confrontation with "boyfriend" Dave at her mother's place. It seemed like a century ago now, but I still remembered thinking that if Gina remained with Julia, sooner or later those 'boyfriends' would stop looking at Julia when there was a beautiful young daughter in the picture. Even if Gina no longer visited Julia, had my worst fears come true? Yet, what could I do? Nothing. I could do nothing. I was no longer involved. I must accept it.

Chapter Forty-Five

Our summer at Sandy Bay in 1978 was a very happy one. In July, Dorrie came over and spent two weeks with the kids and me. We enjoyed picnics at the beach, endless games of table tennis and the barbecue was always on the go. Steve commuted on most weekends and took two entire weeks in August. He started giving Ben golf lessons and we enjoyed many evenings at our neighbour's, the Noonans, where the boys' enjoyed games at Al Noonan's pool table, and Fran Noonan who had a spinning wheel began teaching Amy how to spin her own wool. Other times, we just lazed around in the garden and read books.

From time to time I would think about Gina and the pregnancy and wonder what was happening to her. Not knowing anything was the hardest part. One afternoon, I went up to the Sandy Bay drugstore on the pretext of getting some suntan lotion. Gina's grandmother was still working there, and I guess I thought that if I just happened to be there, Lillian might just say something to me about her. It turned out to be a wasted expedition. When I took my bottle of suntan lotion to Lillian, who was running the cash register, she rang it up, put it in a bag and handed it to me without any comment whatsoever. She didn't appear to recognize me at all. Or maybe she didn't want to recognize me, I thought. After all, Gina was no longer with us and I was probably in her 'bad books'. Maybe I would hear something after we returned home and school was back in. Maybe.

As it turned out, that's exactly what happened. About a week after school returned, Amy came home one day, dumped her books on the kitchen table, and announced "Gina's back at school, mum, I saw her today."

"She is?" I waited hopefully for more news.

256

Amy continued, "Yeah, we had a chat. She's repeating some of the courses she didn't complete last year because of having the baby."

"So she had her baby?" I said.

"Uh-huh, she had a little girl She says her baby is really cute."

"How does she manage to look after her and do school at the same time," I asked. It was a logical question.

"She says the baby is at another foster home and she goes and spends her weekends with her."

That certainly didn't sound like an ideal set-up to me, but it was probably the only arrangement that would work.

"How is Gina herself?" I asked.

"She looks great, mum, really. She's not big anymore. You know what I mean. She looks just like she always does." Amy picked up her books and walked down the hall. Then, just as she started to do down the stairs, she called back to me.

"Gina said to say "hi" to you from her.

Even though it wasn't an 'in person' hi, that message from Gina felt so good, I think. because it was the first communication I had received since we said goodbye at the ferry terminal with Isabella over a year ago. However small, it was something positive. After living for a year with the negative of Gina's absence, that meant a lot. While everyone around me, my mother, my husband, Bette Vogt, Alyssa, other friends who were aware of Gina joining our family--- all of them --- had gone out of their way to be kind, to assure me that nobody could have done more for Gina than I, that nobody HAD done more for Gina than I, all this well-meant kindness hadn't helped. I think it was because they didn't seem to understand that I hadn't given Gina a home because I wanted everyone to think what a great person I was. No. I had given Gina a home because, having come to know what her life had been up to when I met her, I wanted her to experience what a normal home was like -a home where she was safe – a home where she was loved, no matter what. Yes, her behaviour hadn't turned out as I had expected or wanted, but the objective wasn't to have her grovel with gratitude. Gratitude is always nice to receive, but my instinct told me that children with a background similar to Gina's probably need a bit of time before they begin to feel the difference, and some may never come to recognize the difference at all. But they deserve a chance! All I wanted was for Gina to have her chance. So it had been a failure. As I saw it, I could hardly hold Gina responsible for that --- but I did feel that I had failed her, and that knowledge weighed on me all the time. Despite all the kind people, I just couldn't shake it. So I would just have to live with it. The big question was, **could I live with it**?

Time passed. A family time full of soccer games, paper routes, school concerts, science projects, sleepovers, shopping trips, arguments and pranks. Steve was busy at work which meant he was happy, he walked Tessa, spent a lot of time at Ben's soccer games, attended Amy's piano recital and filled up most of his remaining spare time with golf, except when he was entertaining me!! I was busy and enjoying my work world of legal briefs, pleadings and trial dates. At Christmas, we all went to the ballet, Dorrie included. In early January we had a huge snowstorm and my boss gave us the use of his ski cabin at Whistler, where Steve, Ben and Amy enjoyed the skiing while, not being good at doing anything on a slippery surface, I kept the fire going and the hot chocolate on tap.

Since my conversation with Amy back in September, I had heard nothing more about Gina. Neither Ben nor Amy had said anything and I was sure they would have told me if they heard anything more than what I already knew. Looking back, it seemed like those past five years had all been a kind of dream. Had they ever really happened?

PART XIV

Love Always Finds a Way

Chapter Forty-Six

Everything changed one day in May of 1979 when I went down to the drugstore to get a few odds and ends. As I loaded my buggy and searched in my purse for a credit card, I heard a vaguely familiar laugh. When I reached the check-out desk, I saw that the source of the laughter was a young woman with fair hair. Her back was towards me but as I began putting my purchases on the counter, she turned around and I found myself once again looking into a pair of violet eyes. It was Gina!

"Hi there mom," she smiled. "What a surprise!"

"Yes, it is," I agreed. "It's been a long time. How are you doing?"

"I'm doing pretty good," she replied. "I'm back at school sort of catching up on the courses I missed last year".

"That's good," The cashier handed me my bag of purchases and we both began walking towards the door. On impulse, I asked her, "I don't suppose you have a bit of time? I was thinking we might go next door to the Mocha Bean and maybe have a cup of coffee and catch up on things?"

"That'd be great. It's a while before my bus comes."

At the Mocha Bean, Gina grabbed a table for two beside the window while I got two lattes and a brownie each. I sat down and looked at her, not quite knowing what to say. I stirred my latte. Gina was the first to speak.

"I guess you know that I had a baby?" she asked.

"Yes, Gina, I know. Ben told me about it."

She wasn't at all hesitant, even though we hadn't spoken to each other for over a year. "You know, mom, I never thought that I would get pregnant," she said, "I guess I just thought that kind of thing happened to other people. I didn't believe it could happen to me."

I tried to think of something to say as she kept going, "It was such a shock --- when I found out I was pregnant, I mean."

"I guess it was..........."

"At the group home, we had a kind of council, you see, and all of us had to talk it out and decide what to do. And I had to meet with Mrs Mercer and the group home 'mother'. Anyway, in the end, they, well I...... well I guess everyone agreed that the best thing would be for me to have a termination."

I said, "I see."

Gina continued, "So anyway, they made an appointment for me to see a doctor at this clinic – you know - where they do terminations. I had to go there all by myself. I was pretty nervous." Her forehead wrinkled up.

"I can understand that," I hoped I sounded as sympathetic as I felt.

"Anyway, while I was sitting there, another girl came in and sat down beside me. I guess she was my age or maybe a few years older. After a while, she turned to me and said, "Hi. You look nervous," and I said something like 'Yes, I'm totally nervous.' And then she asked me, 'are you having a termination?' When I said I was, do you know what she said to me?"

"No. What...?"

Gina's expression was angry." She said, "Well, you shouldn't be nervous. There's nothing to it! Believe me, I should know. I've had two already! Can you believe that, mom? That girl had had two terminations!"

"That doesn't sound good to me," I said.

"Mom, I freaked out. I freaked out. I thought how could anyone do THAT twice. So do you know what I did?"

"What?"

"I got up and I walked out. I decided I wasn't going to do it at all. I was going to have my baby!"

"That was a big decision...." I began, but Gina continued.

"So I told everyone what I had decided and I went ahead and had my baby." She stopped for a second, her eyes softened, and she said, "Mom, I had the loveliest little girl!"

I smiled, "Yes, I know."

"Did you know that I called her Ruby?"

"No, I didn't know that. Ruby's a lovely name, Gina."

"Yes, Ruby was born last July. After that, she had to go to another foster home, being a baby and all that, because I had to go back to school. But all summer I was able to spend weekends with her. It reminded me of when I was taking care of Scott and Lucy when I was in Winnipeg. Lucy was just a baby back then."

"So how is Ruby doing these days?" I asked.

"Well, mom, I don't have my Ruby anymore."

"You don't?" I hadn't heard about that. "What happened?"

"Mom, I gave Ruby up for adoption!" her eyes were sad.

"You did?"

"Yes, I did, when she was six months old. You see, as the time went by, I began to wish that Ruby had a regular kind of family --- like a mom and a dad --- you know. I thought about how it was when I visited with my dad and Laura and Teddy, and about how good it felt all the time when I lived in your family. I wanted my Ruby to have that kind of family. I didn't want her to have a life like I had with my mom. You know I love my mom, but her life isn't good for kids. I couldn't give my Ruby your kind of life. I'm too young. There's no dad. So I decided to give her up so that she could grow up in a real family."

I sat there, speechless, my mind slowly grasping what Gina had just said. For over a year I had been carrying around a bundle of sadness in my heart because I felt I had somehow failed this little girl who was now a young woman, a young woman who at the same time had been faced with an extremely hard decision. I will never forget what it meant to me when Gina said, "I thought about how it was when I visited with my dad and Laura and Teddy and about how good it felt all the time when I lived in your family, and I wanted my Ruby to have that kind of life." Maybe, just maybe, I hadn't failed at all! Gina had come to see how such things could be different, but not just for herself! She had chosen that kind of life for her little girl, even though it meant giving that lovely little baby away.

I took a sip of coffee as Gina chattered on. "I don't know exactly who Ruby's new parents are, but I do know that they couldn't have kids of their own. The wife- Ruby's new mom -was working but she was going to stop working and be a stay-at-home mom when they got Ruby. The dad had a good job and Ruby would be loved and taken care of always. I just told the social workers that I would like it if they would keep her name as "Ruby" and they promised they would do that.

For a while, I felt very sad." She swallowed, "You know – I missed Ruby a lot. I went down to Rock Beach to stay with some friends for a while until I didn't feel so sad. And now I'm back and trying to catch up on school and do some courses so that I can get a job when I graduate next year."

"Well, Gina," I said, "you have had a lot to deal with, haven't you? I'm glad you had some friends to be with after Ruby was adopted. I'm sure it was very hard."

She sighed, "Yup, mom, it was hard. But I think I did the right thing. Don't you?"

I said, "Gina, I don't believe it matters so much what I believe, or what anyone else believes. What truly matters is what you believe in your heart and if your heart is at peace about Ruby, that's what's important,"

For a while we sat quietly, eating our brownies, sipping the creamy lattes. Then I said, "If only we had been able to talk, maybe I could have helped you,"

"I sometimes thought about that." Her face was sad, eyes cast downward." But I made such a mess of things."

"No, Gina," I said, "I think I was the one who made a mess of things."

She shook her head.

I continued, "You remember, when you came back from visiting Kelsey at Seal Bay, you seemed kind of wild – like a different person. Remember, in the car, you grabbed the steering wheel from me. It was scary."

"That was such a dreadful summer, mom. I sometimes felt like I wanted to die."

"But why, Gina? You had a good time at Kelsey's didn't you?"

"Not really, mom. It started off okay but then Kelsey told me all this stuff that her mom had told her."

"What stuff?" I was curious.

"Well, you know that Kelsey's grandma lives at Sandy Bay and she knows my grandma – and they're kind of friendly. Anyway, Kelsey told me that her mom told her that my grandma had told her grandma that all that summer before I came to live with you, my grandma had been trying to get rid of me. They didn't want me living with them at Sandy Bay. They had somebody important coming to visit and they didn't want them to know about my mom and everything that happened, and they didn't want them to see me."

I started to tell her I knew about that, but she kept on going, telling me what Kelsey's mother had told Kelsey.

"And do you remember I told you about all those little holidays I had that summer – like when I went to my Nana's house and then up to visit my uncle and aunt's ranch….. well those weren't holidays at all --- I was on trial to see if they would keep me --- but they didn't want me either! Then they sent me to my dad's and he said no … and that's where I was when my grandma called and told me you wanted me to live with you."

"Yes, I remember," I said.

"Well, all those visits were a lie! Even my dad didn't want me! That's what was really going on."

"Oh Gina, I know, I know," I exclaimed

"You know!"

"Yes, Gina, your grandmother told me about it when she came over with your grandfather to our cottage at Sandy Bay, to tell me that they would like to take me up on my offer to have you come to live with us. I knew, but I didn't tell you about it."

"Why not!" she was angry.

"Because, Gina, I didn't want you to know. I knew it would hurt you and I didn't want for you ever to be hurt. I only ever wanted you to be happy. I didn't think you would ever find out." I hoped she would understand.

"Well, I did find out. And my grandma said that when you came to see her and said you would like to have me live with you, you told her you wanted to be a foster mother because you needed the extra money."

"That's not true," I said, "I just wanted you to have a home where you were safe and happy and from what your grandparents told me, it might be a long time before your mother could take you back. I didn't even think of being a foster mother. I didn't know anything about being a foster mother. Gina, I just wanted you to be happy. I love you."

"Oh mom," she said, "when Kelsey told me all that stuff, I was so sad and I was angry too. I thought "if all those people think I am such a monster that they don't want me, or else they want to be paid to have me, then I WILL BE A MONSTER." So I guess I started being a monster when I got back to Sandy Bay." She was wiping her eyes.

"I'm sorry I was angry with you," I said, "but I just couldn't understand why you were so difficult. I thought maybe you would be happier when Isabella came but everything just got worse!

Gina grimaced. "I was still in a bad mood when Isabella arrived. And I told her the whole story about my mother and Scott and Lucy and Rosalie and all about coming to live with you."

"You did?"

"Yes. Up until then, Isabella thought you were my mom. When I told her what Kelsey had said, Isabella said I should leave your family. She said she would take me to live with her. It all sounded great. You know they have a lot of money and a big house and Isabella can have just about everything she wants…. and we were such good friends. Isabella said I would be able to go on trips – like when we went to Whistler -and visit their villa in Mexico….."

"So that's what the two of you were discussing when you went out and didn't come back on time? "I was beginning to understand everything now. "But it didn't work out, did it?"

"I guess Mrs Mercer told you?"

"Yes. But why did you do the shoplifting:"

"Part of our plan was for me to go to Mrs Mercer and complain about you. I told Isabella that I didn't think Mrs Mercer would believe me because she knew I had always been happy at your house --- so Isabella said I should do something really bad – and then you really wouldn't want me – so we decided on shoplifting. I **wanted** to get caught!"

'Oh – Gina. What a mess!"

She gave me a crooked smile. "It sure was. But it only got worse because when Isabella told her mother, it all went wrong. Mrs DeSantos was shocked that you weren't my mother. Then when I told her about my real mother and the court and Mrs Mercer and Scott and Lucy, Mrs DeSantos kind of freaked out. She said I was just like a "peon", I think it was. Isabella says a "peon" is a kind of low life peasant in Mexico. Anyway, the DeSantos's said No. **They** didn't want me either!"

"But surely you and Isabella are still friends," I asked.

"No. We're not. After all the trouble, the DeSantos's sent Isabella to a private school in Vancouver, and later, Marco had to go back to Mexico to finish university."

"But why? Marco wasn't part of your plan with Isabella?" I was puzzled.

"Mom," Gina looked up at me sadly, "Marco was Ruby's dad." She turned her head away "I know he really loved me but they wouldn't listen....."

I just sat there for a minute, saying nothing. What could I say?

"But why didn't you call me?" I finally asked, "you didn't even come up to pick up your things."

She said, "Mom, I was so ashamed! I was such a jerk. I just couldn't face you. I wanted to crawl away." Her eyes were full of tears.

"Never! Never in a million years." I put my hand over hers and squeezed it. We were quiet for a few seconds.

"Know something, Gina?" I asked.

"Nope. What?"

"We're gonna be all right,' I said. Then, just as we had done that long-ago day on a bus stop bench, we gave each other damp smiles.

She looked at her watch and stood up abruptly. "I gotta go, mom, it's almost my bus time." Leaning over, she gave me a quick hug, then disappeared out the door.

It was a while before I left the coffee shop. I bought another latte, returned to our table and just sat there, savoring the memory of what had passed between us. Amazing! The lingering mystery of what had happened was finally resolved and it had just taken twenty minutes!. Everything made sense now. All the pieces had finally been put together in the right order – just like one of our summertime jigsaws at Sandy Bay. Fitting the pieces together in the right order, maybe that's what life is all about? What a thought!

Chapter Forty-Seven

I didn't see Gina for quite along time after our chance meeting, but somehow life felt different. A weight had been lifted. I really did feel 'okay' and I knew Gina was 'okay' too. When the opportunity arose, I told Steve and Dorrie about the adoption etc. They were glad to hear she was getting on with her life and I knew they were glad to see me in a happier frame of mind. For them, it was all about something past and gone but they knew it meant a lot more to me.

We had another chance meeting in the spring of 1980. I was hurrying back to work on my lunch hour and, as I came around the corner to cross the street to my office building, who should be coming towards me, but Gina - hurrying too.

She was wearing black tailored slacks, knee-high black leather boots, a smart little black suede jacket with a row of silver buttons and a pretty silver-grey scarf. Her hair was still long – and it still had highlights. She looked great!

We stopped in front of each other. Gina smiled, "Hi mom, how are you doing?"

"How are **YOU** doing!" I exclaimed, "I hardly recognized you. You're looking very smart."

"Oh, I guess --- the clothes," she twirled around. "I'm working now. I'm rich!!!" She rolled her eyes.

"Working --- where?" I asked.

"I'm secretary to a guy at the Stock Exchange,"

"That's great," I said, "so I guess those courses you were doing were a big help?"

"Uh-huh," she went on, "it's a pretty good job, but I'm going to night school as well. I want to work into a better job. Maybe not be a secretary all my life…"

"That's what I did," I said. "Are you still out at Glenoak?"

"Oh no, I'm all through with that. I'm sharing an apartment with two girlfriends. I'll soon be nineteen!!"

"How's that working out?"

"Pretty good" She continued, "I've got a boyfriend too. He's a bit serious but I don't want to move in with him or anything. I don't think I'm ready."

"It's good to take your time," I agreed. Then I asked, "Have you seen your mom?"

Her expression changed. "I saw her quite a while back. There was a lot of trouble where she was living. Some guy molested Lucy and the Ministry took Lucy and Scott away permanently. I'm trying to find out where they are….." Her voice trailed off.

I began to realize that time was running out and I needed to get back to the office.

I said, "I'm sorry, Gina, but I've got to get back to work. I just wanted to find out how you are….."

She nodded, "I've gotta get going, too."

"Goodbye…." I began.

She stepped closer, wrapped her arms around me and murmured in my ear. Then she turned around and melted quickly into the swirling tide of people on the sidewalk. But her presence remained, the warmth of her breath on my cheek, and the softness of her voice as she whispered, "I'll always remember you, mom. Love you forever."

As I waited for the lights to change, I thought: "I **CAN** live with that!"

The End

Train up a child in the way she should go;
Even when she is old, she will not depart from it.
(Holy Bible, Proverbs 22:6)

Epilogue

Gina continued her studies and now teaches Grade One. She married a computer programmer when she was 24 and they have two daughters. It's a happy marriage.

Her brother Scott was moved to a foster home. He became an electrician and went north to work on construction. He sees Gina when he's in town.

Lucy was also moved to a different foster home. She still suffers from the trauma of being raped and is in and out of treatment. Gina tries to help but there is little contact between them.

Julia Niemann moved back to Winnipeg with Rosalie after she lost custody of Scott and Lucy. No one in the family knows where she is.

Gina continues to have a warm friendship with her dad and Laura, and with Teddy who is now a lawyer.

She has no contact with the rest of her family.

Ben is an aeronautical engineer. Amy is a physiotherapist.

Maura Kerry is now retired and writing books. But that's another story!

www.ingramcontent.com/pod-product-compliance
Lightning Source LLC
Chambersburg PA
CBHW021615120626
46545CB00001B/230